Big Ralph:
Reflections Of A Black Police Chief

Carl A. Patton

Psyche Publishers
Atlanta, Georgia

TO RALPH HENRY COTHRAN
PEACE TO ALL THE SAINTS

Big Ralph: Reflections Of A Black Police Chief

Copyright ©1997 by Carl A. Patton. All rights reserved.
Printed and bound in the United States of America.
No part of this book may be reproduced in any form by any electronic or mechanical means without permission in writing from the publisher.

This does not include book reviewers are researchers who may quote passages and note the source.

Library of Congress Catalog Number 97-65057

Published by Psyche Publisher's,
P. O. Box 91697,
Atlanta, Georgia 30364-1697.
ISBN 0-9656467-0-X

Dedicated To The Memory Of Big Ralph

Ode To Ralph Cothran My Husband
By Catherine Cothran May 24, 1996

You live!
You live!
You live!

Now, even in death, because in life,
You had the courage to give, give, give,

It is your breath of good will that death
is unable to still, the breadth of it an
enormous field

You live!
You live!
You live!

A life so vibrant, vital, voluminous,
filled with never-ending goals. A life
always concerned with the outcome of other
souls, blossomed to unfold.

You live!
You live!
You live!

The works that you have done, evoke the
praise from many tongues. Your will and way was bold,
understanding and patience untold.

You live!
You live!
You live!

A part of your heart is entwined in the heart
and hearts of Chattanooga, As as long as hearts beat,

You live!
You live!
You live!

Acknowledgments

I pay the highest tribute to Almighty God for the completion of the book Big Ralph. If not for my rebirth, the completion of this book would not have been possible. I also would like to thank Big Ralph for the time he gave me during his last days. I also thank my beloved brother-in-law Big Ralph for the time and resources he extended to me over the years.

This list of acknowledgments would not be complete without mentioning my big sister Catherine. Thank you very much for your kindness, understanding and the resources to make this book possible.

I also thank my parents for my birth right too free speech. It is for certain that my posture as an independent thinker extends from the blood line of my father and mother as it is the will of God. Thank you mother Ruby. My father passed away in 1965, thank you Big Billy. I also thank my God father Emerson Augustus McGuire who continued to instill the principle of independence in my soul. Mr. McGuire understood the sacrifice of an artist, he was always supportive up to his death in 1995.

Computer skills are very necessary in this technological age. I owe a deep debt of gratitude to my cousin Ann Cooper's husband Clint. Clint, who is computer expert assisted me in the purchase of the proper equipment and was always available to assist me with any problems in operating the equipment.

I owe a special thanks to brother Khalfani Sharrieff for his timely criticism of the research effort. Thank you my brother and may the Creator extend you peace and paradise for everlasting.

My two children William A. (Billy) Patton and Psyche Z. (Zannie) Patton have always supported their father and believed in me. Thank you Billy and Zannie I love you. Thanks also to Lou the mother of Billy and Zannie. I greatly appreciate all the support you have given me down through the years.

Thanks to my brother Gerald for his technical help. Thanks for the gift of my first computer. William Patton III my older brother has always been supportive. Thank you Bay-Brother and many thanks to your wonderful wife Loretta. May you both continue to look to Almighty God for the answers to life's dilemmas.

Mary Elizabeth you have been such a inspiration for many years. Thanks for your spirit and confidence. Louise thank you for your technical assistance. Our brief consultations were always beneficial to the completion of this work.

Finally peace and prosperity to my sister in Christ, Minnie. Thank you for your spiritual guidance, patience and understanding. May the song birds of Peace and Paradise forever sing their songs in your presence. May these songs sing praises in a place that knows no time, for there life never ends.

As a last gesture of thanks. Many thanks to Kenneth (Doc) Neely of Doc-It Express for his timely typesetting services. Thanks Ken I couldn't have made it without you.

Foreword

I have the impression that throughout Ralph Cothran's life, he always tried to help someone. He said, "you haven't done much to help someone unless you go out of your way and scarifice." On the other hand, it was startling, that everywhere he went, he made and amazing impression on people.

In 1964 I was initially shocked when my husband told my father that he would like to be a police officer. However, I very quickly overcame this reaction, realizing he had decided to pursue the job. Thus, throughout the years of being married to a career police officer, I found myself continuously adapting to change. I also attempted to adapt to the stress that comes with the life of a police officer.

Chief Cothran felt the need to write a book many years ago and began compiling notes and had a potential writer engaged. This person eventually left the city with his notes. I'm sure the idea of writing a book remained in his mind.

My brother, Carl was like a son and a brother-in-law. About a year before my husband died, he asked me to write some notes, several times. He said, "I want Carl to write a book." He knew that Carl had the ability and that he could trust him.

I believe Chief Cothran felt this book is important because he wanted the truth as he saw it to be revealed. He wanted facts to be made public that he would have been unable to reveal during his lifetime, from his knowledge and experience as a law enforcement officer.

Ralph would say, "I have lived my life, done my work, now I want to explain the meaning of it all. This book will help somebody. I look forward to the book being an eye-opener. It will stimulate the mind and cause your ears to perk up." Truly his being was crying out, let this be known. His strong will and determination to succeed are continued as the dream of his biography becomes a reality.

From 1964 and on into the early years of my husband's life as a police officer, there was ongoing stress. By the grace of God we were able to withstand the rigors and pressures of the job. We each had to anticipate and try to ward off dangerous errors on our jobs. I would frequently tell him, "I'll pray for you" and he would tell me to "be alert." We were young and full of vim and vitality. He was a patrol officer first and eventually a narcotic's detective. I am a licensed practical nurse who worked in the most stressful areas in the hospital where I worked. The Emergency Room and Delivery Room are always filled with activity and the atmosphere is often intense but I also had a job to do. So we were two people who obviously thrived on being "where the action was."

Overtime, it became more difficult to cope with the stress so easily. As my husband gained rank he became busier and busier. I thought he worked too hard. I would tell him, "you're not made of iron." Often I was a sounding board when he was frustrated about a particular situation or problem in the department. Sometimes he would ask my opinion about what action to take or decision to make. I must admit, I was concerned about his health and welfare a lot and he cared about what was good for his people more than he did for himself.

Police officers are called on for just about everything. When people have a problem, they usually think of the police officer first. I've even had patients to call the police Department instead of calling the nurse. On the other hand they are not always given the respect that they deserve. A police officer has a dangerous and often thankless job.

Chief Cothran thought of himself as a peace officer and he believed this was a calling from God. He placed much emphasis on crime prevention with programs such as D.A.R.E. He loved children and never tired of being involved in their activities. He was careful to be fair to the men and women in the department despite race or creed. Ralph was very liberal and believed in being fair.

On a positive note after Ralph became Chief, I enjoyed going with him to various civic and social events in the community. At these events I was able to meet the people, I was also able to travel with Ralph extensively, which was great. I was very proud of his accomplishments as he continued to succeed.

In 1989 when my husband was appointed Chief of Police he was "bright eyed and bushy tailed." He was genuinely happy and enthusiastic, not because of the prestige, but he was eager to have a chance to make a difference in Chattanooga's government. He was glad to have the opportunity to cause changes in law enforcement for the betterment of the community. Ralph Cothran loved Chattanooga.

Eventually the combination of day and night work of a police officer and the Chief's mounting health problems made him lose his stamina, but never his will. The S.W.A.T. calls, deaths and murders in the late hours took a toll on his strength. The constant grind in bad weather, the ice and snow also took a toll. God only knows how many times I prayed as he traveled, when we lived on Pearl Street (hill) and since we moved to Chickamauga Heights. The stress was transferred to me, as I worried about his health.

I wished that he had not worked so hard and had been able to spend more time with the family. I would say, "why does a Chief have to do this and that and he would often say he couldn't trust anyone else to do it."

It has been a challenge being married to a police officer. When Ralph was hired in 1964, it was the beginning of a new era in Chattanooga history for Black police officers. They were equal with the white officers. So the Black officers were looked up too and respected. We (as Black people) were proud of them.

Finally to be married to the first Black Police Chief of Chattanooga was an honor. Although Ralph said "I am a Police Chief who just happens to be Black," it goes deeper than that. Being the first Black Chief gave him the opportunity to pave the way for posterity.

As a person, Ralph was one that you could depend on and he would not let you down. He had a strong shoulder for you to lean on. I miss him. My protector is gone, my dear husband and my friend. I now know the feeling of being alone. I know how the people of Chattanooga feel who love him too. Our strong protector is gone. It is so wonderful though that when a person dies love does not. Now Deuteronomy 33:27 comes to mind: "The eternal God is thy refuge, and underneath are the everlasting arms."

Finally, I want this book written, because my husband felt it was important. I feel obligated along with my brother, Carl to carry out his wishes to the best of my ability. With the arrival of this book, Chief Cothran continues to fight crime and keep peace as these printed words reach and penetrate the minds and hearts of the masses.

Preface

We will always remember Big Ralph as an honest and dedicated law enforcement officer for the city of Chattanooga, Tennessee. Through his leadership as the Chief of police he brought an atmosphere of racial harmony to Chattanooga that had never existed. Big Ralph gave his life to the city he loved. This book tells his story in the way he wanted me to tell it.

Thanks be to God the Creator of all things, for giving me the strength to follow my divine mission as a scribe. Thanks also, to the written word of God and the peace of prayer as the verbal communication to the Creator. Peace and Paradise to all those that read and are delivered, may God have mercy on the souls that this text further confuses.

Wisdom, truth and knowledge are housed first in the Creator. This trilogy is parallel to the Holy Trinity. So be it, so, it is so.

This biographical work pays special attention to the historical circumstances and events that affect Big Ralph's life. Thus we begin with the historical events that set the table before the birth of Big Ralph. Chapter one is the introduction and in this chapter we note The Seeds of Protest. This first chapter makes up all of Part I which reveals The Mysteries of Our Past.

The historical development of Black people in America is dealt with in the initial chapter. The European intrusion in the New World helped give birth to the institution of slavery. Thus, many scholars argue that the initial presence of free Blacks in North America was brief. Therefore the most significant North American presence of Black people is rooted in a previous condition of economic incarceration.

This lowly and dehumanizing condition of slavery bred a group of people who were conditioned by their captors to be inferior. Racism soon developed to justify the primary economic motives and clear the conscience of the slave master who at times professed to be a Christian.

The most wretched and vile experience of human existence became entangled in the controversy of regional differences. The south had become comfortable with the slave system and the economic, political and social existence of the south reflected the priority of the slave system. The northern states did not rely on a economic system based on slavery. The north wanted the United States of America, meaning all the states, north and south to move toward industrial development. The agricultural south disagreed and like a spiteful child they chose to leave the union and become rebels. Thus, the Civil War came to be fought over the right of the slave states to keep intact the slave system.

During the Civil War countless men died over the question of slavery. It is for sure that the armed struggle over whether America would be slave or free firmly rooted racism in America. The end of the Civil War, even with a northern victory did not end racism. After a short-lived period of Black freedom in the south, racist laws were again placed on the books. Jim Crow emerged and white terrorist organizations were established.

During slavery Blacks had not merely accepted bondage. Thus it is a myth that Blacks did not move toward the natural impulse to rebel against oppression. For the record, in all instances of oppression there are cowards and Uncle Toms that fear their oppressors and will not rise against them. For the natural warrior oppression breeds resistance and the more the oppression the more the resistance. In this case resistance is only terminated when death meets the oppressor or death meets those oppressed. Often slaves revolted and historic Black role models and heroes were realized in the leadership of those who led revolts against slavery in every way they could.

The militant and independent protest against slavery and the sub-human treatment of Black people was virtually silenced. Racism eventually produced a model for Black leadership that would be advantageous to white America and detrimental to Blacks in America. Thus, the emergence with the support and public relations efforts of a sick racist society was ungodly traitors like Booker T. Washington. He set the paradigm and created the precedent for the dependent attitude of so-called Black leadership.

Sadly, the weak among the Black community emerged to lead our people toward disrespect. The courage to die for freedom, independence and manhood was lost to those who included the ways of Judas and were paid and given concessions over their people.

This attitude also produced Black organizations established by white people who claimed to be liberals. Some were liberal, but the organizations as control factors became supported by racists and those who sought to deny Black people independence and freedom.

Some understanding of these factors are very important in placing the events of the life of Big Ralph in proper perspective. The various facets of racism most likely had the most serious impact on the various circumstances of Big Ralph's work in law enforcement. Finally chapter one attempts to give a historical development of the various factors that affect Big Ralph's life.

In Part II Chapter 2 we look at the birth of Big Ralph and his environment. He was born into a segregated and discriminatory society, but he was too young to realize the situation he was in.

In the second chapter of this section my intent is to show the reality of segregation and Jim Crow. The third chapter is centered on Big Ralph's high school years. The most important aspect in this chapter is the fiasco called school desegregation. The historic justification of Jim Crow and segregation is rooted in various Supreme Court cases. These cases are also examined and finally we review the 1954 Brown v. Board of Education decision.

In this chapter we also look at the paradigm for integrationist philosophy and the confusion of integration and equal rights. This confusion still exists and it is anybody's guess when the confusion will end.

This section concludes with a chapter that gives some evidence of the so-called white liberal. It also takes a close look at the presence of passive resistance. Passive resistance and non-violent protest became the order of the day for the civil rights movement. What were the pros and cons?"

As we move on to the third section of our manuscript the first chapter continues to review the madness of school desegregation. We also analyze the massive civil disobedience movements. The sit-in and freedom rides were the ultimate testimony to civil disobedience. Thus, I make a special effort to discusss these movements in this chapter. Big Ralph is placed in this setting in some respect. But simply what I attempt to do is note the crucial historical events that have a direct bearing on his life as he lived through these events.

The second chapter of the third section of the manuscript mentions civil rights organizations and leadership. When I set the table, I noted information about the initial presence of Black leadership and Black organizing. The importance of this chapter as we conclude is the critique of civil rights organizations and Black leadership.

Moving on, the third chapter in this section takes a close look at civil rights. Thus, I attempt to define civil rights and integration. In these definitive statements, I attempt to note if civil rights and integration are one in the same. Also it is very important what the Black leaders are saying about these two points of interest.

The third section concludes with a chapter that attempts to view some results of the civil rights movement. The impact of traditional Black institutions is a clear indication of what has the civil rights movement brought to the table of Black freedom. Thus, what has been the role of the Black family? What has the Black church offered a despised and hated people? I know that some that read these words may become confused when I use words like hate. You become confused because you practice hate and think that since I label some people as hatemongers I also must hate someone. You could not be further from the truth.

Just because I note the reality of hate in the hearts and minds of those that practice racism does not mean that I hate them. Although they hate me, I don't hate them. If I did, I would be confused and not be able to make the correct analysis. The high road of truth and wisdom is found in the unprejudiced scribe who is free of malice and hate.

In this case may; I please quote the following most powerful scripture references. Colossians 2: 3,4,5,8,9,10. Verse 3 says "In whom are hid all the treasures of wisdom and knowledge. Verse 4 "And this I say, lest any man should beguile you with enticing words. Now let us note Verse 8 "Beware lest any man spoil you through philosophy and vain deceit, after there tradition of men, after the rudiments of the world, and not after Christ."

The school as an institution is also assessed in this chapter. The tragedy and folly of school desegregation is viewed and the role of Black colleges is reviewed. Education is so very important to a people once kept in chains. The present reality is a planned mis-education of Black people organized by racist and carried out by the most part by so-called Black intellectuals.

The dominant culture has a keen awareness of the power of media. Thus, there is a clear policy on the destruction of any independent "Black media source. Here we see the philosophy of Black newspaper publishers for example. Again the interests of Black people are controlled by payoffs and economic concessions.

What is the role of the Black politician? Can he be independent and truly represent the interest of Black people in a racist society? We bring even more clarity to our discussion as we move through the manuscript and as we progress to the present time.

The last section in our manuscript is the fourth section. The first chapter attempts to deal with the kind of atmosphere of the city and the attitude of the police toward Blacks before Blacks came on the force. Here we are better able to understand the impact of the first Black police officers. Here also I note why Big Ralph joined the force and his early impressions of law enforcement.

Chapter two of section four notes that Big Ralph is moving up in the ranks. We continue to review the ongoing dilemma of school desegregation. No doubt the battle over school desegregation causes the segregationist and the integrationist to lose sight of their goals. This is especially true for those in the minority community who initially had some thoughts about equal and quality education.

Also, important in this chapter is the discussion of political violence. The history of political violence is discussed and the types of protest movements are brought up for review. The protest movement involved many facets. Culture and power, are two of the factors defined. Urban rebellions and the violence they provoked are also discussed.

If there is violence there must be some theories also on self-defense. Finally we seek to reconcile and compare the ongoing conflict of civil rights and liberation.

The third chapter in this section takes a close look at specific theories developed by our character. These theories affected his police work and clearly established our character as a great thinker.

The most important principles discussed in this chapter are our character's theories on prevention v. detention. The Chief without a doubt believed that broad based recreational programs would help prevent crime.

It is unfortunate that politics and racism caused a break down in the recreational facilities in Chattanooga. It is even more tragic that the city fathers would not listen to the Chief as he pleaded for organized and planned city-wide recreational programs.

Another important element in this chapter is how the Black community reacted to the police department. This attitude of fear and disrespect by many Blacks results from racism. More specifically it results from police violence. To get a handle on police violence we review the police view of man.

To those outside law enforcement the police view of man is looked upon as a negative reaction. This negative reaction toward man also affects the police response to mass protest. No doubt the question of civilian review boards has had great support among those who have felt victimized by police violence.

The last and final chapter reveals that our character has now been appointed Chief of police. In this chapter we note additional theories of Chief Cothran that has a great impact on his life and his philosophy of law enforcement.

The Chief felt that school desegregation ushered in the downfall of quality education in the school system in Chattanooga. In the process prayer was taken out of the schools and many support services were limited and/or excluded. So while Blacks argued for the right to attend school with white people, the white community was busy establishing private schools throughout the city.

The Chief joined the force during the civil rights era. Thus, he soon came face to face with the civil rights movement. The civil rights movement was a great advocate of mass protest and civil disobedience. Here law enforcement came in direct contact with organized groups that challenged certain laws. These laws were judged to be unjust by the demonstrators and often discriminatory. Thus they felt they had a right to challenge the law and commit acts of civil disobedience.

Surely Jim Crow laws deprived Blacks of rights as human beings. No one can deny this truth, but the Chief also saw another truth. The planned and organized efforts of civil disobedience also established a particular philosophy toward authority. Here the Chief notes that this psychological conditioning also resulted in the criminal behavior of later generations. This criminal behavior sometimes is rooted in the attack on authority and basic institutions in our society.

The Chief often noted that the use and sell of drugs were the leading cause of criminal behavior. He also knew that one must be aware of why people got involved in the use and sell of drugs. The Chief was hard on criminals but he also had compassion for his fellowman. Thus, he looked for ways to prevent crime. He also knew the problem of drugs was at our borders and that any city could be cleaned up of drugs.

Police brutality had been an ongoing problem within the Chattanooga police Department. The Chief's record speaks for itself. He knew that this was a problem and he immediately dealt with this issue and won the support of the Black community for the police department.

This chapter also gives important information regarding the corruption in the narcotic's division. Ralph H. Cothran was the first Black Chief in the history of the Chattanooga police Department. He was also most likely the first honest Chief. These two factors, his race, and his honesty had a direct impact on how he was perceived by his superiors and those who made a career out of criminal activity.

The allegations of Chief Cothran being involved in the mis-use of drug funds came about during his illness. Those who were most affected by his principles most likely started the allegations. Tragically the ugly head of racism does not care if a man is on his death bed, or not far removed from passing on.

Those who made the unfounded charges knew of the health of Chief Cothran. They also knew he was innocent. They also knew that the chemical treatments he received for his illness would hasten his death.

The Chief loved his city and by the grace of God his name was not tainted in the scheme of corruption. Big Ralph was willing to dedicate his life to Chattanooga and elements in Chattanooga were willing to take his life because he was Black and because he was honest. It is a crying shame that those inspired by the devil do not realize the power of God as the protector of those that believe.

TABLE OF CONTENTS

Foreword		i
Preface		v
PART ONE:	**THE MYSTERIES OF OUR PAST**	
Chapter One:	Introduction: The Seeds Of Protest	1
PART TWO:	**SEGREGATION AND INTEGRATION**	
Chapter Two:	Bushtown 1938	39
Chapter Three:	Orchard Knob School	53
Chapter Four:	Howard School 1954	65
Chapter Five:	Black Integrationist And White Liberals: The White Backlash	87
PART THREE:	**THE CIVIL. RIGHTS MOVEMENT**	
Chapter Six:	College Experiences: Blacks Challenge Discrimination	109
Chapter Seven:	Little Rock Air Force Base: Civil Rights Organization And Leadership	131
Chapter Eight:	The Cultural South: Does Civil Rights Mean Integration?	159
Chapter Nine:	Youth And Civil Rights: Some Results Of The Movement	177
PART FOUR:	**CRIME IN AMERICA**	
Chapter Ten:	Chattanooga Police Department 1964: Politics And Crime	199
Chapter Eleven:	Moving up In The Ranks: Protest And Violence	211
Chapter Twelve:	Police Reviews: Detention vs. Prevention	243
Chapter Thirteen:	The Leadership Ranks: Parallels Of Crime And Civil Rights	269
Concluding Thoughts		293
Endnotes		298
Appendix		357

Part I. The Mysteries Of Our Past

Chapter One

The Seeds Of Protest
**Fleeting times gone, that show records
by the scribes of struggle, confusion and suffering,
Hence we grow with this knowledge to understand
the present and future.**

On the third of May 1938 when Ralph Henry Cothran was born, the world was on the eve of another world war. Holly Street where Ralph was born is on the eastside. Black people in Chattanooga call this area of Chattanooga "Bushtown." Bushtown is north of the Highland Park community that is on the southern side of east Third Street. Located in Chattanooga, Tennessee, right over the Third Street viaduct, Bushtown was a world away from Europe and the rise of Nazi Germany.

Bessie Hilda Neal Cothran and Charles (Charlie) Henry Cothran were hard working and Ralph was the second child. His sister, Hilda had been born a few years earlier. Charlie would soon join the army to fight for world peace. In March 1938 Hitler's Nazi troops occupied Austria and by September Hitler was preparing to occupy Czechoslovakia.

In as much as Hitler made his greatest impact as a conqueror of Europe he also established a particular philosophy. As we address the issues of the day that would affect Ralph later in life, we cannot leave out the father of white supremacy. It for sure, that even in the 90's, many groups, hold the philosophy of Hitler in high esteem. Many of those that share Hitler's beliefs are organized and threaten the security and safety of institutions and individuals in this country. The agenda for these white

• Big Ralph

supremacy groups now includes persons, places and institutions on their hate list and not merely just nonwhites. Soon young Ralph would grasp the essence of these concerns as they would eventually affect the Black American experience.

Ralph was still a baby and was not aware that soon his father would be thrust into the madness of war. Charlie Cothran served with high distinction and was awarded the bronze star for heroism. Charlie was a big man, strong, and at least six foot five inches tall. Ralph would grow to the stature of his father and inherit his courage and strength.

The world as a changing place was one thing but so were the changing conditions in America. In view of the Black experience significant changes had taken place. Most importantly how did Blacks get to this point?

One must set the table to review aspects of the life of Ralph Henry Cothran. Ralph eventually confronts the serious questions of his day as a law enforcement officer.

The birth of Ralph H. Cothran in Chattanooga, Tennessee in the United States of America was a result of the most dramatic and impacting episode in human history placed on a race of people. In Jamestown, Virginia, August 1619, twenty Blacks of Spanish surnames were sold, and exchanged for food and supplies.

"The twenty Black seeds of Jamestown were farmed out to various officials of the colony and they were farmed out as servants and not as slaves. In court and church records, the first Black Americans were listed as servants. This is a point of immense significance in the history of America. The first Black immigrants were not slaves; nor were the first White immigrants free." [1]

Thus North America is not the original home of the people who were the ancestors of the people called Black Americans in. These original people came from Africa. Nor is North America the original home of the people who had already began to settle along the eastern shores of the area called North America. These people were Europeans, who came to settle and claim land inhabited by the native Americans that became known as American Indians.

Chapter One

These circumstances were a distant mystery of the past on May 3, 1938. It would be sometime before Ralph would realize that the historical development of Black people in North America would be necessary to unravel the social problems of his day.

To set the stage for this biographical reflective work I feel that there are particular circumstances and events that must be discussed. First a description of slavery is very important. At this point I feel obligated to make a particular observation. There are those that seek to discount the knowledge of history in an assessment of present and future problems that plague people throughout the world.

Evidently those that subscribe to this view are the cadre of human beings that have an ongoing duel with ignorance. The human being that does not think and develop his mind remains ignorant and flirts with stupidity occasionally. Some thinkers argue that these people are dumb, stupid and blind. Despite the ignorance of those that seek to discount the validity of history and knowledge, there are at least some human beings that seek to think and develop their mind.

With that point made I now will continue the discussion on particular historical points of interests as the introduction to this biographical work. As I previously mentioned, a description of slavery is very important. The first significant presence of Blacks in America was as slaves. This system of bondage has had a devastating effect on Black people. Thus, the legacy of slavery is a root cause of many contemporary problems with which Black Americans are confronted.

Thus, I argue that often present day problems in the Black community depict a clear historical development during the days of slavery. Therefore, a clear and intelligent understanding of slavery will benefit our understanding of present and future problems and concerns.

Secondly, Black leadership is very important. What type of leaders did Black people have during and after slavery? What was the philosophy of these leaders? There are always varied leadership styles and postures in the various histories of people. The Black experience in North America is no exception.

The third and last topic of discussion in this introductory section will

• **Big Ralph**

look at significant periods after slavery. reconstruction will be a topic noted along with organizations for Blacks. This discussion will end at the time in which Ralph Cothran was born.

"The slave system made the Negro grovel before his master. It destroyed his personality and initiative and his family life. So completely dependent was the slave upon his master that in return for even small favors, he gave support to the very system of slavery that was destroying him."[2]

It is documented that the psychological effects of slavery have had a great impact on Black people overtime. This premeditated system of mental control has seen no rivals. But there has been some comparative analysis made between slavery and Jews being held in Nazi concentration camps. *Charles Silberman* in his book "Crisis In Black and White" quotes *Stanley M. Elkins* who did a probing study of slavery, entitled "Slavery: A Problem In American Institutional And Intellectual Life."

Elkins in a probing study of slavery has "pointed out the parallels between the way the Nazi concentration camps changed the personalities of the prisoners who survived and the way in which slavery in the American south altered the personalities of Negroes brought from Africa and shaped the character of Negroes born here."[3] Concerning personality changes *Elkins* gives us further information on these changes with a more detailed description.

"The most striking aspect of the concentration camp inmates behavior, *Elkins* writes after surveying the extensive literature on the subject "was its childlike quality." Many inmates ---among them mature independent, highly educated adults--were transformed into fawning, servile, dependent children. Infantile behavior took a variety of forms: The inmate's sexual impotence caused a disappearance of sexuality in their talk; instead, excretory functions occupied them endlessly. They lost many customary inhibitions as to soiling their beds and their persons. Their humor was shot with silliness and they giggled like children when one of them would expel wind. Dishonesty was endemic; prisoners became chronic pathological liars; like adolescents, they would fight each other bitterly one moment and become close friends in

Chapter One

the next; "dishonesty, mendacity, egotistic actions,... thefts were commonplace."[4]

The crude and cruel results of concentration life without a doubt have also had an effect on the Jewish people over time. Concentration camp inmates were transformed into servile children in months and years. "The American Negro has been subject to a system designed to destroy ambition, prevent independence, and erode intelligence for the past three and a half centuries."[5] Professor Kenneth Stampp makes the following comment on slavery "there were plenty of opportunists among the Negroes who played the role assigned to them, acted the clown, and curried the favor of their masters to win the maximum rewards within the system."[6]

The docile role practiced by many slaves eventually had a direct affect on slave uprisings and rebellions. "From 1619-1865 slaves staged over 30 separate insurrections against their masters. *Nat Turner* on August 22, 1831, led the most significant of these uprisings."[7]

Although there is evidence to support the lack of unity and various other problems in many slave rebellions, I would argue that all slave rebellions were significant. *Professor Stampp* makes the following assessment of slave rebellions. Professor Stampp also cites a view by Professor Aptheker.

"The two best organized---those led by *Versey* and *Gabriel*-were suppressed quite easily, and the most dramatic, the *Nat Turner* rebellion, was little more than aimless butchery. The remaining "revolts," even under *Professor Aptheker's* sympathetic description, are clearly insignificant--little more than outbreaks of local vandalism. More to the point, the rebellions were suppressed easily, in part because they involved only a handful of slaves, and in good measure because fellow slaves almost invariable informed on the rebels."[8]

So slavery did cause a rebellious attitude among many slaves. Usually man will rise to confront oppression and inhumane treatment, but all revolts are not successful in the sense that they accomplish what they set out to do. In the Black experience all the rebellions and uprisings against oppression have had a definite significance. The most dramatic revolt is one that causes change or a change in the political, economic and social arenas to include those oppressed.

What was this system of slavery? What was so different about American slavery from slavery throughout the history of man? What was unique about the American slave system that still has many Black people confused during contemporary times? Yes, even 130 years after slavery we can still detect the root causes of many of our problems to be a result of the most dehumanizing episode in the annals of humanity.

Silberman in "Crisis In Black White" quotes *Tocqueville* as a means to determine the realities of American slavery and race/color and the stigma of slavery. "There is a natural prejudice that prompts men to despise whoever has been their inferior after he has become their equal." [9]

The statement by *Tocqueville* stands with sound reasoning and logic. The natural tendency of man is to form class lines and distinctions. Freedom, civil rights and laws do not, and cannot change attitudes and rid man of certain prejudices about other people.

Propelled by the stigma of color, slavery in the U.S. and colonial outposts throughout the Western Hemisphere was totally unlike slavery that had existed anywhere else in the world. *Silberman* notes that *Tocqueville* saw the distinctions between the slave system in the west and ancient slavery. "The only means by which the ancients maintained slavery were fetters and death; the Americans of the south have discovered more intellectual securities for the duration of their power. They have employed their despotism and their violence against the human mind." The ancients, *Tocqueville* pointed out, took care to prevent the slave from breaking his chains. The Southerners, by contrast, have adapted "measures to deprive him even of his desire for freedom." [10]

The question can be asked, what happened to transform the heroic African into the submissive slave? "For one thing, the process of enslavement subjected the African to a series of traumas that tended to sever him from his culture and institutions and destroy his sense of identity." [11]

"The Romans (as did most other ancients) saw slavery as a normal condition of man –the result of accident and misfortune, rather than of

Chapter One

human nature. In this view, slavery affected only the body of the slave–that is, only his labor: his mind and soul remained free. Spiritually, the slave was his master's equal; intellectually, he could be his superior."[12]

"When Negro slavery began in Spain and Portugal in about the mid-fifteenth century–a century and a half before it was introduced into North America–the slaves found not just a tradition of slavery but an incredibly elaborate body of law and custom designed to protect the slave's status as a human being."[13]

Professor *Frank Tannenbaum* says "for all practical purposes slavery in South America became a contractual arrangement that could be wiped out by a fixed purchase price"---a contract, moreover, in which a master owned a man's labor, not the man himself."[14]

Sambo and other myths about Blacks became prevalent in the U.S. and served to entrench the deep psychological results of slavery." Sambo never took roots in South America. But he flourished in the U.S., however. For on this continent, slavery developed in such a way as to convince the whites that Negroes were inherently inferior and incapable of freedom."[15]

Silberman notes two reasons for the crude form of slavery that developed in America. "Slavery took its peculiar and brutal form in the U.S. (and all other English colonies) precisely because there was no precedent either in tradition or in common law."[16]

Slave laws were evidence of the cold stark brutality of slavery. Especially dehumanizing was slave law that governed marriage and the status of children, but the forced breeding of slaves was even worst.

"Slave law not only refused to recognize marriage, it reversed the common-law tradition that children derive their status from their father, maintaining that "the father of a slave is unknown to our law." To have held otherwise would have raised the embarrassing question of what to do with the children born of a white father and a slave mother; the old common law would have created a large class of free mulattoes."[17]

Europeans had sexual relationships with slave women for a variety of reasons. The men to women ratio in the settlements had a direct affect on these illicit relationships. "The shortage of slave women, moreover-

--with the interferences imposed upon the slave trade in the late 18th and early 19th centuries---led to the ultimate perversion; the breeding of slaves like cattle." [18]

For one group of human beings to breed another group of human beings like lower animals takes a certain attitude. Therefore the Europeans who enslaved Blacks conditioned themselves to accept the inferior status of Blacks as lower animals.

"Having erected the system of slavery on the assumption of Negro inferiority, and having produced the behavior that seemed to justify the assumption, it was inevitable that America would refuse to admit free Negroes to full membership in their society. slavery became associated with race, and race with inferiority; the two concepts merged. And so Black meant inferior: meant Black." [19]

So as this decadent system flourished voices of leadership arose to meet this challenge. Leadership has always, been important in the history of Black people in North America. So when we talk about early Black leadership we can begin to grab a handle on the historical development of Black leadership and its particular philosophy.

Black leadership arose to combat the conditions of slavery. "As a result of the slave trade, white Europeans became a single group opposed to the rest of the world, and a new and terrifying idea was invented: the idea of subordination and superordination based on skin color." [20]

racism as a thought pattern came into existence to justify the slave system. In so doing Europeans justified their actions by convincing themselves that Blacks were an inferior race of sub-humans. "Slavery, contrary to the general impression, did not spring from racism; racism sprang from slavery. The concept of race was a direct outgrowth of the slave trade. And it was deliberately invented by an exploiting group that needed a theology to maintain and defend privileges on naked force." [21]

Early significant Black leadership in North America was shown by *Frederick Douglass, Booker T. Washington, W.E.B.DuBois* and *Marcus Garvery. Prince Hall, Charles L. Redmond, Charles Sumner, George T. Downing,* the latter two even though not well known, also had an impact on Black leadership.

Chapter One

Also one cannot discount the leadership projected by those that led slave revolts and rebellions. All attempts of rebellion against the criminal slave system were acts of independence. For reasons based on their ethnic orientation European scholars in recounting the period of slave rebellions try to evaluate the merits and impact of slave rebellions by using purely the scientific method of analysis. From the Black perspective any revolt against the white man in this instance was positive. Because, the system of slavery, as noted by these same European scholars, was designed to destroy the Black man's will and desire to revolt. I would argue that the system was designed to turn Black people into docile, submissive Uncle Toms with the genes of Booker T. Washington, guaranteeing the white man a race destined to serve him. Meanwhile this system produced many Blacks that were content and happy to serve the white man and felt licking his boots was an honor and privilege. Snitchers and traitors were bred like cockroaches. In fact Black traitors that informed the white slave masters caused many slave revolts to be hampered and disrupted. One has to realize that this country was born by revolt against oppression and tyranny.

By 1776 with the colonial revolution on the horizon calculated and organized Black leadership began to unfold. "In 1776, American patriots held some five hundred thousand human beings, some of them whites in servitude. And yet they chose to make a revolution in support of human equality. By this incredible act, the partriots sowed the seeds of continuous conflict."[22] This conflict still rages as Blacks still fight for full citizenship and the right to live as human beings. " Negroes, as a group, did not exist before the revolution. The development of a national Negro group with a common viewpoint and a consciousness of common fate was a product of a syndrome that recurs repeatedly in the history of the American Negro---the sudden dilation of the Negro mood under the impact of a war for freedom and the sudden contraction of the mood in the wake of postwar reaction became a reality." [23]

The Negro freedom movement began to evolve during the period the patriots revolted against their colonial rulers. "The Negro church, from which came the current freedom movement, the first Negro newspaper, the first Negro mass meeting, the first Negro convention: all date from the pioneer period between 1780-1830." [24]

"*Richard Allen* was the first national Negro leader, a pioneer Negro abolitionist, and the organizer and president of the first Negro convention held in the western world." [25] "*Daniel Coker, Richard Allen's* great rival, and *John B. Russwrum*, the first Negro college graduate, were among the first converts to the colonization cause." [26]

The colonization movement however stirred opposing viewpoints. "Out of the ferment of the defensive anti-colonization movement came the first militant • abolitionists and the first Negro newspaper, Freedom's Journal, which was published for the first time on March 16, 1827, by *Samuel E. Cornish* and *John B. Russwrum*. In its first issue, the paper struck a note of militant protest: we wish to plead our own cause. Too long have others spoken for us. " [27]

"Another sign of internal stirring was the Negro convention movement that began in 1830, three years before the founding of the American antislavery society. After 1830, northern Negroes met in convention and hammered out pleas and admonitions to their white brothers." [28]

Frederick Douglass became the leading black abolitionists of his day. *Douglass* escaped from slavery in 1838 and soon after began a career as an activist for freedom and human rights for Black people. The prominence and impact of the *Douglass* personality is a gauge to judge and compare Black leadership styles overtime.

There are some social thinkers that accept the notion that during slavery and Jim Crow Blacks had to take a submissive attitude. Those that share this view evidently have discarded the militant posture of the rebellious personas of *Nat Turner, Denmark Versey, and Gabriel Prosser*, and all other Black men that rose to bear arms in defiance of slavery. Also, these particular social thinkers have not placed the time of *Frederick Douglass'* activism adequately. To get to the point, *Douglass* came before *Booker T. Washington* who accepted the submissive role of Blacks while *Douglass* spoke for pride and did not concede to white supremacy.

As we briefly critique the leadership styles and impact of *Douglass, Washington, DuBois and Garvey* it is of note that we began with the

Chapter One

hallmark of *Washington's* argument. This argument resides in the direction of Black people to manual arts and not intellectual goals.

Douglass also spoke of the need for Blacks to develop manual and mechanical skills, but he did not speak of these vocations in the context of the *Booker T. Washington* philosophy. In a letter to *Harriet Beecher Stowe*, March 8, 1853, *Douglass* asserts that "poverty, ignorance and degradation are the combined evils; or in other words, these constitute the social disease of the free colored people of the U.S." [29]

Douglass continues in the letter to *Stowe* to describe just how white America can help Blacks eliminate the social disease of poverty, ignorance and degradation. Thus, removing Blacks from this threefold malady would put them on equal standing with whites.

"First, not by establishing for our use high schools and colleges. Such institutions are, in my judgment, beyond our immediate occasions and are not adapted to our present most pressing wants. High schools and colleges are excellent institutions, and will in due season be greatly subservient to our progress; but they are the result, as well as they are the demand, of a point of progress which we, as a people, have not yet attained. Accustomed as we have been to the rougher and harder modes of living and of gaining a livelihood, we cannot and we ought not to hope that in a single leap from our low condition, we can reach that of ministers, lawyers, doctors, editors, merchants etc. These will doubtless be attained by us; but this will only be when we have patiently and laboriously, and I may add successfully, mastered and passed through the intermediate gradations of agriculture and the mechanic Arts." [30]

On the surface it seems as if *Douglass* is preaching the industrial education views of *Booker T. Washington*. *Douglass*, however is simply making logical statements in assessing the conditions of a people whose majority is still enslaved. At this point refining basic necessities was most important and basic education would lay the foundation for intellectual pursuits in the future. Also, no where in *Douglass'* dialogue do you see any acceptance of the Uncle Tom syndrome and the alleged inferior role of Black people.

There are two good examples in the writings of *Booker T. Washington* that reveal his inferiority complexes. The prominent and most well known

• Big Ralph

is "The Atlanta Exposition Address" in 1895. In this address we see the classic reasoning for second -class citizenship and the broken spirit of *Booker T. Washington* as a Negro with a slave mentality. Let us now digest the accommodations thought of *Washington*.

"We will enter into a new era of industrial progress. Ignorant and inexperienced, it is not strange that in the first years of our new life we began at the top instead of at the bottom, that a seat in Congress or the state legislature was more sought than real estate or industrial skill; that the political convention of stump speaking had more attractions than starting a diary farm or truck garden." [31]

In this instance *Washington* is most likely referring to the emancipation of Blacks as slaves and the constitutional rights of citizenship and the right to vote and hold elective office. These gains came soon after emancipation and ushered in the reconstruction era.

Washington uses the terminology "we began at the top and not at the bottom." In this instance *Washington* implies that Blacks are destined to be on the bottom and that this is the rightful place for Blacks. He does not consider the need for Blacks to enter all ranks of society and not the acceptance of farming etc. as the only means for Black survival. During the time of Booker T. Washington the reconstruction era was over and Jim Crow was on the move and Blacks were being lynched and murdered throughout America. So during the period when Black people were lynched as if it was legal and lawful, *Washington* spoke and tried to influence Black people to accept a role of serving white people as their permanent domestic servants/slaves.

The south, the land of slavery was not the only region guilty of the wholesale carnival spectacle of lynching. For the record Black people were lynched all over the United States. *Washington* continues in his Atlanta address and further reveals the subordinate position he takes concerning Black people.

"To those of my race who depend on bettering their condition in a foreign land or who underestimate the importance of cultivating friendly relations with the southern white man, who is their next door neighbor, I would say: cast down your bucket where you are--cast it down in making friends in every manly way of the people of all races by whom we are surrounded. Cast it down in agriculture, in mechanics, in commerce,

Chapter One

in domestic service, and in the professions."[32]

Although Washington was an educator he felt Black people would prosper more by working with their hands. Sure there is dignity in any honest profession but an entire group seeking dignity from agriculture in a vastly changing world is a people accepting slavery and the plantation mentality.

The following passage clearly reveals why white people loved *Washington* and loudly applauded his speech throughout America and the world.

"No race can prosper till it learns that there is as much dignity in tilling a field as in writing a poem. It is at the bottom of life we must begin, and not at the top. Nor should we permit our grievances to overshadow our opportunities. While doing this, you can be sure in the future, as in the past, that you and your families will be surrounded by the most patient, faithful, law-abiding, and unresentful people that the world has seen. As we have proved our loyalty to you in the past, in nursing your children, watching by the sickbed of your mothers and fathers, and often following them with tear-dimmed eyes to their graves, so in the future, in our humble way, we will stand by you with a devotion that no foreigner can approach, ready to lay down our lives, if need be, in defence of yours, interlacing our industrial, commercial, civil, and religious life with yours in a way that shall make the interests of both races' one. In all things that are purely social we can be as separate as the fingers, yet one as the hand in all things essential to mutual progress."[33]

This should be enough to assess the subordinate slave position that *Washington* took, but, one more excerpt from his address is even more revealing. No doubt *Washington's philosophy* would encourage and condition Blacks to fetch the lynch rope and relish and accept the whip as rightful punishment for Blacks. It is for sure that *Washington's* views are sickening but, the greatest crime is the system of racism created by white people that produced this demeaning and insulting attitude by Blacks like *Booker T. Washington*. "The wisest among my race understand that the agitation of questions of social equality is the extremist folly, and that progress in the enjoyment of all privileges that will come to us must be the result of severe and constant struggle rather than artificial forcing."[34]

• **Big Ralph**

The previous quotation from *Washington's* Atlanta address speaks for itself. The more you read about *Washington* the more confused you get because he was a man of blind vision. To bring into focus what I believe to be blind vision, we will draw upon another writing by *Washington*. The writing is titled "Industrial Education For The Negro" and was printed in the book "The Negro Problem" in 1903.

"It has been necessary for the Negro to learn the difference between being worked and working--to learn that being worked meant degradation, while working means civilization: that all forms of labor are honorable, and all forms of idleness disgraceful. It has been necessary for him to learn that all races that have gotten on their feet have done so largely by laying an economic foundation, and, by beginning in a proper cultivation and ownership of the soil." [35]

It is true that Black people need an economic foundation, This was true during the days of *Washington* and is still true in the present world. We still do not have an economic foundation because of the confusion of leadership like that of *Booker T.Washington*. It is illogical to think that a people who accepts a slave mentality will ever have economic parity with the dominant group in America or have any other semblance of parity with white America.

Washington continues with his blind vision as he further illustrates the need for Blacks to work in an exclusive service capacity. "Our knowledge must be harnessed to the things or real life. I would encourage the Negro to secure all the mental strength, all the mental culture--whether gleaned from science, mathematics, history language or literature that his circumstances will allow, but I believe most earnestly that for years to come the education of the people of my race would be so directed that the greatest proportion of the mental strength of the masses will be brought to bear upon the every day practical things of life." [36]

As *Washington* continues his plea for Blacks to work in industrial education we see clear evidence of his confusion. In an oppressive society, with this oppression based on economic exploitation and justified by racism, how can one enter the commercial arena? Also *Washington* unconsciously exposes his inferiority complex as he often uses the word shiftless in describing a major problem among Black

Chapter One

workers. How could a Black man at the turn of the century, who recently had been a slave be shiftless. Unfortunately *Washington* was such a clone Uncle Tom that he had also picked up the white man's terminology. Most likely white plantation owners etc. began calling Black slaves shiftless when they were creative in keeping the white man from working him to death on slave plantations.

Let's allow *Washington* to continue to get more details of his vision. "I would not confine the race to industrial life, not even to agriculture, for example, although I believe that by far the greater part of the Negro race is best off in the country districts and must and should continue to live there." [37]

"I plead for industrial education and development for the Negro not because I want to cramp him, but because I want to free him. I want to see him enter the all powerful business and commercial world. Many seem to think that industrial education is meant to make the Negro work as he worked in the days of slavery. This is far from my conception of industrial education. If this training is worth anything to the Negro, it consists in teaching him how not to work, but how to make the forces of nature--air, steam, water, horsepower and electricity work for him. If it has any value it is in lifting labor up out of toil and drudgery into the place of dignified and the beautiful. The Negro in the south works and works hard; but too often his ignorance and lack of skill causes him to do his work in the most costly and shiftless manner, and this keeps him near the bottom of the ladder in the economic world." [38]

I would argue that *Booker T. Washington* was the supreme architect of Black Uncle Tom thinking. Surely there were Uncle Toms among Black people before *Washington* arrived on the scene but no one among the Black race in America sought to develop Uncle Tomism into a science like *Booker T. Washington*. The cornerstone of Black inferiority solidly implanted by *Washington* is the only sanctioned leadership philosophy accepted, promoted and supported by white America even today.

Those that take an independent stance are destroyed and are not noted by white America as leaders for Black people. For example the traditional civil rights organizations and their leaders are considered the top Black

• **Big Ralph**

leaders by white America. These organizations carry the torch of *Booker T. Washington* as they play a confidence game on Black people and are financed by white corporations and the federal government.

To further illustrate that Black leadership before *Washington* was independent we will return to *Frederick Douglass*. In an article titled "The Present And Future of the Colored race in America" *Douglass* advocates full equality for Black people.

"Save the Negro and you save the nation, destroy the Negro and you destroy the nation, and to save both you must have but one great law of Liberty, Equality and Fraternity for all Americans without respect to color." [39]

"There are at least four answers, other than mine, floating about in the public mind, to the question, what shall be done with the Negro?

1. It is said that the white race can, if they will, reduce the whole colored population to slavery.

2. The next and best defined solution of our difficulties about the Negro is colonization, which proposes to send the Negro back to Africa.

3. It may be said as another mode of escaping the claims of absolute justice, the white people may emancipate the slaves in form yet retain them as slaves in fact just as *General Banks* is now doing in Louisiana.

4. The white people of the country may trump up some cause of war against the colored people, and wage that terrible war of races and exterminate the Black race entirely." [40]

Douglass is already on record for his utility of the idea of agitation for Blacks to achieve equal rights. In the following quotation in this instance *Douglass* notes that equality for Blacks will not only save Blacks but also America.

"There is but one way of disposing of the colored race, and that is to do them right and justice. It is not only to break the chains of their bondage and accord to them personal liberty, but it is to admit them to the full and complete enjoyment of civil and political equality." [41]

The first thing to consider in the comparative critique of *Douglass* and *Washington* is the time in which they lived. *Douglass was* born in 1818, escaped from slavery in 1838 and soon after became an

Chapter One

abolitionist, writer, spokesperson and activist for the equality of Black people in North America. *Douglass* died in 1895 and was a strong symbol of Black pride and uncompromising resistance to oppression.

On the other hand *Washington* was born a slave in 1856. He was educated at *Hampton Normal and Agricultural Institute*. In 1881 he was chosen to head the *Tuskegee Normal and Industrial Institute*, which was modeled after *Hampton Institute*.

At *Tuskegee, Washington* attempted to carry out his vision of Blacks developing practical skills for survival. He died at *Tuskegee* on November 14, 1915.

In view of the times in which they lived even though they overlap-- *Douglass* defeats the theory that agitation was not realistic during slavery or early Jim Crow. *Douglass* endured his experiences as a slave but was never psychologically broken to the point where he would hand his master the whip and lynch rope. While *Washington* was broken in spirit and fit the mold of the happy, brow bending, Negro, *Douglass* was just the opposite. Form my analysis of Washington's writings I would argue that he accepted slavery as if it was a privilege.

There are those that might say well at least *Washington* didn't marry a white woman. It is true that in later years *Douglass* took as his second wife a white woman. Most likely from this experience *Douglass* gained even more insight into the attitudes and motivations of white America.

So as Douglass faded from the scene *Washington* was steam rolling ahead as the leading spokesperson for Black America. *Washington* would soon meet his most serious challenge as the leading spokesperson for Black people. W.E.B. *DuBois* became involved in the cause of Black equality because of the insulting conciliatory tactics of *Booker T. Washington.*

DuBois was born in 1868 in Massachusetts, and received a Ph.D. from Harvard in 1895. He became one of the founders of the NAACP and as a teacher, scholar and writer he was an activist for Black equality until 1963 when he died at the age of 95.

DuBois had a significant impact as the editor of the *Crisis*, a magazine published by the NAACP. As a writer for the *Crisis, DuBois*

• Big Ralph

reveals his philosophy toward Black equality, in an article titled "The immediate Program of the American Negro."

"The American Negro demands political equality, industrial equality and social equality; and he is never going to rest satisfied with anything else."[42]

DuBois sounds a lot like *Frederick Douglass* but there is no comparison to *Booker T. Washington.* To get a full view of the thinking of *DuBois* I will note detailed excerpts from this article and offer another article up for review.

"In social intercourse every effort is being made today from the president of the United States and the so-called Church of Christ down to saloons and bootblacks to segregate, strangle and spiritually starve Negroes to give them the least possible chance to know and share civilization.

The practical steps to this are clear. First we must fight obstructions; by continual and increasing effort we must first make American courts either build up a body of decisions that will protect the plain legal rights of American citizens to oppress a few.

We must secondly seek in the legislature and the congress remedial legislation; in national and in public school education, the removal of all legal discriminations based simply on race and color, and those marriage laws passed to make the seduction of Black girls easy and without legal penalty.

Third the human contact of human beings must be increased.

Fourth only the publication of the truth repeatedly and incisively and uncompromisingly can secure that change in public opinion that will correct these awful lies. *The Crisis*, our record of the darker races, must have a circulation not of 35,000 chiefly among the colored folk but of a least 250,000 among all men who believe in men. A voice that thunders fact and is more anxious to be true than in pleasing."[43]

DuBois in his explicit style clearly reveals what he views as the major obstructions to the cause of Black equality. He continues to articulate his program for Blacks as he lists what he calls the concerns of constructive effort.

"Let us now turn to constructive effort. This may be summed up

Chapter One

under (1) Economic cooperation (2) A revival of art and literature (3) Political Action (4) Education and (5) Organization.

Under economic cooperation we must strive to spread the idea among colored people that the accumulation of wealth is for social rather than individual ends. In art and literature we should try to loose the tremendous emotional wealth of the Negro and the dramatic strength of his problems through writing etc. In political action we should organize the votes of Negroes in such congressional districts that have any number of Negro voters. In education we must seek to give colored children free public school training. We must watch with grave suspicion the attempt of those who, under the guise of vocational training, would fasten ignorance and menial service on the Negro for another generation. Our children must not, in large numbers, be forced into the servant class; for menial service is still in the main, little more than an antiquated survival of impossible conditions."[44]

All of the previous points made by *DuBois* are very important for Black progress, but the position *DuBois* takes on, education is more significant. Mainly because *Booker T. Washington* had confused the need for Blacks to educate themselves with his servant mentality. Clearly *DuBois* and *Washington* stood on opposite poles and the friction between them heightened as *Washington* resented any threat to his assigned leadership role as the major spokesperson or leader for Black people in North America.

DuBois concludes with another important point. Unfortunately though the *NAACP* eventually also succumbed to white sponsorship and domination.

"I thank God that most of the money that supports the *NAACP* comes from Black hands; a still larger proportion must so come, and we must not only support but control this and similar organizations and hold them unwaveringly to our objects, our aims and our ideals."[45]

Booker T. Washington set the precedent for manipulated and controlled Black leadership, which is often described as Uncle Tomism. In so doing, *Washington* also set the precedent for payoffs, and the white sponsorship of Black organizations, institutions, etc.

• Big Ralph

Undoubtedly the white power structure has groomed what white people call, good Black leaders by donating money to their causes, organizations and institutions. It is only human nature to control what you buy. So white America controlled *Tuskegee* because they gave *Washington* the money to operate the school.

As the debate between *Washington* and *DuBois* came to a close with the death of *Washington* in 1915, there was soon another significant figure on the scene. Here we can draw certain parallels between *Douglass, Washington, DuBois* and *Marcus Garvey*. These parallels I would argue reflect the specific precedents that each established regarding a major philosophical posture.

In the case of *Douglass* he set the standard for Black leadership to be uncompromising in the pursuit of freedom, justice and equality for Black people. *Washington* discarded this philosophy and adopted a accommodationist and subordinate role. Thus he set the precedents for Black leadership to be brow benders, who relish the manipulation and control by white people.

DuBois related to *Douglass* in his interest in arguing for the cause of Black equality. Specifically *DuBois* set the precedent for the logical approach to defining segregation. This definitive statement by *DuBois* logically also gives a definitive description to integration. This statement by *DuBois* was made in the *Crisis* in 1934, but by 1954 the question of what is segregation and what is integration loomed over America like a dense and endless thunder cloud.

Before we get back to *DuBois* and his article we must conclude our discussion of the significant precedents set by our leaders with *Marcus Garvey*. *Garvey* adopted the style of *Douglass* as he was militant. He did not get along to well with *DuBois* because he was more militant and to the left. In this instance *Garvey* set the precedent for Black Power that would prove to be a moving and dynamic concept of race pride by the 60's.

Now before we discuss *Garvey*, let's return to *DuBois* and his article "Segregation," *The Crisis,* 1934. "The opposition to racial segregation is not, and should not be any distaste or unwillingness of colored people to work with each other, to cooperate with each other, to live with each

Chapter One

other. The opposition to segregation is an opposition to discrimination. The experience in the United States has been that usually when there is racial segregation there is also racial discrimination.

But the two things do not necessarily go together, and there should never be an opposition to segregation pure and simple unless that segregation does involve discrimination. Not only is there no objection to colored people living beside colored people if the surroundings involve no discrimination, if streets are well lighted, if there is water, sewage and police protection, and if anybody of any color who wishes can live in that neighborhood." [46]

There is no difference in the degree of race pride held by *DuBois* and *Garvey*. Because *DuBois* clearly reveals that Blacks should be opposed to segregation only when it discriminates. As *DuBois* continues, he makes specific arguments regarding the school and education.

"The same way in schools, there is no objection to schools attended by colored pupils and taught by colored teachers. On the contrary, colored pupils can by our contention be as fine human beings as any other sort of children, and we certainly know that there are no teachers better than trained colored teachers. But if the existence of such a school is made a reason and cause for giving it worse housing, poorer facilities, poorer equipment and poorer teachers, then we do object, and the objection is not against the color of the pupils' or teachers' skins, but against discrimination." [47]

DuBois concludes his statement with a statement that gives us a clear understanding of what Black people should mean when they talk about segregation-integration.

"Americans stand ready to take the most distinct advantage of voluntary segregation and cooperation among colored people. Just as soon as they get a group of Black folk segregated, they use it as a point of attack and discrimination.

Our counter attack should be, therefore, against this discrimination; against the refusal of the south to spend the same amount of money on the Black child as on the white child for its education; against the inability of Black groups to use public capital; against the monopoly of credit by white groups. But never in the world should our fight be

• **Big Ralph**

against association with ourselves because by that very token we give up the whole argument that we are worth associating with." [48]

Marcus Mosiah Garvey is the last significant Black leader we will discuss. *Garvey* was born in Jamaica in 1887. He moved to New York as a young man and launched his "Back to Africa movement." *Garvey* was the first Black leader in history to capture the support of the masses. His thoughts concerning race pride and the right for Blacks to bear arms to protect themselves set him apart from the other Black leaders of his day. It is also important to note that his contribution to Black Power, is more significant than the impact of his philosophy on separatism.

Garvey unlike *Douglass, Washington* and *DuBois* wrote only one book. His writings were complied by his wife *Amy-Jacques-Garvey*. This work is titled "The Philosophy and Opinions of Marcus Garvey." Within this manuscript we find the thinking of *Marcus Garvey*.

We will begin with an article by *Garvey* titled "An Appeal to the Conscience of the Black race to See Itself." "The evil of internal division is wrecking our existence as a people, and if we do not seriously and quickly move in the direction of a readjustment it simply means that our doom becomes imminently conclusive.

Industrial and commercial progress--Is such a progress that the Negro must attach to himself if he is to rise above the prejudice of the world. *The Universal Negro Improvement Association* teaches our race self-help and self-reliance, not only in one essential way, but in all those things that contribute to human happiness and well-being. The Negro needs a nation and a country of his own, where he can best show evidence of his own ability in the art of human progress." [49]

Unity, self help and self-reliance are clearly some important elements for Black progress but *Garvey* goes further. Here most importantly we see that *Garvey* clearly felt that Blacks needed a nation or country of their own.

He proceeds and discusses the need for Blacks to organize and remove themselves from an environment of prejudice. *Garvey* uses the term universal prejudice, here we gain from the Caribbean origins of *Garvey* as he sees the plight of Black people in a global context.

Chapter One

"It is unfortunate that we should so drift apart, as a race, as not to see that we are but perpetuating our own sorrow and disgrace in failing to appreciate the first great requisite of peoples-organization.

No Negro, let him be American, European, West Indian or African, shall be truly respected until the race as a whole has emancipated itself, through self-achievement and progress, from universal prejudice." [50] I am obligated at this point to bring into focus *Garvey's* position on divisions, and groups within the Black race.

In view of the confusion of Black people even in 1997 concerning what name they should be called and their ignorance to the distinct Black racial group born in North America, one can gain from the logic of *Garvey*. Here *Garvey* clearly sees the different racial stock among Black People in the Diaspora. In so doing he notes the geographical situation of each group. Thus Black Americans must distinguish themselves from Africans who become African-American when they gain American citizenship.

The African is a distinct group, so is the Black man in Europe and the West Indies. But no culture and personality is more distinct than the Black American among the Black race. The ethnicity of Black people encompass African, Native American and western cultures into a unique blend. This factor along with the United States being a high stage of technological advancement help make for the Black American distinction. *Garvey* continues his discussion and gives more knowledge and information.

"The Negro will have to build his own government, industry, art, science, literature and culture, before the world will stop to consider him. Until then, we are wards of a superior race and civilization, and the outcasts of a standard social system.

But the world of white and other men, deep down in their hearts, have much more respect for those of us who work for our racial salvation under the banner of *The Universal Negro Improvement Association*, than they could ever have in an eternity for a group of helpless apes and beggars who make a monopoly of undermining their own race and belittling themselves in the eyes of self-respecting people, by being 'good boys" rather than able men." [51]

• Big Ralph

Garvey as a dynamic spokesman for Black people also documents his opinions and philosophy on questions like propaganda, slavery, education, miscegenation, prejudice, government, poverty, power, race assimilation and the list goes on. But one of the most important testimonies by *Garvey* is his opinion on traitors.

"In the fight to reach the top the oppressed has always been encumbered by the traitors of their own race, made up of those of little faith and those who are generally susceptible to bribery for the selling out of the rights of their own people.

As Negroes, we are not entirely free of such an encumbrance. To be outspoken, I believe we are more encumbered in this way than any other race in the world, because of the lack of training and preparation for fitting us for our place in the world between nations and races.

The traitor of other races is generally confined to the mediocre or irresponsible individual, but, unfortunately, the traitors among the Negro race are generally to be found among the men highest placed in education and society, the fellows who call themselves leaders.

For us to examine ourselves thoroughly as a people we will find that we have more traitors than leaders, because nearly everyone who essays to lead the race at this time does so by first establishing himself as the pet of some philanthropist of another race, to whom he will go and debase his race in the worst form, humiliate his own manhood, and thereby win the sympathy of the great benefactors, who will dictate to him what he should do in the leadership of the Negro race. It is generally "you must go out and teach your people to be meek and humble; tell them to be good servants, loyal and obedient to their masters. If you will teach them such a doctrine you can always depend on me to give you $1,000 a year or $5,000 a year for the support of yourself, your newspaper or other institution you represent. I will always recommend you to my friends as a good fellow who is all right." With this advice and prospect of patronage the average Negro leader goes out to lead the unfortunate mass. These leaders tell us how good Mr. so and so is, how many good friends we have in the opposite race, and that if we leave everything to them all will work out well.

Chapter One

This is the kind of leadership we have had for the last fifty years. It is nothing else but treachery and treason of the worst kind. The man who will compromise the attitude of his country is a traitor, and even so the man who will compromise the rights of his race can be classified in no other way than that of a traitor also.

Not until we settle down as four hundred million people and let the men who have placed themselves in the lead of us realize that we are disgusted and dissatisfied, and that we shall have a leadership of our own and stick by it when we get it, will we be able to lift ourselves from this mire of degradation to the heights of prosperity, human liberty and human appreciation."[52]

Garvey evidently had people like *Booker T. Washington* in mind when he developed his position on traitors in the Black community. *Garvey* does not say what should be done to traitors. In most countries crimes of treason are punishable by death, but Black Americans do not have a country.

Our third major area of concern in this introductory chapter is a look at historical periods in Black American history. The study of history for any people is best served by a review of the historical development of significant events etc. In this instance a chronological look at events, places, persons and themes will be explored.

Prince Hall was one of the organizers that drafted a petition presented to the Senate and House of Representatives of the Commonwealth of Massachusetts Bay in 1787. In this year *Prince Hall* founded the *Negro Masonic Order.*

This petition is an early document that reveals that Blacks wanted equal education for their children. The petition noted that since they pay taxes they have the right to enjoy privileges of free men. Their children, they pointed out, do not receive the benefit of the free schools. "We therefore pray your honors that you would in your wisdom make some provision . . . for the education of our dear children. And in duty bound shall ever pray."[53]

Equal transportation was also a concern for Blacks that lived in the free states before the end of slavery. It is of interest to note that even

• Big Ralph

before the end of slavery Blacks who held pseudo citizenship rights in the free states were actively seeking equality. *Charles Lennox Redmond* delivered a speech against segregated transportation before a committee of the Massachusetts House of Representatives in 1842. *Redmond* was an active leader of the American Anti-slavery Society. The following are excerpts from his speech to the Massachusetts House of Representatives. "Our right to citizenship in this state has been acknowledged and secured by the allowance of the elective franchise and consequent taxation; and I know of no good reason, if admitted in this instance, why it should be denied in any other.

Concerning the wrongs inflicted and injuries received on railroads by persons of color, I need not say they do not lend with the termination of thought, but, in effect, tend to discourage, disparage and depress this class of citizens. All hope of regard for upright conduct is cut off. Vice in them becomes a virtue. No distinction is made by the community in which we live. The most vicious is treated as well as the most respectable, both in public and private.

But it is said, we all look alike. If this is true, it is not true that we all behave alike. There is a marked difference; and we claim a recognition of this difference."[54]

The major significance of the early documents by *Prince Hall, Lenox Redmond* and others is in the context of understanding why Blacks felt discriminated against. Thus we see precedent setting statements regarding major issues we will explore throughout this work. For example the question of quality education and the segregationist and integrationist philosophy will be set in better focus by an understanding of the positions set in place by some of our early leaders.

The pre Civil War thinking on education is further revealed to us by *Charles Sumner. Sumner argued his case* before the Supreme Court of Massachusetts in Sarah C. Roberts v. City of Boston Dec. 4, 1849. This case laid the basis for the separate but equal doctrine of *Plessy V. Ferguson* in 1896. *Sumner's* argument is reflected in the U.S. Supreme Court decision in Brown v. Board of Education in 1954. Both of these important cases will be discussed later. I have chosen to continue to quote long passages verbatim so the reader can grasp a better

Chapter One

understanding of what the original writing said. Here is what *Charles Sumner* had to say about quality/equal education for Blacks.

"Can any discrimination because of race or color be made among children entitled to the benefit of our common schools under the constitution and laws of Massachusetts? This is the question that the court is now to hear, to consider, and to decide.

On, stating the question with more detail, and with more particular application to the facts of the present case, are the committee having superintendence of the common schools of Boston intrusted with power under the constitution and laws of Massachusetts, to exclude colored children from the schools, and compel them to find education at separate schools, set apart for colored children only, at distances from their homes less convenient than schools open to white children?" [55]

Sumner continues and makes three points in arguing his case:

"1. The separate school for colored children is not one of the schools established by the law relating to public schools. It has no legal existence therefore cannot be a legal equivalent.

2. The separate school is not equivalent. It is the occasion of inconvenience to colored children, which would not arise if they had access to the nearest common school. The matter, taught in the two schools may be precisely the same, but a school exclusively devoted to one class must differ essentially in spirit and character from that common school known to the law, where all classes meet together in equality. It is a mockery to call it an equivalent.

3. Admitting that it is an equivalent, still the colored children cannot be compelled to take it. Their rights are found in equality before the law; nor can they be called to renounce one jot of this. They have an equal right with white children to the common schools. A separate school, though well endowed, would not secure to them that precise equality that they would enjoy in the common schools. The Jews in Rome are confined to a particular district called the Ghetto, and in Frankfurt to a district know as the Jewish Quarter. It is possible that their accommodations are as good as they can occupy, if left free to choose throughout Rome and Frankfurt; but this compulsory segregation from the mass of citizens is of itself an

• **Big Ralph**

inequality that we condemn. It is a vestige of ancient intolerance directed against a despised people. It is of the same character with the separate schools in Boston. Thus much for the doctrine of "Equivalent" as a substitute for equality." [56]

As Blacks petitioned for civil and equal rights the United States, the white majority continued to maintain the non human status of Black people, especially those still held in slavery. The *Dred Scott* Supreme Court decision of 1856 distinctly declares the noncitizen status of Black people. We begin with the question put before the court.

"Can a Negro, whose ancestors were imported into this country, and sold as slaves, become a member of the political community formed and brought into existence by the constitution of the U.S., and as such become entitled to all the rights, and privileges, and immunities, guaranteed by the instrument to the citizen?

We think they are not, and that they are not included, and were not intended to be included, under the word "Citizens" in the Constitution, and can therefore claim none of the rights and privilege which that instrument provides for and secures to citizens of the U.S.

Upon these considerations, it is the opinion of the court that the act of Congress which prohibited a citizen from holding and owning property of this kind in the territory of the U.S. north of the line therein mentioned, is not warranted by the Constitution, and is therefore void; and that neither *Dred Scott* himself, nor any of his family, were made free by being carried into this territory; even if they had been carried there by the owner, with the intention of becoming a permanent resident." [57]

In a few years after the *Dred Scott* decision the United States was cast into the dark days of Civil War. When the war ended in 1865, the question of slavery had been put to rest as an institution in name. But, the question of what to do with Black people remained like a yoke around the neck of the white man. Blacks were still worked like slaves throughout the south as sharecropping and tenant farming became institutionalized as a post slavery form of peonage and exploitation.

Three amendments to the Constitution allowed Blacks a semblance of citizenship although short-lived. This experience of citizenship by Black people provoked white people. Blacks were considered a burden

Chapter One

but when it came to labor power, just like in the days of slavery, the white man used the Black hands that continued to pick cotton on southern plantations.

The 13th amendment was established Dec. 18, 1868. It stated "Neither slavery nor involuntary servitude, except as a punishment for crime whereof the party shall have been duly convicted, shall exist within the U.S., or any place subject to their jurisdiction." [58]

The Civil War Amendments were enacted to protect the rights of the newly freed slaves. Especially the right to vote and against infringement by the states. A few years later came the 14th Amendment, July 28, 1868, it stated the following:

"All persons born or naturalized in the U.S., and subject to the jurisdiction thereof, are citizens of the U.S. and of the state wherein they reside. No state shall make or enforce any law which shall abridge the privileges or immunities of citizens of the U.S.; nor shall any state deprive any person of life, liberty, or property, without due process of law; nor deny to any person within its jurisdiction the equal protection of the laws." [59]

Black people gaining the right to vote most likely angered white people more than any of the Civil War Amendments. The 15th Amendment was declared in force March 30, 1870. The Amendment stipulated that "the right of citizens of the United States to vote shall not be denied or abridged by the United States or by any state on account of race, color, or previous condition of servitude." [60]

Even with the passage of the 13th, 14th and 15th Amendments Black people still had to petition and protest for equal rights as citizens. *George Downing*, Chairman, National Civil Rights Convention presented a petition to Congress in 1873. The petition stated---"We regret the necessity which compels us to again come before you and say "we are aggrieved." We are authorized to say to those in authority, to Congress, to the people whom it represents, that there are nearly five millions of American citizens who are shamefully outraged; who are thus treated without cause. The recognition's made within a few years respecting in part our rights, make us more sensitive as to the denial of the rest." [61]

• **Big Ralph**

Downing continues and refers to those Civil Rights that Congress has the authority to take action on. "We shall take it for granted that action will be had by Congress, protecting us from invidious distinctions in the enjoyment of common carriers, hotels and other public places of convenience and refreshment, in public places of amusement, and in enjoying other Civil Rights; but there are indications that there may be some objection made to federal action against discrimination as to race and color in the management of public instruction, and in impaneling juries, the objectors alleging that it is unconstitutional for Congress to legislate to affect these cases." [62]

So as the Black community in America searched for equal rights as human beings through the halls of Congress and the courts other significant factors occurred. White hate groups like the *Klu Klux Klan* had emerged in the south after the Civil War to deny Blacks the constitutional gains made through Civil Rights legislation.

Also, in 1877 a political, economic and social decision was made by the two dominant political parties in the United States. abolitionist *Wendell Phillips* is quoted as saying "the Emancipation Proclamation freed the slave but ignored the Negro." For a time after the Civil War, it appeared that the Federal Government might insist on a thorough reformation of southern society to guarantee the freed men equality. But, in 1877, as a part of a deal to elect *Rutherford B. Hayes* President, the Republicans agreed to the withdrawal of federal troops, the dissolution of the Freedmen's Bureau, and a general acquiescence in the white south's demand that the Negro be restored to his proper place. [63]

Lerone Bennett calls the *Hayes-Tilden* decision the climax of the revolution that failed. "The essence of the bargain of 1877 was a defacto suspension of Constitutional safeguards that protected the rights of Negro citizens in the south. The south called off the filibuster, and *Hayes* was elected. On April 10, 1877, federal troops were withdrawn from Columbia, South Carolina, and the white majority took over the state government. Eighty years and five months would pass before federal troops would enter the south again to uphold the dignity and majesty of the U.S. constitution." [64]

C. Vann Woodward in his very important work on Jim Crow also places the decision of 1877 in perspective. "The phase that began in

Chapter One

1877 was inaugurated by the withdrawal of federal troops from the south, the abandonment of the Negro as a ward of the nation, the giving up of the attempt to guarantee the freedman his civil and political equality, and the acquiescence of the rest of the country in the south's demand that the whole problem be left to the disposition of the dominant southern white people." [65]

The decision of 1877 became a dramatic result of Black pseudo-enfranchisement in the south. With the close of the Civil War, while the predicament of Blacks in the north remained unchanged, Blacks in the south witnessed a short-lived political freedom.

In the south Blacks could vote and hold elective office at the local, state and national levels during reconstruction. The white southern plantation owners and those filled with hate and racism toward Black people were repulsed at former slaves having rights as citizens. Their response to Black enfranchisement came in various measures. For example, organized white hate groups emerged. And eventually the white south and the white north came together and agreed to limit Blacks to 2nd class citizenship.

The emergence of *Jim Crow* was another phenomena that was a part of the white backlash to Black Civil Rights. Before we discuss *Jim Crow,* we will review a very important Supreme Court decision. Black people in the north had petitioned Congress about segregated transportation even before the start of the Civil War. The following is an excerpt from another document that questions segregated transportation.

"There has been universal discrimination here in Alabama, and, indeed, all over the south, in the treatment of the colored people as to cars they are permitted to ride in.

We simply ask for equal accommodation and protection with the white people in riding on the railroads." [66]

The Supreme Court case of *Plessy V. Ferguson* of 1896 legalized segregated transportation throughout America. The dissent on the court came from Justice Harlan, he argued that the arbitrary separation of citizens based on race presents a badge of servitude, inconsistent with the equality before the law established by the 13th, 14th and 15th Amendments to the constitution.

• **Big Ralph**

"The case turns upon the constitutionality of an act of the general assembly of the state of Louisiana, passed in 1890, providing for separate railway carriages for the white and colored races.

The first section of the statute states that all railway companies carrying passengers in their coaches in this state shall provide equal but separate accommodations for the white, and colored races, by providing two or more passenger coaches for each passenger train, or by dividing the passenger coaches by a partition so as to secure separate accommodations: Provided, that this section shall not be construed to apply to street railroads. No person or persons, shall be admitted to occupy seats in coaches, other than the ones assigned to them, on account of the race they belong to.

So far, then as a conflict with the 14th Amendment is concerned, the case reduces itself to the question of whether the statute of Louisiana is a reasonable regulation, and with respect to this there must necessarily be a large discretion by the legislature.

We consider the underlying fallacy of the plaintiff's argument to consist in the assumption that the enforced separation of the two races stamps the colored race with a badge of inferiority. If this is so it is not the act--but Blacks choose to place this on themselves. Also the question of the proportion of colored blood necessary to constitute a colored person is left to the states." [67]

No doubt the *Plessy V. Ferguson* decision solidly implanted *Jim Crow* as the law of the land. Not only in transportation but in every conveyance Blacks were segregated. The *Jim Crow* laws became public symbols and on-going reminders of the inferior position of Black people.

"The origin of the term " *Jim Crow*" applied to Negroes is lost in obscurity. *Thomas D. Rice* wrote a song and dance called " *Jim Crow*" in 1832, and the term had become an adjective by 1883. The first example of " *Jim Crow law*" listed by the Dictionary of American English is dated 1904." [68]

But whatever its origin *Jim Crow* became the contemporary laws of apartheid and segregation. segregation codes that became *Jim Crow* laws were comparable to the Black codes of the slave regime. Therefore segregation logically was based on the old pro-slavery argument and

Chapter One

had its origin in the slave period.

Tennessee was the only state that had a *Jim Crow* railroad law before 1881. Soon after the civil rights decision of 1883 all southern states enacted *Jim Crow* legislation. By 1899 most southern states required *Jim Crow* waiting rooms.

Just like slavery the system of *Jim Crow* was a means to exploit the economic power of Black people. *Jim Crow* laws kept Blacks in their place while sharecropping as a neo-slave system came into existence. Most Blacks were confined to Black Belt plantations by crop liens and vagrancy laws. The sharecropping system was an organized system that held Blacks as workers for plantation owners who supplied tools and gave them credit for food and clothing. The sharecropper and the planter were supposed to divide/split the proceeds from the crop. But the books were kept by the planter who also sold the crop on the market.

Most, if not all, newly freed slaves that were now neo-slaves on sharecropping plantations could neither read nor write. What little reading and writing the planters could do was enough to cheat and swindle the Black sharecroppers and each year they slipped deeper into debt.

Strangely though segregation did not grow up contemporaneously with slavery. "One of the strangest things about the career of Jim Crow was that the system was born in the north and reached an advanced age before moving south in force." [69] Although there was no slavery in the north, that part of the country was steeped in prejudice toward Black people. Here Black people in the north just like Blacks in the south were reminded that American society held white people superior and Blacks as inferior.

As the system of segregation preceded the system of *Jim Crow* the major political parties were convinced that Black people were incapable of entering into the mainstream of white society. So one way to confine Blacks to their place was through segregation.

Alexis de Tocqueville was amazed at the depth of racial bias he encountered in the north. "The prejudice of race, he wrote, appears to be stronger in the states that have abolished slavery than in those where it still exists; and nowhere is it so intolerant as in those states where servitude has never been known." [70]

• **Big Ralph**

There has always been a different racial climate in the south and north. The oppression was different in the two regions but the north was ranked right up with the south concerning racism. The period soon after reconstruction saw Blacks operating all types of businesses. Often Blacks had to sell to each other because they were not allowed to patronize certain white establishments. Also there were many service jobs that Blacks had traditionally held. Many of these jobs resulted in Black owned businesses in white communities or downtown and often with an exclusive white clientele. During the twenty-year period 1880-1900 the Black business community included barbers, boot and shoe makers, butchers, restaurant owners and caterers flourished. *Jim Crow* put a serious dent in Black business of this type. In any event Black Businesses were regulated to the Black areas of town as white land owners refused to rent to Blacks wanting to conduct business in the white downtown areas. It is for sure that the white man's power to license had a serious affect on Black business.

"Since white men controlled the power to license, it was relatively easy to push Negroes out of coveted grades. In this way, the Negro lost his monopoly over barbering and catering." [71]

Legally and through any other means Blacks were kept out of the mainstream white community. *Bennett* looks at the exclusion of Black people in a unique way. "From birth to death, they were enclosed in a system of maximum insecurity. They awoke to the world under a sentence that could be extended any time by the white man. The ultimate sanction was lynching which reached staggering heights in the 1890's when a Negro was lynched somewhere every day or two. As the years wore on, lynching became more barbarous and lynchers became more sadistic. • • • Negroes were burned at the stake, mutilated, hacked to pieces, and roasted over slow fires." [72]

During the 80's and 90's lynchings reached the highest level ever recorded. Brutality, violence and racial conflict were widespread. The southern white man strongly believed in intimidation of the Black man to keep him in place. Lynching became the most important element in this system of southern intimidation that of course knew no regional boundaries because Blacks were lynched throughout America and not

Chapter One

only in the south.

This racist system sought to penalize the Black man for standing in defense of his home, himself or his family. Built into this system were rewards for the passive and ignorant Black man, while death was sought for the aggressive and independent Black man.

Henry Grady in the 1880's became the architect of the "New South." "The Negro, *Grady* said bluntly, must be led to know and through sympathy to confess that his interests and the interests of the south are identical."[73]

Booker T. Washington with his blind vision came to accept the notions of *Grady*. Here *Washington* just like *Grady* identified the interests of Black people with the interests of the oppressors of Black people. "Washington, like *Grady*, spoke often and eloquently of "humble" Negroes, the most patient, faithful, law-abiding, and unresentful people that the world has ever seen."[74] Thus southern Negro leaders like *Booker T. Washington* conferred with southern white leaders like *Henry Grady* and said if there was a problem it must be worked out with the Negro and his "best friend," the southern white man.

During *Washington's* Atlanta Compromise speech in 1895 he totally accepted the program outlined by *Grady*. In this case *Washington* advised Black people to accept the domination of white people, and to be grateful by showing a spirit of meekness.

But, there were some Blacks in leadership that clearly saw that *Booker T. Washington* did not speak for the true interests of Black people.

"To the people of Great Britain and Europe the undersigned Negro-Americans have heard, with great regret, the recent attempt to assure England and Europe that their condition in America is satisfactory. They sincerely wish that such were the case, but it becomes their plain duty to say that if Mr. *Booker T. Washington*, or any other person, is giving the impression abroad that the Negro problem in America is in process of satisfactory solution, he is giving an impression which is not true."[75]

Washington set the standards for accommodating an Uncle Tom style Black leadership. Meanwhile, Blacks were being lynched daily throughout America and Jim Crow prevailed.

The southern conservative thinkers believed that all societies had a

• **Big Ralph**

particular class structure of superiors and inferiors. These same conservative thinkers did not relate the inferior status of Blacks to discrimination. Regardless how, and if, discrimination resulted from the label of Black inferiority--Blacks were discriminated against as a rule of society. The evidence of class was a significant variable in various causes. Blacks realize that there are two basic classes among the whites, the "well-raised gentlemen" and "poor white trash." Both groups treated Blacks harshly and since poor white people had to interact with Blacks more, they in turn felt more threatened and responded even more harshly toward Blacks.

    Black people would become scapegoats again. Used as the scapegoat during reconstruction, Blacks now became the scapegoat in the reunion of the solid south. White supremacy was the distinct formula used to control Black people and the first step toward implementation of the formula was disfranchisement. Ingrained in the thinking of disfranchisement was the commitment of white unity north, south, east or west in support of keeping the Black man in subordination.

    C. Vann Woodward in his powerful research "The Strange Career of Jim Crow" says Mississippi was the pioneer in inventing means to disenfranchise Black people. In this case Blacks were prevented from voting by the grandfather clause and the poll tax. The white primary also locked Blacks out of the political process in the south." The effectiveness of disfranchisement is suggested by a comparison of the number of registered Negro voters in Louisiana in 1896, when there were 130,334 and in 1904, when there were 1,342. Between the two dates the literacy, property, and poll-tax qualifications were adopted. In 1896 Negro registrants were a majority in twenty-six parishes--by 1900 in none."[76]

    As the Black man floated in this sea of degradation white intellectuals discussed his state of affairs. They concluded that the Black man and woman were subhuman and that they were incapable of self-government, did not need to vote and could only be taught basic skills.

    Booker T. Washington again stepped in to second the motion for the white man. In 1912 *Washington* said "we are trying to instill into the

Chapter One

Negro mind that if education does not make the Negro humble, simple, and of service to the community, then it will not be encouraged." [76]

Meanwhile *Jim Crow* laws became entrenched in southern society. Most *Jim Crow* laws by 1900 had only represented passengers aboard trains. These first laws applied to separation within the cars. In Montgomery in 1906 a city ordinance was passed to require a completely separate Jim Crow street car. The law eventually affected 1st class and 2nd class coaches.

The growth of Jim Crow produced a multitude of signs that noted the separation of the races ("whites only," "colored only") all over the south. Many of these signs were a result of city ordinances but many came to appeal to southern custom, which became accepted as law.

Unlike Booker T. Washington, W.E.B. DuBois stood up against Jim Crow and the laws of bigotry. The "Niagara Movement was the forerunner to the NAACP and DuBois was said to have written "The Niagara Movement --Declaration of Principles" which took a firm stand against inequality. [78]

After the Great Depression and Great war, Blacks were still appealing for rights as citizens. The call of the National Negro Congress in 1935 makes a significant statement about Black equality in the following excerpts.

"For Negroes the six terrible years of depression have meant an intolerable double exploitation both as Negroes and as workers. The Negro farm population in the south is fast becoming landless. In the last 15 years Negroes not only have not gained land but have lost more than four million acres of farm land. What will the Negro Congress do? The National • • • Negro Congress will be no new organization, nor does it seek to usurp the work of existing organizations. The Congress seeks unity of action among existing organizations."

1. The right of Negroes to jobs at decent wages and for the right to join trade unions.
2. Relief and security for every needy Negro family.
3. Aid to the Negro farm population.
4. A fight against lynching, mob violence and police brutality.

• **Big Ralph**

5. The right of Negro youth to equal opportunity in education.
6. Complete equality for Negro women.
7. To oppose war and fascism--independence of Ethiopia." [79]

These historical factors would come to dominate the existence of **Ralph Henry Cothran.** As a Black man, like so many other Black men he would learn how to deal with a racist society. Ralph was able to cope with racism and have a positive impact on humanity. His story lies ahead with its unique circumstances.

Part II. Segregation And Integration

Chapter Two

Bushtown 1938

**Life comes to another soul of humble inception,
as so many countless souls have done,
With pride, dignity and the will to
succeed and survive did this man come.**

Bushtown is still a conservative low to middle income neighborhood in Chattanooga. This is where *Ralph Henry (Big Ralph) Cothran* was born on May 3, 1938.

Doctor Edgar Scott delivered Ralph in a small shotgun house on Holly Street. Ralph was big even as a baby because he weighed a hefty 13 pounds. There were three rooms in the house, a kitchen, living room and bedroom. An out-house in the back yard served as the toilet. In later years the back porch was converted to a bathroom. This action had more to do with local and federal health codes than a convenience to poor people who had to live in these run down houses.

Many of Ralph's characteristics like bravery came from his father. Charlie Cothran was a kind man. He was also brave and dedicated and there is no doubt Ralph inherited these traits from his father.

Ralph took his large frame from his father who was a tall, big man over 6 feet. five inches tall. Charlie Cothran, his father, and Bessie Neal Cothran both came from Georgia. Charlie was born in Georgia about 30-40 miles south of Chattanooga. Bessie was born in Fort Oglethrope which is less than a mile from the Tennessee state line with the state of Georgia.

Ralph was only two years old when his father went into the army to fight in WWII. Those early years had a lasting impression on his life.

Big Ralph

Ralph did not remember his father. During the years he was away Ralph had a boyhood fantasy that his father was a cowboy. Bushtown was a close knit neighborhood and everybody knew everybody that lived there. Mother Ricks was a faith healer who lived next door. Ralph would see various people with different ailments coming and going from her house. There was a great mystery about the house and Mother Ricks. But kids in those days seldom were given the opportunity to ask grown-ups many questions about grown-up affairs.

So when kids in the neighborhood were taken to Mother Ricks they seldom ever asked any questions. Anyway she also was a healer for the kids in the neighborhood. Parents throughout Bushtown and the city took their kids to Mother Ricks for counseling and prayer. She received excellent wages for her services and some people in those days made claims that Mother Ricks was wealthy. Tommie Brown was another friend of Ralph when he was growing up in Bushtown. Tommie was Mother Ricks' granddaughter. Tommie Brown is now a state Representative and she still lives in the house on Holly Street.

Naturally the kids of the same age group came together. Some of Ralph's early playmates became life long friends. Frank Newson was one of Ralph's boyhood friends who also became a police officer. Frank and Ralph knew each other as babies. As Ralph would fondly say "we ate out of the same garbage can." Ralph's father and Frank's father would often baby-sit the boys together when their wives were busy or working. Frank also had two brothers, Richard Newson was a great athlete who fell to several social problems. Richard was a very talented athlete who excelled as a boxer and football player. He developed an intravenous drug problem and died of Aids. Frank's other brother was a talented artist who is a legend in Chattanooga for his artistic accomplishments, paintings, murals etc. Nunny, (John Newson) as they called him, was also a well known homosexual and in some circles is more remembered for these activities than his artistic genius.

Ralph had a lot of respect for John (Nunny) Newson. First, and foremost Nunny was very intelligent and an artistic genius. Ralph always had a sense of compassion for people. This compassion was a part of Ralph's

Chapter Two

personality and he expressed these feelings despite one's station in life or life style. Nunny made a number of artistic contributions to Chattanooga's artistic community. Friends recall that at the time he passed away they were certain that he had truly accepted God and Jesus Christ as his savior.

Hugh Lynn Johnson another close boyhood friend that grew up with Ralph, left Chattanooga at an early age. Hugh Lynn recently died in California. When they were growing up, he lived across the street from Ralph. Hugh Lynn and Ralph were very curious young boys. So one day they decided to find out if cats really had nine lives. They filled the wash tub at Ralph's house full of water and placed several cats in the tub to see if they really had nine lives. They had heard grown-ups say that cats had nine lives and they wanted to find out. Well unfortunately they found out that the nine lives story was not true after drowning at least three cats in the process. Lee Derrick was also an early playmate. Lee was big and muscular and an accomplished swimmer. He was also an outstanding football player for the "Big Blue Tigers" of Tennessee A&I State University.

Edward Fain, another Bushtown buddy, like Lee Derrick still resides in Chattanooga. Presently Fain is the principal at Howard School. There were many more kids in the neighborhood though and plenty to make up two good baseball teams.

Ralph and his friends played ball at Bobby Greens field on Greenwood Avenue. The field was named in honor of Bobby Green because Bobby Green lived in a house next to it.

The church was also a big influence during these early years. Bessie Cothran was a faithful member of Orchard Knob Missionary Baptist Church. Orchard Knob is located on 3rd and Hawthorne Street on the southwest corner. The church is still located on this site but a new church has been built and a large parking lot accommodates the church's large membership.

Mrs. Cothran worked as an usher, she had a great rapport with the people she worked with. No doubt she had outstanding leadership attributes. Ralph not only looked like his mother, he had the freckles, the long fingers but he also inherited her leadership qualities. If Bessie Cothran had gone to college and obtained a formal education she most

Big Ralph

likely would have had a greater impact on her community. She was a classmate of former educator and state representative C.B. Robinson. Friends and relatives at Orchard Knob Baptist Church recall that when Ms. Bessie found out the city named a bridge after C.B. Robinson she had a fit. Ms. Bessie said "I helped Clarence with his homework when we were in school, so how did he get to be so smart."

Ms. Bessie worked diligently with the youth of the church. She kept a scrapbook of all her young people over the years. They loved Ms. Bessie because she had taught them so much and had such a profound impact on their lives. For example people like Howard Roddy who grew up in the church and went on to become a quiet success story. The scrapbook consisted of pictures, letters, cards etc. The young people sent Ms. Bessie letters and cards after certain achievements. On the back of one such picture a young lady signed the back of the picture by saying, Ms. Bessie was a "hip soul sister. That was during the 70's and "hip, and soul sister " were terms frequently used. Ms. Bessie reputation is still legendary at Orchard Knob Baptist church though she died back in 1984. For example older church members back in the usher's pew may tell another usher "I bet you wouldn't do that if Ms. Bessie was here."

Ms. Bessie also had a great impact on the community where she lived. The people in Bushtown loved Ms. Bessie and relished her charismatic personality. Again there were parallels in Bessie's personality and Ralph. Catherine remembers that Ms. Bessie volunteered to keep Cyzanne when she was a baby so she could finish some additional training in nursing. Here Catherine recalls that Ms. Bessie had this great stamina that her husband also possessed. During that time Ms. Bessie broke her foot, but she still kept Cyzanne in a wheel chair.

Parents were really strict about kids attending church in those days, especially Ralph's mother. Bessie Cothran, was a long time member and a faithful church worker. No doubt Ms. Bessie considered church as a way of life. If you did not attend Sunday school and church on Sunday you were not allowed to take part in any other activities on that day.

So, if you were sick, which was the only acceptable excuse for missing church, you had to stay in your room all day. You could read a

Chapter Two

book but that is about all. Rev. Joe Johnson was the minister at Orchard Knob when Ralph was growing up.

Ralph remembers that he and the other young boys in the church took turns taking Rev. Johnson to the Barber Shop. Rev. Johnson was not your normal minister and Ralph always viewed his experiences with the minister as unique.

Rev. Johnson was blind. Ralph had fond memories of leading the minister every Saturday morning up to the Barber Shop and Shoe Shop on the corner of 3rd and Holly Streets. Since Ralph was well aware that Rev. Johnson was blind he was amazed when on Sunday morning Rev. Johnson made it to the church without any assistance.

Rev. Johnson lived on Greenwood Avenue. He had a daughter who lived with him and took care of the house. Ralph remembers as most of his playmates that Rev. Johnson had a loud booming voice. Ralph recalled that Rev. Johnson's voice was so loud that when he called his daughter, you could hear him for blocks throughout Bushtown.

No doubt when Rev. Johnson preached, the members of Orchard Baptist Church could clearly hear every word of his sermons. Since kids did not ask many questions of grown-ups Ralph did not know how Rev Johnson came to know so much about the Bible although he was blind. To Ralph it seemed as if Rev. Johnson had memorized the entire Bible.

Ralph's sister Hilda was nine years older than Ralph. So she really was a big sister although small in stature in contrast to Ralph who grew to be 6 feet six inches tall and well over 200 lbs.

Ralph remembers that Hilda was a great singer. She joined the Air Force when she finished high school. In the Air Force Hilda traveled all over the world singing with the Air Force Band.

Family values were very important to Ralph. When he was growing up family values were at the center of his life. So Hilda and Ralph were raised in the old-fashioned way. I use "old-fashioned" because that is the best way to describe this kind of child rearing in the Black community. Under this system during Ralph's generation children were raised to respect their elders and institutions of authority. Common

Big Ralph

courtesy was a mainstay of old-fashioned child rearing. You were taught in those days to respect other people's property. During an interview Ralph reflects on the principles of family values. He renders his thoughts and applies the situations of his youth to the time in which he became Chief of police.

"In this case how you were raised was very important. There is a big difference in rearing children today than yesterday." For example during the 1940s and 1950s when Ralph was growing up in Bushtown the whole community was involved in a young person's development.

"Neighborhood drunks would even lecture kids back then, on the pitfalls of life." Ralph and his playmates would respectfully listen to these street corner lectures because they were taught to respect all elders or grown-ups. Despite one's station in life and blood relationships young people often followed the customs and practices that clearly marked the distinction between youth and adult.

Ralph also recalled that "homosexuals that lived in the Bushtown community would also take time out to lecture the kids. Meanwhile kids became clearly aware that all elders were due respect."

From Ralph's point of view times have changed. "Kids don't have the respect for adults that kids had when I was growing up. Respect, and laws have changed with the times and presently kids don't respect anything. Well; what happened to respect? Did the change in certain laws influence this change in attitude? "

During the days when Bushtown and the areas north and south of East 3rd Street were bustling with people, times were hard. Black people were underpaid and over worked. During 1940 and 1950 there was a pay scale that was a throw back to the days shortly after slavery. Domestic workers made fifty cents to a dollar a day. Most grown Black men working 8-12 hours a day, five days a week, could make 30-50 dollars a week at the most.

Ralph remembers that in his Bushtown neighborhood even before most people had telephones if you did wrong your parents would find out. There was an automatic "neighborhood watch" for young people and neighbors would tell parents about the negative behavior of their kids. They had what some say is telewoman.

Chapter Two

Family values were strong in those days. Ralph was steadily growing up and his father had returned from the service. Adults in the neighborhood would whip Ralph and his playmates if they caught them doing something wrong. Then the grown-up would tell Ralph's mother and father and he got another whipping.

No one in those days had any reason to think that their neighbors or friends would physically abuse their children. There was a sense of belonging and the essence of the extended Black family caused mature adults to be responsible toward all the kids in the neighborhood.

Parents had a different idea of discipline in those days. First they believed in corporal punishment. They had the right as responsible parents to discipline their children and they exercised this right.

The most serious challenge to discipline occurred in the public schools. Ralph recalls that "corporal punishment was a reality during his school years." Ralph was not a disciplinary problem and he remembers that Mr. George Key the principal at Orchard Knob School never had to whip him. There were a few instances when Ralph did cause a problem. One Sunday when he was about 12 years old, he, and some of his friends chose to play football instead of going to church. He cut his knee really badly and lost a great amount of blood Ms. Bessie thought she was going to lose her baby that day but he survived. Ralph recalls that he was severely disciplined for this infraction.

Eventually the laws were changed. Integration became the law of the land with the Supreme Court decision of 1954 that outlawed segregated schools.

The law regarding school desegregation was slow to take affect. When the law did take affect, corporal punishment was a relic. Black and white schools, had used corporal punishment as a means to discipline kids in school. With integration on the scene white parents were very concerned about a Black teacher physically whipping their child. Blacks felt their children would also be abused by white teachers if they were allowed to use corporal punishment.

So laws changed, sometimes for the good and sometimes for the bad. There were negatives, and positives about new laws. Here discipline began to reach a never ending low in 1954 with the move to desegregate

Big Ralph

the public schools in America. Corporal punishment was done away with and chaos and confusion set in to play havoc with and misdirect the learning process and seriously undermine the public school system.

Organized recreational activities were also an impacting experience on Ralph at a young age. During these so-called "old-fashioned days" the basic institutions in society were distinct. Ralph's home life was steeped in the basic tenets of home rearing that drew the distinct line between elders and children. Respect for this age difference was ever present.

Besides the home, the church is also an established institution. Thus many thinkers argue that the church has historically been a refuge for the Black man and woman in North America. Kids were taught the value of religion and church attendance was usually mandatory .

Ralph was very seldom disciplined in school. The school is also a basic institution in our society; consequently, it plays a vital role. Education was and is very important because the need for knowledge for Black people still has an everlasting appeal. This appeal can be described as man's great thirst for water, the fluid of life. I use knowledge in the past tense because during the present time Black people (our youth) do not consider education as a vital part of their life. Even before the school experiences there were other organized institutions in the community.

Bushtown was not unique to any other section of Chattanooga when it came to organized athletics. During this time Chattanooga had a highly organized citywide recreational program. Ralph reflects on the great experiences he had at Carver Community Center and in retrospect the quiet dedication of the various center directors.

Carver Center is still located on Orchard Knob Avenue on the golf course. The center Director at Carver when Ralph was growing up was Mrs. Pearl Vaughn. Mrs. Vaughn was not the only strong Center Director. All the Centers had outstanding Directors who took pride in their work and were filled with the competitive spirit.

In every distinct Black neighborhood or community there was a community center. Carver Center was the Center that served Blacks in Bushtown, and Churchville. (At this time Blacks had not moved into the

Chapter Two

Avondale area that was farther east and an all white neighborhood).

Lincoln Park Community Center was right over the viaduct going west on Third Street from where Ralph lived in Bushtown. This Center was also within walking distance. Mrs. Bea Scrgggs and Mrs. Pearl Vaughn were the Center Directors and this center served the Fortwood community.

College Hill Courts on the westside was most likely the most famous Community Center in town if I might say so. The westside at this time still housed most of the Black people that lived in Chattanooga. Many Black people that lived elsewhere in Chattanooga had been born on the westside, so many Blacks had roots in the westside and College Hill Courts. The westside Center was very competitive and the center was very successful in many city wide tournaments because the most gifted athletes in the history of Black Chattanooga came from the westside.

Alton Park is south, past Howard School a mile on South Market Street. Alton Park is a community of homeowner and has the largest public housing unit for Blacks. When Ralph was growing up, College Hill Courts on the westside and Alton Park Projects were the public housing units assigned to Blacks. Now since the days of segregation are over, no public housing units are segregated but very few, if any, white people now live in public housing in Chattanooga. Blacks now live in the public housing units in the city that once were reserved for white people. The Bethlehem Center, with a day care and recreational facilities, is located across from Alton Park projects on 38th street. The city recreation department also operates a center located inside the projects.

North Chattanooga is a community across the Tennessee river going north. To get to the historic Black community you go north across the Market Street bridge out North Market Street. At the crossing of North Market and Dallas Road bear left back to North Market Street, then North Market resumes being a two-way street and you are taken directly into the Hollow. The Hollow sometimes called "Blue Goose Hollow" is where Black people lived in those days.

In those days the old Spears Avenue School was the Black grammar school in North Chattanooga. Spears Avenue School was at the north end of Spears Avenue where the street came to a dead end. In the basement was the community center that was probably the smallest

Big Ralph

Black community center in town. Mrs. Georgia Hairston ran the center back then and she fit the mold of her city-wide counterparts, with dedication and commitment toward the youth of her community.

Most likely Chattanooga was a unique southern city during Jim Crow. Black establishments were definitely not on the same level with white establishments, but they were not as inferior as facilities in most other southern cities. For example most southern cities in the southeast and throughout the south did not have segregated swimming pools for Blacks. Most southern cities had no swimming facilities for Blacks at all. So the southern cities that provided a small Black park did not also provide a swimming pool during the days of segregation.

Chattanooga had Lincoln Park, Lincoln Park also had a big swimming pool. So Blacks although restricted to a segregated park, still had facilities. During the summer season Black tourists came to Lincoln Park by the busloads from Birmingham, Huntsville, Knoxville, Atlanta, Nashville and all around the southeast. None of these cities had a Black park that came anywhere close to matching the facilities at Lincoln Park.

Along with the pool, which had two diving boards and a diving platform, there was a small zoo. A Ferris Wheel, merry-go-round and at least two other rides made the park a fun place with a carnival atmosphere. The park had a tennis court, fields for baseball and softball that could be played at night, a large concession stand, dance hall and ample picnic grounds.

Ralph eventually became an accomplished swimmer. As a youngster he started taking swimming lessons at Lincoln Park. During the summer season swimming classes were taught every Tuesday. Ralph's elders told him to take swimming lessons and in those days you did what your elders told you. Also, there was another special incentive.

On the days that swimming classes were taught you were able to get in free for the rest of the day. With his tall frame and long legs Ralph became an excellent swimmer and thought little about it. Yes, swimming was just another athletic and fun thing to do as a kid.

As Ralph grew up he would interact with other Blacks from different environments and come to realize distinct differences. First, most Blacks even those in the medium to large southern cities were not

Chapter Two

exposed to a swimming pool when they were young. It must be noted that poor Black kids raised in the country did learn to swim in the ponds and lakes where they lived. Blacks in the urban areas usually had no ponds or lakes and had very little opportunity to learn how to swim.

Ralph had a natural aptitude toward table games and swimming. He became a champion at various table games. Catherine remembers that even later in life Ralph could play almost any table game like an expert. Richard Newson and George Haslerigh were also excellent swimmers during this time. Ralph remembers that swimming with his friends at Lincoln Park was some of the greatest fun he had as a kid.

By 1943 Ralph would attend school. Hilda, Ralph's older sister had taken Ralph to school for an entire year, when he was only five and not yet old enough to enroll in first grade. In those days many older children brought their younger siblings to school when no one was available to baby-sit. Ralph was left in a first grade room while his sister attended her classes. This was not an unusual practice in those days. Here Ralph got a first hand look at the public schools at an early age.

Ralph when he was 5 years old

Hilda & Ralph as toddlers

Neighborhood Picture of Kids In Bushtown

Front Charlie Cothran & Bessie Cothran & Neighbors

Charlie & Bessie Cothran & daughter Hilda

Charlie Cothran during WWII

Mother Ricks Faith Healer

Ralph's cousin Ora Jeannett Neal age 9

Hilda Cothran high school graduation 1948

Aunt Ruth Derricks Neal & Uncle Ralph Neal
at Wedding

Chapter Three

Orchard Knob School

**These foundations and preparations did unfold,
hampered by restrictions that proved in time to
bring positive appeal,
Hail the great Kings who have toiled to achieve,
never to falter as time moves the unwise to the wise.**

One of the first things Ralph remembers about his school days was when he did some work for Mother Ricks. It was early in the morning before he went to school, it was cold outside and the sun had not come up. In those days most people had a coal bin and place alongside where they stored wood for heating and in some cases for cooking. Mother Ricks had asked Ralph to bring in some wood and coal before he went to school and she in turn would fix him a big lunch. Ralph knew that Mother Ricks was well off because most people in Bushtown considered her wealthy. Ralph anticipated a big delicious lunch because he loved to eat and had already developed a hefty appetite that would last for the rest of his life.

This is the famous neckbone story, one of the funniest stories Ralph ever told about his early childhood. Ralph couldn't wait until lunch time

Big Ralph

so on the way to school he opened the lunch bag. When Ralph saw what was in the bag he was grossly disappointed because Mother Ricks had prepared him two neckbone sandwiches. He was so frustrated that he threw the sandwiches in the branch and he had no desire for neckbones for rest of his life. This is unique because he was a meat eater and loved pork as well as beef. Catherine recalls how Ralph would eat the ham hocks out of the turnip greens before they could finish cooking. But you couldn't pay Ralph to eat a neckbone.

Ralph got off to a poor start when he enrolled at Orchard Knob School. Ralph was an introvert and had very little to say. He was easy going, shy and quiet and at times let other kids take advantage of him. His family thought he was slow not only in movement but slow in mind. They also felt he had very little potential and had dim hopes for his future. This did not prove to be the case because Ralph became a great thinker and one of the great sons of Chattanooga and made everlasting contributions to humanity. In contrast his sister Hilda was very sharp when they were growing up.

Hilda was multi-talented in academics and the arts. She had outstanding potential but for some reason Hilda never put it together. Hilda played in the band in school and she had a beautiful singing voice. She socialized when she attended college and did not keep up with her studies and eventually dropped out. She joined the Air Force and worked in nursing, but she never got her license when she was discharged from the service.

Because of his lack of communication Ralph believes he was put in a remedial reading class the first few years in school. This was a traumatic experience for Ralph and had a great impact on his self-esteem and pride. Ralph was fortunate because he had some help. His aunt, Ester Neal, taught at Orchard Knob and became aware of his dilemma. She gave Ralph extra tutoring after school at his house for at least six straight weeks. This extra effort helped Ralph prove that he was not slow and not a candidate for the remedial program.

Many kids were retarded that were in the remedial program. Ralph played a lot during this time because he would finish his work and there was nothing else for him to do. Often kids were disciplined by being

Chapter Three

placed in a remedial program. Sometimes kids that were unruly or caused disciplinary problems were placed in remedial programs.

Evidently there was no correct testing. The evaluation methods set in place resulted in many kids being harmed for life because of this experience. But Ralph said "I don't blame it on incompetent and irresponsible teachers but mostly on my failure to communicate." Thanks to Aunt Ester Ralph became more expressive and assertive.

Orchard Knob school is still located on the corner of 3rd Street and Orchard Knob Avenue. In Ralph's day Orchard Knob had classes for grades 1-9, but presently the school has classes for grades 1-6. A junior high school, built during the 70's now handles classes 7-9.

Orchard Knob got its name from the days of the Civil War. During the war all the high ground in and around Chattanooga held a strategic importance in the defense of the city. Knob is defined as" a rounded lump or mass or a prominent, isolated, rounded hill or mountain." The land area called, Orchard Knob covers about five acres of land. It is bound on the east by Orchard Knob Avenue, and on the west by North Hawthorne Street, East 5th Street makes up the north boundary while Vine Street bounds the area on the south.

This five-acre plot of high ground gave its name to an adjoining street, a school and even the church Ralph's family belonged to. In fact Ralph recalls that the large white influential Highland Park Baptist Church wanted Black Orchard Knob Baptist to drop the name Orchard Knob so they could rename their church Orchard Knob.

Highland Park Baptist Church is one of the largest churches in Chattanooga. The church also sponsors a religious college and they do missionary work throughout the city. Ralph noted that he even attended services at Highland Park occasionally though he was a member of Orchard Knob Baptist Church. He noted that the white people at the church treated him courteously and he enjoyed the new experience.

It is great that Ralph's experiences at Highland Park were pleasant. But, many Black people felt intimidated by the big buses from Highland Park Baptist Church. These big new shiny buses drove through the Black neighborhoods Sunday and through the week soliciting Blacks for church and bible study. Thus some Blacks came to conclude that the

Big Ralph

general mission of the church, though it had some merit, was flawed and steeped in the old time slave religion. This conclusion was reached due to the parentalistic attitude of the missionaries that sought after Black people to attend the church. Therefore, many Black people would not allow their children to go to Highland Park Baptist Church. Many kids in the projects were poor and hungry. These kids more often than not attended church to get food. They always returned with a small bag of candy, fruit and nuts.

School was fun most of the time and Ralph had a strong church in his family. Bessie Cothran had no intentions of letting Ralph attend Highland Park regularly. He had gotten the experience of seeing a big white church and that was enough.

School was a place to learn and also a place to have fun with your friends. School also had it's hard moments. But, there was an award for attending school in Chattanooga during these days. The Knothole League was organized by representatives of the Chattanooga Lookouts, the baseball team that played in Chattanooga. The Lookouts are in the Southern Conference and they play all of their home games at Engle Stadium. Engle Stadium is right over the Third Street viaduct going west on Third Street. The Stadium sits to the left soon as you come down off the viaduct.

Ralph and his friends could easily walk the few blocks from Bushtown over the Third Street viaduct to Engle Stadium. They definitely could attend many games because Knothole cards were given to students to be used to gain admission to see the Lookouts play.

Knothole cards were blue, white and pink and were awarded for good conduct, good grades and good attendance in school. All of Ralph's boyhood friends enjoyed Knothole privileges as they relished the opportunity to see the Lookouts play baseball.

Summer camp was a highlight of the summer. Ralph and his friends enjoyed the summer and going to camp was high on their excitement list. Camp Cedine is operated by a religious group. They offered free camp to kids in those days. They took kids that were bad or good. The bad kids had extra bible lessons though but everyone had a lot of fun.

Boy Scout Camp was another summer camp that Ralph had the good

Chapter Three

fortune to attend. Ralph always seemed to excel at anything he attempted to do. He was an outstanding Boy Scout and became an Eagle Scout and a Boy Scout leader in the city. William Patton (Bay-Brother), Catherine's brother is a great story teller. The following is one of his fondest Ralph Cothran stories.

Bay-Brother recalls that "one day at Boy Scout Camp all the scouts were going through a swimming exercise. At first they were all swimming and having fun and completing the swimming exercises assigned to them. But, then a swimming instructor put a greased large watermelon out in the lake and told them to swim out and fetch it. Well all hell broke loose, because no one could hold on to the greasy watermelon. Finally Ralph who was an excellent swimmer swam out and retrieved the watermelon like it was a loaf of bread to everyone's surprise."

George Key was the first principal Ralph remembers at Orchard Knob School. During this time grammar school and Junior High schools were combined. Ralph, like most of his classmates, hated to take books home. Mr. Key was always lurking outside somewhere after school and would always make the kids go back inside and get their textbooks.

Another fun memory of Ralph's early school days is the story of the herb bags. Ralph's mother like most Black mothers' in those days had many home remedies for colds etc. Ralph like some of his classmates wore a bag of smelly herbs and potions around his neck during the winter months. Ralph remembers that he and his friends saved money in these bags after they were used.

The money that they saved was to buy new play ground equipment at Orchard Knob School. George Key is alleged to have stolen the money In this case Mr. Key went on record as a thief and a crook and a person with no morals or principles. Unfortunately this uncivilized attitude became a permanent part of his personality because he has made a career out of wretched ways of deceit, dishonest, and bowed low-life fraud. For example in later years as the president of the local NAACP Mr. Key sold Black people out to the highest bidder. He used the discriminatory plight of Black people that he was supposed to be helping for his own self-monetary gain. He has also made a career out of accepting payoffs from the local political power brokers to split the Black vote during

Big Ralph

political campaigns.

I arrived at the previously mentioned conclusions from my personal observation of George Key overtime. Honest white people will admit, if called upon that Black leaders like George Key have made a career out of taking bribes from white political and economic power brokers. I can also cite another example, when I ran for mayor of Chattanooga in 1990 no one was in the race but me and the incumbent mayor Gene Roberts. But, on the last day of filing George Key decided to enter the race. For the reacord another white candidate entered the day before George Key. It is for sure that the political dynamics of Chattanooga have sponsored vote splitting as a on-going tactic to maintain power in the hands of those that control the economic and political arenas in Chattanooga.

Mr. John Franklin was the physical education teacher at Orchard Knob and very popular. Mr. Kennedy, Mrs. Easterling, and Mrs. Fait were all well known and Mrs. Holder was the music teacher back then. These teachers and the principal, Mr. Key, enforced the rules around the school. The first bell that you heard during recess all students were supposed to freeze wherever they were was one such rule. When the second bell would ring, all students were then to head immediately back inside the school house.

Ralph and his buddies were like most boys and liked to play way out on the playground. So, when the first bell would ring to get back to the building on time they would start running and not wait on the second bell. School monitors (snitchers) would always tell on all the kids that broke this rule. So once inside the school house and back in your classroom all kids in violation would be called downstairs to receive a whipping. Ralph and his friends always got caught and came to believe that grown-ups, especially Mr. Key, always knew what you were doing.

Mr. Kennedy had a great influence on Ralph's life. Mr. Kennedy was one of his favorite teachers and Ralph always had fond memories of his classes. Mrs. Holder was another beloved teacher. Ralph thought Mrs. Holder was the most beautiful lady he had ever seen. Mrs. Holder was a roving music teacher. Ralph felt close to Mrs. Holder throughout his life and viewed her as his favorite teacher.

Chapter Three

   After Ralph finished the 6th grade his relatives in Flint, Michigan, on his father's side, came to visit Chattanooga. They took Ralph back to spend the summer. He could have stayed longer but he wanted to come back home and attend school. Ralph rode the bus back to Chattanooga. This is when he first saw and realized that segregation existed.

   Ralph had to use segregated facilities when the bus made its stops on the way south to Chattanooga. Eventually he just stayed on the bus as the transition to Jim Crow gradually unfolded soon after he left Flint, Michigan. Since Ralph grew up in an all Black neighborhood he had not given racial differences much thought, but now he began to think. He enjoyed his stay in Flint and knew it was a new and interesting experience.

   Ralph's family consisted of his mother and father and his older sister Hilda. They lived in a small three room shotgun house. In Flint, Ralph witnessed the large extended family. The whole family, mother, daddy, grandmother, uncles, aunts, sisters and brothers all lived in one big house. The house had four levels and the entire family ate together and did other things that families do.

   Charlie Cothrans' folks had all come from Cassville, Georgia to Flint, Michigan back in the early 30's. Charlie, Ralph's father stayed in Flint for a while and drove an ambulance but he went south to Chattanooga after a few years. Back then the automobile industry was booming and Blacks flocked to cities like Detroit and Flint to take the well paying jobs on the automobile assembly lines

   Ralph was anxious to get back to Chattanooga and start school with his friends. He would now be in Junior High School. Kids by now knew what was expected of them and there was a host of dedicated and sincere teachers who took a genuine interest in the students. The segregated schools even with some problems were filled with an atmosphere of belonging. This feeling was characteristic of the teachers as they went about the business of education. No doubt it was expressed in their sincere efforts to discipline the kids justly, and teach them to the best of their knowledge.

   Many things became clear as Ralph's awareness came alive. Sex was

Big Ralph

something Ralph became aware of as he grew into his early teens. Now he could understand the feelings he got when he saw females. Ralph also became aware of the pitfalls of juvenile delinquent kids.

Pikeville was a Juvenile Detention Center when Ralph was growing up. Only real bad kids went to Pikeville and good kids were warned to limit any association with kids that had been confined at Pikeville.

There were positive role models for kids in those days. These role models warned of the evils of juvenile delinquency. Mr. Provine was Ralph's homeroom teacher when he attended Orchard Knob. Mrs. Provine was also one of the legendary Center Directors at Lincoln Park. Mr. Provine taught shop and was also as dedicated as his wife in working with the kids. Mr. Provine was very fair skin and could pass for white. By this time Ralph and his classmates knew that many Black people were different colors and some were the color of white people.

Orchard Knob had the honor roll like other schools, but Orchard Knob also had the dishonor roll. If you failed, you were also called on stage during assembly and you were recognized for your lack of achievement. Mr. Provine gave out punishment for bad grades. If you were in Mr. Provine's homeroom you got five licks for an "F" and four licks for a "D."

The honor roll was good because honor roll students got concessions. They worked in the office and delivered messages throughout the school. Schools did not have the intercom systems when Ralph attended Orchard Knob. Since the messenger carried messages throughout the school the job of messenger was well sought after by many students.

Junior High was the period that Ralph became introduced to organized sports. Already, tall he took to basketball and enjoyed swimming, tennis and a good round of ping pong at Carver Center.

Home life was stable and respect for your parents were an ongoing reality. Everybody was poor. Well, the people that Ralph knew and those that lived in his neighborhood. Ralph never felt cramped in the three room shotgun house on Holly Street. Ralph remembers that they always had plenty to eat. Most people like the Cothrans' had a small garden and Ralph and his father also raised chickens in the back yard. Ralph also caught a rabbit in his back yard.

Chapter Three

Ralph was determined to catch the rabbit so he devised a method to catch the rabbit. Then Ralph discovered that the rabbit had a hole that he would eventually go into. By being patient and waiting he was able to catch the rabbit by observing his habits. Big Ralph would later in life catch many crooks by learning their habits and by exercising patience.

The house on Holly Street was heated with a coal stove in the center room. Sometimes money would be short or the coal man had been by and no one stopped him to buy coal. In those days peddlers would come through the neighborhood selling coal and wood. They would holler "coal man," "wood," "kindling," "50" cent a bushel."

Bushtown was close to the rail yards under the Third Street viaduct. Ralph had a small red wagon. Often his father and mother would tell him to go down to the rail yards and pick up a load of coal. Coal often spilled over from the rail cars carrying coal from the Tennessee coal mines.

Walking along side the tracks picking up coal was not too hard but usually by the time you got a load you were over a mile from the house located on Holly Street. Ralph would be cold and by this time hungry and the loaded little red wagon would be heavy and filled to the rim.

Soon Ralph sought to resolve this matter. Whenever he was sent to the rail yards to pick up coal he climbed up on a coal car. He would then throw down enough coal to fill his wagon. He would take his time loading his wagon and head for home. The railroad detectives never said anything. Now Ralph realizes that they had to see him getting the coal but they always let him get away. Now Ralph, also realizes he was stealing coal. Ralph remembers that he would always want to fill his wagon as soon as possible because he would get cold and hungry. The quicker he got back to the house meant he could eat and get warm.

Every Black neighborhood back then had neighborhood grocery stores. The grocery stores allowed credit. The grocery store that catered to the needs of the people in Ralph's Bushtown neighborhood was Dan's Grocery Store. Dan's store was located on Highland Park and Citico. There was another store called Nathan's at Highland Park and Cleveland.

Since children did not ask grown-ups about money Ralph and his playmates just had a vague notion about credit. Charlie Cothran a big

Big Ralph

strapping man over six foot five inches worked at Signal Mountain Cement Company on Suck Creek Road. Suck Creek Road is an isolated area inhabited by real live hillbillies. No Blacks lived in the mountainous area around Suck Creek Road.

Charlie Cothran was well liked by the people who worked at Signal Mountain Cement Company. So Ralph remembers going with his father at an early age deep into the mountains of Suck Creek where no Black people lived. The mountain people accepted Ralph because he was Charlie's boy and Charlie was well liked by these people though he was to them a "Nigger."

They made good whiskey back in the mountains and Charlie Cothran was very fond of good mountain white whiskey. Charlie operated a Cement Packer back at the Cement Company. In reality he filled bags with dry cement. This job was very dusty and chemicals were constantly in the air.

Ralph later concluded that this hazardous work around chemicals was not good for his fathers' health. This work experience and some of his father's habits like drinking mountain whiskey most likely contributed to his father's ill health in the later years of his life. Charlie Cothran passed away June 9, 1978.

Bessie Cothran was a hard working woman who liked to take a nip every once in while herself. She was average size and Hilda, Ralph's older sister, took size after her mother. Ralph of course took after his father and eventually outgrew him in height. Mrs. Cothran did domestic work in private homes. Ralph remembers that his mother worked for a lady named Mrs. Watson. He was influenced by Mrs. Watson in a way Ralph cannot explain. But Black families that have had the mother taking on domestic chores for a white family have traditionally been influenced by the white employers.

Whites seem to respond to a paternalistic duty while the Black maid and family accept a subordinate role that reflects days of bondage, servitude and the whip.

Of course most of these conclusions were as far from Ralph during this period as the moon. He and his friends, like most boys, just loved to

Chapter Three

have fun. His good friend Frank Newson had an aunt on the Westside who owned a funeral home. On Saturdays Frank and Ralph would go over to Mrs. Buchanan's funeral home down on West 9th Street. She would give them a money bag with her weekly receipts to take to the bank. On the way to the bank through alleys Ralph and Frank tossed the money bag like a football. Ralph recalled that "no one ever tried to rob us." No one realized that the two kids playing with a bag like a football actually had over two hundred dollars or more in the bag.

Many things went on in the neighborhood back in those days. Most of the time Ralph and his friends would be required to be in the house as these things happened at night. But one day Ralph and his friends happened to be out just before it got dark.

Not far from Ralph's house a man on Smartt Street got in trouble with the police and barricaded himself in his house. The police shot up the house and tossed in tear gas that the man tossed back out. When the man finally surrendered the white policemen wanted to physically abuse him. But two Black political leaders stood up to the white police officers and would not allow them to beat the man with their blackjacks. The two community leaders were Percy Billingsley and Harry Cook. They also got other Blacks that had gathered to support their cause.

This was the first time Ralph saw Black men stand up to the white man. This experience definitely made a lasting impression. How this incident influenced Ralph's life remains to be seen.

A lasting impression was also made when Ralph saw his first antidrug film. He had not quite made it to Junior High, and while he was in the 5th or 6th grade Mr. Key the principal at Orchard Knob showed a film about drugs. The film was about heroin addiction. It showed in graphic detail the tragedies of a drug addict in New York.

Ralph and his friends were frightened by the realities of the picture. They vowed to never use drugs. But now when the Chief looks back he notes that he never thought Chattanooga would also develop a drug problem.

The impact of the church also had a lasting impression on Ralph. His mother raised Ralph up in the church. That is why the Highland Park

Big Ralph

Church experience did not confuse Ralph. At Orchard Knob Baptist Church Ralph was involved in various activities. He was a member of the Jr. Usher Board and worked with youth groups to sponsor various social events for the youth in the community.

Junior High soon came to a close as life moved on and Ralph passed to the 10th grade. Life was becoming more than just time to play. Ralph was now becoming a young man and there were certain responsibilities. To most kids of that day, assuming responsibilities of young adulthood was a natural reaction. Today the word responsibility to young adults has very little meaning.

Chapter Four

Howard School and 1954

**Oh, the joy of life, friendships and all things of the beautiful and majestic Creation, as you meet the golden years of youth,
Yet debts to be paid as your
foundation of learning is still to be laid.**

The old westside still existed as Ralph enrolled at Old Howard. Old Howard is the name Black Chattanoogans called the school when it was located on the westside on Carter street. This was 1953 and Ralph was entering the 10th grade.

The ride or walk from Bushtown over on the westside was not bad. Because the excitement and adventure of going to high school was a high point in the life of Ralph and his friends.

Old Howard was closed after Ralph finished the 10th grade. A new school was built on South Market street that had grades 1-12. Mr. Davenport was the principal at Old Howard and he had a strange way of rendering discipline.

For example, one day, Ralph left the school grounds to get a hamburger. Mr. Davenport caught Ralph slipping back on to the school grounds. Mr. Davenport decided that for the next two weeks the entire school would eat hamburgers every day. Every morning Ralph had to go down to Buehler Brothers Food Market and get 50 to 100 lbs. of hamburger meat. That experience broke up Ralph's interest in leaving the school grounds.

Big Ralph

To Ralph and his friends high school was exciting and fun. Athletics were organized on a higher level and kids were now treated like young adults. But some kids still did not want to cooperate. In those days kids that refused to go to school and those that caused on-going problems were recommended for military service.

Even though Ralph was a maturing young man he was not aware of many problems that existed while he was growing up. He had already grown taller than his father and at times he had to wear his father's clothes. Since he was taller than his father he kept his hands in his pockets to push down the pants so they would not appear to be high water.

Ralph was just a normal, Black kid born and raised in the south who accepted certain facts of life. Jim Crow was one fact of life. Even though Ralph didn't feel directly confronted by Jim Crow it was present and real. The Jim Crow laws became a fact of life in America by 1905. During this year the Chattanooga Times reported that "Negroes and whites fight on rapid transit. The Negroes were thrown off the rail car and they take revenge by throwing rocks." [1] The dispute came about regarding the seating arrangements of Blacks and whites that led to whites forcing Blacks to sit in the rear of the rail car.

So by the early part of the 1900's Jim Crow was established and enforced throughout the south. Blacks reacted to this discriminatory system symbolized by Jim Crow in various ways. One direct result of this form of white bigotry was the Garvey Movement. The Garvey movement of the 1920's reached an indeed dedicated and spirited group in Chattanooga. In 1927 the Times reports that: "Police raid a building housing members of Garvey movement. Headlines read----"Three alleged Reds Taken Into Custody." [2] Furthermore the article notes that there were over 700 members in Chattanooga and the biggest problem the police had with these Garvities was that they attempted to buy 200 30-30 rifles from local arms dealers and various pawn shops.

By the time Ralph finished the 10th grade the year was 1954. In 1954 significant changes would take place to cause Ralph to realize the effects of Jim Crow. After the school year 1953-1954, Old Howard on Carter Street was closed. As previously noted a new school also named

Chapter Four

Howard school was built on South Market Street. Ralph enrolled in the 11th grade at the new school.

During the fall of 1954 Mr. Davenport, who also became the principal at the new school, called an, assembly of the entire student body. During the assembly Mr. Davenport announced that segregated schools were outlawed. At the time, the Supreme Court ruling desegregating public schools had very little meaning to Ralph. But to all that attended that assembly it was obvious that the 1954 decision was very important to Mr. Davenport.

Thus from my estimation, by 1954 with the Brown v. Board of Education decision a great war on the definition of terms was launched. In this case in Chattanooga you see this great and confusing battle going on as reported by the *Chattanooga Times*. The mockery of the English language goes on endlessly and the following terms are at the highlight of review and discussion: Integration, segregation, separate but equal, equal access and Jim Crow.

The *Chattanooga Times* began the series of debates on school desegregation 18 May 1954. "Elimination of segregation in the Chattanooga city school system would affect approximately 75% of the schools under the present zoning alignment."

"Thirty-two out of the 44 schools would have both Negro and white pupils if all students were required to attend the nearest school. Commissioner Trotter noted he is desirous of abiding by the Supreme Court ruling." [3]

In another article printed in the *Times* the same day the NAACP responds to the 1954 Supreme Court decision. "Dr. P.A. Stephens Chairman Executive Committee calls the ruling on school segregation the most momentous decision which has occurred in 80 or 90 years." [4]

Dr. Stephens goes on to give credit to his organization, the NAACP, for bringing about this great change. "It is only the fruits of 45 or 50 years of the work of the NAACP to secure first class citizenship for the Negroes in this time."

"This decision will benefit both white and colored, even the tots, may reap the most benefits there from and there by refute this threat of communism." [4]

Big Ralph

It is very interesting to note that Dr. Stephens parallels racism/segregation with communism. Dr. Stephens, speaking as a classic NAACP integrationist, contradicts the opposing view point. The segregationist has often found integration, and equal rights as Communist inspired. I would argue that both the integrationist and the segregationist are overcome with tunnel vision. But by whatever standards the debate goes on.

The following quote gives us some clarity as to how and why Jim Crow became the reality of the times. "During the period after Reconstruction, law did in fact support inequality: Law did in practice encourage separation; law did in reality make hate legal. Thus, while the 13th amendment to the Constitution of the U.S. freed the slaves, the 14th made the Negro a citizen, and the 15th amendment gave him the right to vote, state law and custom took away from him what the Constitution gave." [5]

"Separate but equal" became a phrase to be defeated. In so doing segregation was ruled separate but not equal and integration came the means to equality. "Not until WWII was the practice of separate but equal openly challenged. And not until 1954, in the case of Brown v. the Board of Education of Topeka, Kansas, did the Supreme Court rule that in schools, at least, separate could not be equal." [6]

Prior to the '1954 decision there were two other prominent Supreme Court decisions that had a impact on the 1954 decision. Dred Scott v. Sanford occurred in 1856. This was before the end of slavery and well before Blacks received citizenship rights, from the 14th amendment.

"The question is simply this: Can a Negro, whose ancestors were imported into this country, and sold as slaves, become a member of the political community formed and brought into existence by the Constitution of the U.S., and as such become entitled to all the rights, and privileges, and immunities, guaranteed by the instrument to the citizen?

We think they are not, and that they are not included, and were not intended to be included, under the word "citizens" in the Constitution, and can therefore claim none of the rights and privileges which that instrument provides for and secures to citizens of the U.S." [7]

Chapter Four

So at this point in time Blacks were not recognized as citizens slave nor free. After the end of slavery a different expression took hold to separate the races. This phrase which came to be separate but equal was initially established in the Plessy v. Ferguson case of 1895.

"This case turns upon the constitutionality of an act of the General Assembly of the state of Louisiana, passed in 1890, providing for separate railway carriages for the white and colored races.

The first section of the statute enacts "that all railway companies carrying passengers in their coaches in this state, shall provide equal but separate accommodations for the white, and colored races, by providing two or more passenger coaches for each passenger train, or by dividing the passenger coaches by a partition so as to secure separate accommodations.

The constitutionality of this act is attacked upon the ground that it conflicts both with the 13th amendment abolishing slavery and the 14th amendment, which prohibits certain restrictive legislation on the part of the states.

We cannot say that a law which authorizes or even requires the separation of the two races in public conveyances is unreasonable, or more obnoxious to the 14th amendment than the acts of Congress requiring separate schools for colored children in the District of Columbia, the constitutionality of which does not seem to have been questioned, or the corresponding acts of state legislatures." [8]

Ingrained also in the Plessy v. Ferguson decision is the assumption that the enforced separation of the two races stamps the colored race with a badge of inferiority. Thurgood Marshall would soon attack the separate but equal clause in a scientific manner. In this instance Marshall would use the assumptions of Black inferiority as the means by which to strike down separate but equal and move the Supreme Court to declare segregated schools unconstitutional.

The south insisted that even though they operated separated schools they were equal. This was a falsehood. But to prove that southern schools were not equal was a long and very expensive legal process.

"Marshall resumed his efforts to enforce the "equal protection clause" of the 14th Amendment. This time he knew how to attack the separate but equal doctrine. The 1896 Supreme Court decision in the Plessy v. Ferguson case which supported the separate but equal doctrine had to be overthrown scientifically. Marshall sent Robert Carter, one of his assistants, to talk with psychologist Kenneth B. Clark about the effects of racial segregation on Black children."[9]

Dr. Clark in his study of segregation argued that Black children placed in segregated situations suffered long lasting feelings of inferiority. He went on to conclude that segregation refers to inferiority and that segregated schools in America are the most prominent offenders.

"Using this evidence along with figures showing the gap between monies spent for white and Black children's education Marshall carried four suits to the U.S. Supreme Court. Kansas, South Carolina, Virginia, and Delaware were the defending states. Thurgood Marshall would challenge them with a document prepared by three psychologists and endorsed by thirty-two outstanding social scientists. Its title was "The Effects of Segregation and the Consequences of Desegregation."[10]

The Supreme Court on May 17, 1954 "directed the states to end school segregation "with all deliberate speed." But there was no fixed time schedule for compliance. The court did not at this time endorse the recommendations of the social scientists, and its final decision carried an air of uneasy vagueness."[11]

The Supreme Court decided that separate education is unequal. "We come then to the question presented: Does segregation of children in public schools solely on the basis of race, even though the physical facilities and other "tangible" factors may be equal, deprive the children of the minority group of equal educational opportunities? We believe that it does."[12]

The opinion by the court then moved to the relationship of inferiority and segregation. Thurgood Marshall had skillfully persuaded the court to accept his theory that segregation breeds and causes inferiority.

"Segregation of white and colored children in public schools has a detrimental effect upon the colored children. The impact is greater when it has the sanction of the law: for the policy of separating the races is usually interpreted as denoting the inferiority of the Negro group. A

Chapter Four

sense of inferiority affects the motivation of a child to learn. Segregation with the sanction of law, therefore, has a tendency to retard the educational and mental development of Negro children and to deprive them of some of the benefits they would receive in a racially integrated school system." [13]

The opinion of the court went on to note the impact of Plessy vs. Ferguson and the earlier ruling on separate but equal. Furthermore the court noted that the 14th amendment applied to all citizens.

"Whatever may have been the extent of psychological knowledge at the time of Plessy vs. Ferguson, this finding is amply supported by modern authority. Any language in Plessy vs. Ferguson contrary to this finding is rejected.

We conclude that in the field of public education the doctrine of "separate but equal" has no place. Separate educational facilities are inherently unequal. Therefore, we hold that the plaintiffs and others similarly situated for whom the actions have been brought are, by reason of the segregation complained of deprived of the equal protection of the laws guaranteed by the 14th amendment. This disposition makes unnecessary any discussion whether such segregation also violates the due process clause of the 14th amendment." [14]

Mr. Davenport clearly knew the great consequences of school desegregation when he told Ralph and his classmates that segregation was outlawed. Many things were taking place and Ralph's 10th grade year 1953-1954 ended not so quietly.

White people in Chattanooga and throughout the south were accustomed to the legal and southern way of dealing with the so-called Negro. Separate schools was just one example of southern racial separation. If white people had no objections to white and Black kids attending the same schools, the Supreme Court would not have had to pass a law giving Blacks the constitutional right to an integrated education.

So white people reacted to the decision by the Supreme Court (May 1954) with a vengeance. The hatred for Black people was a throwback to days of the Klan and white supremacist organizations. Everybody got involved, and the debate continued. White congressional representatives

Big Ralph

voiced their opposition to a legitimate Supreme Court decision with a document called "The Southern Manifesto."

While these segregationist hold up the constitution as the law on one hand, they attempt to defy and rewrite the constitution on the other. The following critical excerpts reveal the shallow analysis of the constitution by the legislators.

"The unwarranted decision of the Supreme Court in the public school cases is now bearing the fruit always produced when men substitute naked power for established law.

We regard: the decision of the Supreme Court in the school cases as a clear abuse of judicial power. It climaxes a trend in the federal judiciary undertaking to legislate, in derogation of the authority of congress, and to encroach upon the reserved rights of the states and the people.

The original constitution does not mention education. Neither does the 14th amendment, nor any other amendment. The debates preceding the submission of the 14th amendment clearly show that there was no interest that it should ; affect the systems of education maintained by the states.

Without regard to the consent of the governed, outside agitators are threatening immediate and revolutionary changes in our public school systems. If done, this is certain to destroy the system of public education in some of the states. We reaffirm our reliance on the constitution as the fundamental law of the land.

We decry the Supreme Court's encroachments or rights reserved to the states and to the people, contrary to established law and to the constitution. We commend the motives of those states which have declared the intention to resist forced integration by any lawful means." [15]

You can see from the Southern Manifesto that white people were angry and if at all possible they would resist the desegregation of the schools. The white southern segregationists was a confused bunch of folk, but they were not alone.

The debate continues as the die heart integrationist also contributed to this confusion. It was a crying shame that Thurgood Marshall could not move the court to accept his arguments of "separate but equal" as not equal for Blacks.

Chapter Four

The "separate but equal" doctrine came out of the Plessy v. Ferguson case at the end of the last century. By 1954 clearly it could be documented that Black facilities were inferior to white facilities, for example Black and white schools. But to litigate this argument in court proved to be long and costly.

A closer look at the angle Thurgood Marshall came up with is important to further explore this question. This angle was Black inferiority. In many aspects this was a unique way to challenge segregated schools but not the way Marshall and his cadre of social scientists decided.

First of all Black people have to accept inferiority for it to work. Secondly one can become inferior or be inferior as a part of one's psychological makeup. But, of course the conclusions are to claim that not being able to integrate with the white man is a measure of inferiority is absurd.

In the question of education it is not so much about inferiority, Black, or white or the nature of the physical building, the important query is quality education. So the separation of Black and white children in education from my view does not make one inferior. But if for some reason you already feel inferior to the group you are separated from, then it is a different story.

The system of Jim Crow and segregation impacts on every aspect of life in America. But still by way of custom and life style Ralph still knew very little and felt very little impact as to what was going on.

There was a certain social fabric and peer pressure at Howard School as Ralph entered the 11th grade. Sports were organized on a higher level and Ralph played basketball for the "Howard's Hustling Tigers" and utilized his height.

Red Gaston was the head football coach then and also a legendary history professor. All students at Howard had to take a history test in order to graduate. Red Gaston gave the history test and it was hard. Ralph's mother's cousin lived one block over from Ralph's house on Greenwood street, she was the school teacher who had helped Ralph with his school work in grammar school. Through her friends at Howard

Big Ralph

she would keep tabs on Ralph and report him to his parents if he did not do well in school.

Kids were still disciplined in school in those days. Even though Ralph was at least six foot six inches tall and well over 200 lbs. he would never get to big to be disciplined by his parents and teachers. Also kids in the 50's still had respect for their elders and that was a carry over from elementary school days.

Meanwhile the debate over desegregation was heating up. Some of the frustrations and confusion by Blacks can be gleaned from excerpts from the following article.

"Over 200 people attending a forum called by the Elks reached a consensus that white and colored pupils should be integrated as soon as possible. C.B. Robinson a leader in the group said that a time limit should be set for complete integration. They agreed to organize delegations to go before the school board and ask for complete integration by 1957." [16]

But the most impacting aspect of this article is the acceptance of the inferiority argument rendered in Brown vs. Board of Education. For example the valedictorian of Howard School is quoted as saying "she believed she could have learned more and been better prepared had she attended school with both white and colored boys and girls."

Robinson also alludes to the question of Black inferiority. "Robinson said that in achievement there are many Negro students equal mentally to the most intelligent white students, but he said there is a difference in background. He said most white children have had better cultural opportunities and advantages, and that Negro pupils can assimilate such things through association with white pupils in the schools." [17]

The debate continues and the argument continues to be covered with confusion and the inability to reason. "City School Board issued a formal statement declaring that it will integrate the schools in compliance with the Supreme Court ruling. But not this year." [18]

The next day, 24 July 1955 the Times reported. "Board of Education announced that it will comply with the law on integration. Commissioner Harry Allen states it is our duty to uphold the law. But the Board will seek the widest counsel and not attempt quick implementation." [19]

Chapter Four

By the fall of 1955 the Chattanooga School Board made more sense as they debated the question of desegregation. "The Chattanooga School Board reaffirmed yesterday it's intent to hold public hearings on racial desegregation and compliance with the law in good faith.

The Board's supplemental statement of policy followed a switch by Chairman Commissioner Harry Allen to one of continued opposition to desegregation. The Board declared that its interpretation of the findings is that the Supreme Court directed the school board to find the best means of ending racial discrimination in the schools." [20]

The stall and delay of carrying out the decision of the court is noted in this last statement reported in the previous article. " The Board is best suited to decide what is best for our children and our community instead of having some drastic action imposed upon us. The court itself opened the way for each community to solve its problem in its own way so long as the effort is carried out in good faith." [21]

By November 10th the "City School Board named 28 white persons and 12 Negroes to an interracial advisory committee." [22] A few days later during a School Board meeting violence erupted. "A tube of tear gas was dropped and broken last night as a tense public meeting of the City School Board and its newly appointed interracial advisory Committee was adjourned." [23]

Ralph recalls that during this time he was learning discipline from playing basketball and learning how to get along with others. Fred White one of the legendary coaches in the history of Howard athletics was Ralph's mentor and confidant. In those days Howard had a strong athletic department and a winning tradition. Segregation had caused Howard to be the only high school in the city of Chattanooga where Blacks attended. So all the good athletes in the city had no choice but to attend Howard. Booker T. Washington High School was the, Black high school in the county. Howard competed with Booker T. but segregation caused southern Black high schools to compete with other segregated schools and these schools were out of town.

So during the days of segregation Howard competed with schools like Pearl High School in Nashville, Austin East in Knoxville, St.

Big Ralph

Augustine and Melrose in Memphis and Parker High in Birmingham. Even though segregation was outlawed, a state of segregation still existed throughout the south.

Also the southern segregationist began to organize to keep segregation in place. The Times reports-- "Two legal actions aimed at ultimately reversing the Supreme Court decision against segregation are in prospect, noted the president of the Tennessee Society to Maintain Segregation.

Segregationist urged, to refuse to obey what was declared a decision dictated by subversive thinking. Instead the south could turn to the 2nd amendment. The 2nd amendment reads: "A well regulated militia being necessary to the security of a free state, the right of the people to bear arms shall not be infringed." [24]

The dispute continues as the School Board takes more decisive action in the spring of 1956 and defies the law. " The Board stated there will be no integration of white and Negro pupils in Chattanooga for probably 5 or more years." [25]

A few days later the NAACP sought to protest this action as the Times reports. "Chattanooga NAACP protested School Board decision to not end segregation. President of NAACP Henry L. Pearson charged the board with not allowing the community to express themselves on the problem." [26]

The jitney cabs that ran a route up and down 3rd Street would take Ralph and his friends to school if they were late. Ralph recalled that the cab drivers would see us on the corner waiting on the bus and realize that we had missed the bus and would be late for school by the time the next bus ran.

Ralph like most kids attending Howard bought school bus tokens at a reduced rate. These tokens could be used to ride the city busses to and from school. A white high school was down on 3rd Street in Fortwood that was called City High School. Also in walking distance to Bushtown was a white county high school located within the city limits called Central High School. At this time, as a teenager, Ralph began to realize the difference between Blacks and whites but you went where you were supposed to go. In this case all Black high school age pupils attended

Chapter Four

Howard no matter where they lived in the city of Chattanooga.

In response to the growing awareness of Jim Crow, Ralph once again notes "you went where you were supposed to go." The problems caused by Jim Crow and segregation caused the government to take certain actions. Thus there were various responses to the discrimination of Black people by the federal government.

C.Vann Woodward in his very influential research "The Strange Career of Jim Crow" has given us a good back ground of federal involvement in the cause of equal rights for Blacks. In 1952 the democratic Attorney General filed a brief with the Supreme Court in regard to the cases before the court involving school segregation. The brief noted that racial discrimination promotes communist propaganda and questions the U. S. as the leader in the principles of democracy. [27]

Woodward argues that Franklin Delano Roosevelt and his wife Eleanor paved the way for Harry Truman in the cause of Black equality. "FDR's first direct commitment, his executive order of June 1941 establishing a Fair Employment Practices Committee to supervise all defense contracts in industries, was made under threat of a massive demonstration, but it set an important precedent." [28]

By 1946 Roosevelt's successor Harry Truman began to evaluate U.S. racial policy. "He created a Commission on Higher Education, which reported the following year that there will be no fundamental correction of the total condition until segregation legislation is repealed." [29]

In two years Truman began to make some unprecedented moves against segregation. "By February 1948 Truman sought to outlaw poll tax and lynching, the elimination of segregation in interstate transportation, a law to enforce fairness in elections, and the establishment of a permanent civil rights commission. In the same year the president issued an executive order to end discrimination in federal employment, and a momentous order to end segregation in the armed services." [30]

With the passing of dominant presidents, like Roosevelt and Truman, the leadership in civil rights on the federal level passed to the federal judiciary. In turn the courts asked for a greater exercise in federal authority.

Big Ralph

"The early decisions were concerned with interstate, not intrastate, commerce. Not until 1946 did the court, in Morgan v. Virginia, throw out a state law requiring segregation of a carrier crossing state lines. Four years later came a ruling against segregation on railway diners. Intrastate carriers remained untouched for a time and Jim Crow continued to prevail for lack of federal legislation, which Eisenhower was reluctant to demand." [31]

"Another entrenchment of Jim Crow, older in north than in the south, was residential segregation. The courts had struck much earlier at housing segregation by law, but the practice continued under the protection of private restrictive covenants written into deeds and agreements. In 1948 the Supreme Court held these private agreements invalid on the ground that they deprived minorities of equal protection of the laws." [32]

We will now look at a concluding statement by Woodward as he seeks to bring clarity to Jim Crow.

"The Negro awakening of 1960 was more profound and impressive than the abortive stirrings of 1867. One of the great uprisings of oppressed people in the 20th century, it could have taken anomaious form had it not been for the extremely fortunate circumstances. One was the Brown decision of 1954 that had prepared the way for redress of grievances by constitutional means. The other was that all the major civil rights organizations, now as well as old, were committed to the philosophy of nonviolence." [33]

Even though one cannot doubt the enormous impact of the Supreme Court decision of 1954, realistically Blacks cannot say the same for the commitment to the philosophy of nonviolence. This is also not to say a philosophy of violence would be better for Black liberation. What we are saying is that a commitment toward the philosophical aspects of nonviolent theories have not been sanctioned by God or some higher power as the best approach to liberation for Black America.

On the contrary nonviolence by Blacks leads to violence by whites. Also the logical result of bowing, pleading, begging and publicly praying for your enemies equals no respect and disrespect for all Black people.

Chapter Four

In Chattanooga sit-in demonstrations as part of the nonviolent movement began in 1966. "Sit-in arrests were made for the third consecutive school day Monday at S. H. Kress & Co. as the students were loaded in the paddy wagon they chanted one, two, three, four, we want freedom; five, six, seven, eight we want to integrate." [34]

You can see the confusion with freedom, justice and equality and so-called integration. No doubt the nonviolent training camps confused the term integration with equal access, equality and basic citizenship rights. But the sit-ins had an impact and this assessment is not an attempt to lessen their importance to the overall movement for Black equality.

By August of 1960 the sit-in demonstrators had taken a heavy toll on lunch counters in downtown Chattanooga. "Negro students were served at seven downtown lunch counters at 4 o'clock Friday afternoon by prearranged plan.

The plan was the result of excellent work by the ministers group here working with the merchants involved. It was the climax of a series of many long meetings." [35]

Even though white merchants eventually gave in to the humane requests of the sit-in demonstrators in Chattanooga all was not well. The Times reports November 1960 that there was an on-going problem with bombings in the Black community.

"The Alton Park Mothers Civic Organization has deposited $116.16 to be paid for information leading to the arrest and conviction of those guilty in bombings here during July and August. The total reward is now $6,821, the bombings were July 16, August 11, August 12, August 17 and August 21." [36]

Louis E. Lomax gives a view of the circumstances that lead to what he describes as The Negro Revolt. Lomax relates "as of May 17, 1954, separate but equal was the law of the land; however, separate but unequal was and still is, the practice and reality." [37] The conclusions by Lomax in most cases are factual and represents a certain consciousness and responsibility. In this case the Lomax book is very useful especially compared to other works that deal with similar historical concerns. Lomax like many other writers evaluates the Black predicament along economic lines.

Big Ralph

"The American Negro of the fifties lived in a state of constant humiliation. His dignity as an individual was not admitted, in the north or south, and his worth was so demeaned that even other nonwhite peoples of the world had little respect for him. School desegregation, disfranchisement, segregation of public facilities and overt police brutality aside, the true condition of the Negro is best reflected by his relative position as a wage earner and professional man in American society."[38]

The particular economic status of Blacks which was assessed by Lomax brings additional factors up for review. In this case there are various forces that produced a depressed economic status of Black America:

"1. Discrimination against Negroes in vocational as well as academic training.

2. Discrimination against Negroes in apprenticeship training programs.

3. Discrimination against Negroes by labor organizations particularly in the construction and machinists crafts.

4. Discrimination against Negroes in referral services rendered by state employment offices.

5. Discrimination against Negroes in the training and "employment" opportunities offered by the armed services, including the "civilian components."

6. Discrimination by employers, including government contractors and even the federal government."[39]

The economic analysis of the Black experience speaks of a desperate set of circumstances. These circumstances get even more desperate when specific statistical data is noted. Once again Lomax's "The Black Revolt" becomes a premiere source for the modern Black experience. The constraints of economic impotence may well be the most impacting in the Black struggle for equal rights.

"This economic strait jacket has everything to do with the breakdown of family life and general morality in the Negro community: it is the basic explanation for the inordinate Negro crime rate: it is the

Chapter Four

fundamental cause of our high welfare rolls and absurd relief chiseling, this is why we live in slums." [40]

Housing is also a factor in this equation. As a necessary aspect of human survival housing in America: in the ghetto, in the Black community is dictated by one's economic means.

"Housing in the south, one out of four nonwhite dwellings (rentals) are dilapidated as compared with one out of ten for white dwelling units. Not only is nonwhite housing of an inferior quality: the nonwhite dweller must pay more for his housing. [41]

Blacks seemed to still experience a sort of modern day slavery as everything in society seems to cost them more. During the contemporary period since 1960 public housing has taken a nose dive and become one of the most wretched housing situations that exist in the urban American landscape.

"Nonwhite families (4.4 members) are on the whole, larger than white families (3.6 members). Whereas public housing has improved the quality of housing available to low-income Negroes, it has not noticeably increased the quantity of good housing available to Negroes. This seemingly contradiction arises from the fact that public housing usually displaces slum units and the former slum dwellers cannot afford to occupy the new units.

These economic and housing factors are reflected in the Negro family characteristics. One out of three nonwhite women above 14 who have married was as of 1960, are separated or divorced from her husband: the corresponding ratio for white women is one out of five. The higher morality rate among Negro males leads to a higher ratio of nonwhite widows. This creates another financial burden. The Negro crime rate which takes the Negro man, principally, from the social scene adds even more of a burden.

Broken homes lead to a broken morality. One out of five nonwhite births is illegitimate, as compared with one out of 50 white births. Adoption is closed to most blacks and 2/5 of welfare goes to Blacks. [42]

In view of these statistics the vast majority of Black people are suffering because of their pitiful economic potential. But there is what

Big Ralph

some call the Black elite. All Blacks are not poor, unemployed and underemployed. So what are these people doing? "The Negro elite is hard at work supporting the NAACP and the Urban League." [43]

Claude Bennett head of Associated Negro Press gives a classic integrationist view of the Black elite. In this case Bennett uses Black newspapers as an example.

"It's a shame that we have a separate Negro society in this country and a separate wire service for Negro newspapers. We are working toward the end that someday there will be no more need for my news service and no need for anything else-including society- which at present the white community does not allow us to share." [44]

The confusion continues and no doubt becomes the foremost principal in the Black struggle for freedom. This confusion is rooted in Black leadership, steeped in a integrationist philosophy believing that integration with white people was crucial in the fight for freedom, justice and equality.

Segregation had historically meant that Blacks did not receive equal treatment when it came to public facilities etc. To offset this trend of discrimination the Plessy v. Ferguson decision of the late 1800's had set the precedent for "separate but equal" doctrine.

But in reality, facilities, and services for Blacks were never equal to those of whites. In this case the contradicting integrationist philosophy gained a new life. The logic that developed was the only way to receive equal rights was to totally integrate with white people. So in this confusion many Blacks lost their identity, culture, economic enterprises and begged and pleaded to enter the white world.

Thus equality got confused with integration. And as the mood to integrate gained momentum so did the resistance to integrate result in violence and a white backlash. Prior to 1954 the Supreme Court cases that dealt with civil rights did not strike down the "separate but equal" doctrine. These cases said that Blacks were entitled to the same treatment as white people in public institutions.

Brown v. Board of Education, Topeka, Kansas May 17, 1954 ruled that separate but equal was unconstitutional, thus segregated public

Chapter Four

schools were outlawed. As the court moved slowly toward implementation of it's order the white people reeled in defiance. Blacks had the bitter taste of war and racism as WWII and Korea came to a close. Lomax also speaks of how naive Blacks were.

"James Eastland senator from Mississippi stated that the south would never accept this decision. He predicted that this decision will bring on a century of litigation.

We heard Eastland say it: we knew there was some truth in what he said: but we did not, refused to, actually believe that Eastland spoke for the south." [45]

Lomax goes further in describing the "confused Black naiveté." While Blacks made a distinction between classes of white people they failed to realize that class did not supersede race.

"Those of us who believed the desegregation order would be carried out were twice bemused, each time by a false faith:

1. We particularly those of us who were southern born--had faith in a class of white people known to Negroes as good white people. These people represented the power structure. It never occurred to us that professional white people would let poor white trash stone the town and take over. Not that the good white people wanted integration---indeed, we know they did not---but we expected them to be law-abiding and to insist that their communities remain that way.

2. The second false faith that bemused us was the belief that local school boards would recognize the court order and submit their own integration schedules. This odd course, did not happen. With few exceptions, Negroes have had to institute court action before local boards submitted integration schedules and when submitted the plans called for "token" integration and did little to unburden the current generation of Negro students, almost all of whom will go forth to life from segregated schools." [46]

Truly this was a climate of confusion. Luckily the country did not resort to total chaos. So it was not unusual for a young man finishing Howard School in 1957 to also be confused.

Big Ralph

Ralph looked toward the future and decided to attend Lane College. He hoped for a chance to play basketball and a career in athletics. In less than two years Ralph made another career move and joined the U.S. Air Force.

Chapter Four

Big Ralph as a young patrol officer investigates a crime scene. Ralph was a skilled investigator, this skill would prepare him for the leadership ranks

Big Ralph

Big Ralph stands at a Chattanooga police cruiser as the Chief of Police. His stern look reveals that Ralph took a hard stand on crime and the criminals that commit criminal acts.

CHAPTER 5

Black Integrationist And White Liberals: The White Backlash

**Neither did they know the irony they posed,
as they hardened already hate filled souls.**

Ralph and Catherine were married soon after Ralph left Lane College. They had been classmates in high school. Catherine was not born in Chattanooga. She was born a few years before her parents, William (Billy) Patton and Ruby (Griffin) Patton, migrated to Chattanooga from Madison County Alabama around 1940. Catherine was two years old when Billy and Ruby Patton came to Chattanooga. The family first lived with Aunt Babe on Chandler Avenue in Alton Park. Aunt Babe's name was Ida, she had married Solomon (Saul) Sanderfur. Ida was Billy Patton's only sister and he was her only brother. Ruby Sue Griffin Patton also had one brother. Uncle Dub was given the name Everette W. Griffin. Uncle Dub to Catherine and her family was also called E.W. He and Aunt Babe left this world during the 90's while Uncle Saul passed away in the 80's.

Billy and Ruby soon found their first house down the street from Aunt Babe on Chandler Avenue. While Catherine was still a little girl the family lived briefly in St. Elmo which was south of Alton Park. They lived on Tennessee Avenue. Catherine remembers that when they lived in St. Elmo they had a big black dog. The dog would always come out to meet her father when he came home from work, always wagging his

Big Ralph

tail. They soon moved to the first public housing project in Chattanooga, College Hill Courts. Located on the Westside, the new brick structures were a great deal more hospitable than the cold water, rundown, shotgun houses most poor Blacks lived in during the 40's.

Catherine has fond memories of living in College Hill Court. She and her friends played games like house, not it and ball games. Catherine recalls that she soon developed a complex about playing ball because she was not apt at the game. Therefore often no one would choose her to play so she lost interest in the game.

The flag pole was located in the center of the projects. This was a place for kids and adults to gather. The flag pole had a good concrete surface to skate on, and Catherine was a good skater. During the summer they turned water on around the flag pole, and the kids in the projects considered this their swimming pool. During those days Catherine notes there was not a stigma attached to public housing. Thus public housing was a step up instead of a step down, because public housing was such a improvement over the available housing for poor people.

Marianne McCann Efiom, was, and still is Catherine's dear and close friend. Marianne grew up in College Hill Courts. In fact Marianne has been as close as a sister to Catherine, she has also been the writer's other big sister. Catherine recalls that she has been blessed to have a devoted, and truly loyal friend over the years. Marianne like Catherine was not born in College Hill Courts. Ralph and Marianne were born in Bushtown. While Ralph stayed in Bushtown, Marianne and her family moved from Greenwood avenue to College Hill Courts. Sarah Reed, and Gwendolyn Wingfield were also close girl friends when Catherine grew up in College Hill Courts.

Billy and Ruby Sue were hard working, good parents. The family grew to include three brothers and four girls counting Catherine the oldest. Though Billy Patton was not fair skinned with white features his blood line was a mixture of African, European and Mulatto ethnic traits. Ruby Sue, who was brown skinned with dark hair, had the African presence and the features of the Native American.

They were both proud and independent and without a doubt they

Chapter Five

stood in awe of only, Almighty God. A few Blacks in the history of Black America have never felt they were inferior to white people or any other people. Ruby and Billy were of this persuasion and they taught their children that they were as good as any other human being. This sentiment of independence and self-pride was evidently passed on to them by their elders. So, while most Blacks held a fear of the white man, the Patton family held fast to their independence and inferiority was unnatural and illogical.

Catherine readily took on this attitude. She was a quiet, unassuming person who, with quiet courage, voiced her opinion on the editorial page of the Chattanooga News Free Press while, still a high school student. Catherine felt a great need to respond to the confusion over school desegregation. This was a courageous act because Blacks were not supposed to speak up for their rights nor write about them to local newspapers. (See Appendix A Catherine's letter, also see response letter and other editorials on segregation)

Catherine's Christian attitude caused her to speak out. Catherine's response to speaking out and writing, the Chattanooga News Free Press reveals her basic principles and values. She said " I admire anyone who has the courage to stand up for what they believe in and will speak out. One should have the courage to die for whatever cause you believe in. That is why I named my first son after Stephen in the Bible who was the first Christian martyr. Stephen was filled with the Holy Ghost and preached the Gospel. For this he was stoned to death. Stephen had love for his people and even when he was being stoned to death he was praying to God to forgive the people."

Catherine was just appalled to witness the unjust treatment of Blacks by white people. Inside of her is this great love and feelings of compassion for all people Black or white. With these feelings in mind she recalled that she had to vent out her frustrations on paper. She got a response from a young white male who was afraid to sign his name to his letter. He didn't sign because his family did not share his views and he was afraid that he might be mistaken for his father. But, this was the climate in the south during the early days of the attack on segregation.

Catherine said that "speaking out has been a natural reaction for her

Big Ralph

as a person. "But, Catherine married Ralph Henry Cothran who rose through the ranks to become the first Black Police Chief in the history of Chattanooga. Then she had to take a different attitude and hold her peace because of the high profile of her husband.

Catherine attended Roosevelt University in Chicago before her and Ralph attended Lane College. Catherine attended Roosevelt for six months during the school year 1956-1957. Her mother Ruby Sue Patton had surgery back in Chattanooga and Catherine had to return home to care for her. Mrs. Patton had no sisters and Catherine was the oldest girl, so she made the decision to come home and care for her mother.

During this time Ralph had taken a basketball scholarship at a small college close to the town of Greely, Colorado. Ralph and Catherine both experienced financial problems their first year in college. Anyway Ralph did not complete the year at the school in Colorado and he also returned to Chattanooga.

Ralph got a job in 1958 at the Henry Branch YMCA teaching swimming. Ralph also worked as the Director of a community center in Dalton, Georgia that is 20 miles south of Chattanooga. This is where Ralph gained his basic knowledge about working with youth that would be part of him for life. These experiences helped form his attitudes about crime prevention and his dream of broad based recreational programs for youth citywide.

Ralph did not meet Catherine until they attended Lane College. The post 1954 era was a challenging period as the nation struggled with the questions of integration versus segregation. White liberals came on the scene in support of integration. Also, many Blacks took on a philosophy of integration. What was this philosophy? Also, what was the philosophy of white liberals during this era?

These questions and concerns are questions to which Ralph sought answers during his life time. In fact the multifaceted problem of race plagued him throughout his career as a law enforcement officer.

Again to bring some clarity to this discussion we will review prominent literature written during this time. The question of liberals and tokenism is brought into focus by Leroi Jones in the following

Chapter Five

quotes.

"A rich man told me recently that a liberal is a man who tells other people what to do with their money. I told him that was right from the side of the telescope he looked through, but that as far as I was concerned a liberal was a man who told other people what to do with their poverty.

I mention this peculiar American phenomenon, i.e., American Liberalism, because it is just this group of amateur social theorists, American Liberals, who have done most throughout American history to insure the success of tokenism.

Slavery was not anything but an unnecessarily cruel and repressive method of making money for the western white man. Colonialism was a more subtle, but equally repressive method of accomplishing the same end. In fact, even though the slave trade, for instance, was entered for purely commercial reasons, after a few years the more liberal-minded Americans began to try to justify it as a method of converting heathens to Christianity."[1]

Jones continues his discussion and seeks to define the Black integrationists as a Black person who would side with reactionaries on matters concerning civil rights. This group of Blacks are found in the middle-class. Often these educated Blacks began to form a distinct integrationist philosophy.

The idea of tokenism in Jones' analysis merges with the integrationist philosophy. Here a neo-colonistic attitude takes hold and the absurd notion that some how a man, usually a Black man must progress to freedom. The attitude that people must get prepared for freedom is just another game to continue the exploitation of Blacks. Many social scientists conclude that tokenism is not an abstract philosophy but a realistic part of American political life.

The question of white liberals and the Black struggle is explored in detail by James Farmer the founder of CORE.

"The issue is not militancy versus moderation. There are militants indeed and there are moderates, too, in both camps. Nor is "integration versus separation" the definitive division. Which is it--integration or separation--when a Black student joins a campus Afro-American

Big Ralph

Association after choosing freely to enter an integrated university? Then, is it youth against age? The young, it is true, carry burdens of the argument on one side, while many of their elders form the bulwark on the other. Is the question, then, "Black power?" How does one debate a slogan without a precise statement of its meaning? What is the way for Black Americans to find a meaning for their existence and to achieve dignity in the American context? Is it through assimilation? Or is it through racial cohesiveness?"[2]

The essay by James Farmer makes several critical arguments. One very important argument is "do Blacks want integration or equal rights?" There is some confusion in the quest for equal rights. As this humane principle gets bogged down in a quest for integration, yes integration merely for the sake of integrating.

Integrating merely for the sake of integrating does not make sense. If this is the interest of the integrationist they also wish to assimilate. In reality there are most likely three aspects are definitive qualities ascribed to assimilation. First white people view assimilation as a way to allow token Blacks into the mainstream and to produce a superficial atmosphere of acceptance. This is an accepted attitude by white liberals who relish their Black friends, who aspire to be like them, which of course is impossible.

Secondly Blacks view assimilation as a means to integrate with white people and be accepted. Their goal is to do any and everything possible to appease whites. They will straighten their hair, lighten their skin, talk like white people and do anything to turn Black souls into what can be described as an honorary white person. In their way of thinking this is progress and equality.

The third view of assimilation comes from Blacks that view this phenomenon as counter productive. These Blacks do not want to give up their racial identity to try to be like white people. They want equal rights but blind integration is not necessarily associated with equal rights. Thus, these Blacks want freedom, equality, dignity and respect. These Blacks are proud of their ancestry and are insulted by those who think it is important to be subservient to white and European culture.

Black Americans cannot compare themselves to the assimilation

Chapter Five

processes of the Europeans here in America. First these people are white and they do not have to deal with the legacy of slavery. For some reason the integrationist philosophy became dominant and Blacks felt they could assimilate just like Europeans. Meanwhile Blacks resisted efforts to maintain Black businesses and institutions by claiming this would keep segregation intact.

This confusion is even more pronounced when we see the paternalistic attitude of the white liberal. Thus, as Blacks have allowed the white liberal to take them by the hand like a child, they have forgotten their own neighborhoods, schools, businesses and institutions. Sadly they have convinced themselves that whatever the white man has is better. Therefore this confused Black person wants to integrate, despite the need and the attainment of equality.

It is very interesting that Farmer concludes his powerful essay with statements on education. Education clearly brought the discussion of segregation versus integration to the forefront. There is some hope evidently because at least some Blacks see a need to consider an option to integration. These Blacks see a need to control the schools in their communities. Though the effort to take control of neighborhood schools was short-lived it is still a very important statement. At least somebody considered that integration or segregation was not the problem regarding education in the Black community. The problem was, and is, quality education. Some came to believe that the only way to improve and maintain quality education was to integrate Black and white children in the same schools.

Some parents believed that integration was not necessarily a panacea for quality education. First the entire U.S. Armed Forces could not force white America to integrate the public schools. Thus, these Blacks concluded that the only sensible thing to do was to take control of their own neighborhood schools. Black parents that took this attitude insisted on having some control of teachers, administrators and the curriculum.

The white liberal's definitive qualities and variables are explored further by Louis Lomax. "Lomax says that as one views the American populace divided along ideological rather than ethnic lines with respect to the Negro revolt--it is likely that in time the western race problem

Big Ralph

would transmute into a class problem. The Negro cause has always been laced with white people. The NAACP, Urban League and CORE were founded by Negroes and whites. The SCLC is a Negro organization but the bulk of its financing is white. And from the outset the student movement has been interracial.

Many Negroes feel that the presence of white people in Negro organizations inevitable leads to "go-slowism." They cite the NAACP and the Urban League as examples. They are refuted by CORE that has a larger contingent of white people and is by far the most militant Negro action group. Many Negroes argue against the presence of white people in Negro organizations on the ground of race pride. "The Jews would die before they would let a Negro rise to the leadership of one of their organizations. So why should we let Jews, or any white man for that matter, head our organizations?" [3]

It is amazing and most interesting to see the clear and correct logic of Lomax in so many aspects of the Black experience. Lomax is credited with a sensible analysis of Jewish and Black relationships.

For example Blacks were upset that in 1961 the NAACP named Jack Greenberg to succeed Thurgood Marshall as head of the NAACP Legal Defense and Education Fund. These protests were clearly pro-Black and had nothing to do with Jack Greenberg being a Jew.

So if some Blacks have a problem with white people leading their organizations they also have a problem with white membership. White people when denied membership in Black organizations use spies in the Black community to infiltrate Black organizations. Blacks have used light skinned Blacks to also spy at white meetings even Klan gatherings.

All of this is true and makes sense but Lomax clearly leaves his previous sense of logic when he justifies why whites should stay in Black organizations.

"1. The first reason is historical. White liberals spoke for us when we were, for the most part, unable to speak for ourselves. They had power, we did not, they had learning, we did not; they were white, we were not, and thus they could speak without the total sense of fear that enveloped every militant Negro in the last days of the 1800's and the early days of

Chapter Five

the century.

2. The second reason is financial. In the early days white people had money, we did not, most of the money for the major civil rights organizations comes from white money.

3. The third and most important reason is that the presence of white people in Negro organizations keeps the Negro revolt from turning into a race conflict." [4]

Maybe Lomax was a militant integrationist. His views on the utility of including the white presence in all aspects of the Black experience, add to the philosophy of integration.

The integrationist philosophy did not dwell in isolation as other views came into play. Kenneth B. Clark in his writings gives us a psychological analysis of aspects of the Black experience. One primary concern is the term "Black Power." What is it, what does it mean for Black progress? How does Black Power also embrace integration?

"I differ with early Gunnar Myrdal only in my belief that the American democratic creed and ideals are not psychologically contradictory to American racism. In terms of dynamics and motivation of the insecure, they are compatible.

The demand for racial justice on the part of American Negroes is balanced by an almost equal psychological reality, of the fear of the removal of racial barriers. The hopes and beliefs of the Negro that racial equality and democracy could be obtained through litigation, legislation, executive action and negotiation and through strong alliances with various white liberal groups, were supplanted by disillusionment, bitterness, and anger which erupted under the anguished cry of "Black Power" which pathetically is sought to disguise the understandable desperation and impotence with bombast and rhetoric." [5]

White backlash stepped to the forefront to answer the cry for "Black Power." Clearly "Black Power" did not cause the white backlash. The historic rhetoric of racism and all its components was well established, since the birth of the nation. June 1966 was the birth of "Black Power" which launched a new contemporary phenomenon that had to be reckoned with.

Big Ralph

Clark says "Black Power'" emerged as a response to the following facts:

"1. A recognition of the fact that of the center gravity of the civil rights movement had moved to the northern, urban, racial, ghettos, where it was immobilized by white resistance for significant change for Blacks.

2. Recognition that successful litigation, strong legislation, free access to public accommodations, open housing, the right to vote to hold office and yet Blacks are still in poverty in the ghetto.

3. Despite the war on poverty and the Great Society Blacks still are regulated to inferior schools, unemployed and underemployed." [6]

"Black Power" advocates had a legitimate concern and right to express a non- accommodation's view point. Here they sought only the right to be granted basic constitutional rights. Booker T. Washington was accepted by white America but militants were not accepted.

Clark on a final note talks about the cleavage between the Black middle class and the masses. In this instance the masses concluded that recent civil rights victories had benefited only a small percentage of the Black community.

The masses live in the ghetto. In a further study Clark analyzes the ghetto and the people in it. The social dynamics of the ghetto are a different sort than the circumstance of those that live in middle-class neighborhoods. Usually whites see Blacks as inferior thus Clark feels that accepting Blacks as equals is what really terrifies the white community.

Ghetto schools in Chattanooga and elsewhere in the U.S. were separate and unequal. Ralph had attended segregated schools all his life. He would always remember the resistance to change. The white backlash is seen most vividly as Blacks and liberals challenge the customs and laws that govern public education throughout the nation.

"School segregation in the south had, for generations, been supported by law; in the north, segregation has been supported by community custom and indifference. It is assumed that children should go to school where they live, and if they live in segregated neighborhoods, the schools are, as a matter of course segregated.

Chapter Five

"Segregation and inferior education reinforce each other. Some persons take the position that the first must go before the second does; others, that the reverse is true." [7]

The confusion of Black integrationist and white liberals has had a direct affect on the reactions of many whites. The white people that often react to the integrationist and liberals are often called racists. Some truly are racists but many of these white people are just responding to custom and law.

So as Blacks and their supporters seek to integrate public schools, whites flee. White people all across America, not only in Chattanooga have sent their children to private or parochial schools. So schools have remained segregated even when Blacks moved into a previously all white community.

The impossible task of integrating the public schools in America put school districts throughout the nation in a dilemma. Since integrationist thought that equality in education for Blacks was only achieved through Blacks and whites attending the same schools, the quest for integration was eternal.

So instead of seeking improved neighborhood schools, integrationist chased the last remnants of the white student population throughout their school district.

"One of the remedies for segregation has been long-distance transportation of elementary school pupils, or "busing." This plan seems to offer immediate desegregation, but in many cases it would lead to bad education and, in the end, therefore to even more segregation.

"Therefore, any effective plan must (1) reduce school segregation; (2) bring better educational services; and (3) hold white pupils, even bring more back into the public school system." [8]

Busing has been considered forced desegregation. White people have organized to counter this tactic to integrate the schools. The result has been to place their children in private schools. Poor whites who have not been able to afford private schools have been left behind.

Logically one would conclude that the quality of education should have nothing to do with income or status. Here ghetto schools should be equal to schools in affluent areas. This promotes people like Clark to

Big Ralph

argue. "The goals of integration and quality education must be sought together; they are interdependent. One is not possible without the other." [9] When this premise is challenged the civil rights activists and integrationist claim that Blacks that want excellent ghetto schools only want to keep segregation intact. What is wrong with quality schools in our own neighborhoods? Why do some Blacks feel that quality education can only be achieved by going to schools with white children?

To answer these questions some Blacks and whites have noted that most Black students are inferior academically to white students. Here they feel that all Black segregated schools are inherently inferior academically. Thus white people that flee integrated schools strongly feel that academically inferior Black students justifies segregation.

Tragically some middle-class Blacks have come to conclude that their children are more adaptable to integration than poor Blacks. The confusion continues regarding integration or quality education. Does integration automatically mean quality education?

Those that became integrationist took on feelings of inferiority. Integration soon also came to be a means to spite white people. Meanwhile, alleged Black inferiority and the childish spite game became the gross contradiction of the integrationist. The reality of Black survival depends on our establishing an economic base. Thus, civil rights should mean economic rights first. White people and even the white liberals and the integrationist Jewish supporters have wanted Blacks to continue to be economically dependent on white America.

"Seventy years ago, for example, both Booker T. Washington, the great apostle of accommodation, and W.E.B. DuBois, the great militant, were urging Negroes to go into business in order to develop the wealth and power they needed to change their position in American society. Their exhortations were in vain; if anything, Negro business is relatively less important now than at the turn of the century.

"Only about 100 thousand Negroes in the U.S. operate their own businesses or hold managerial positions; beauty parlors, barber shops, undertaking, and cosmetic manufacturing are the only kinds of Negro businesses which provide significant numbers of jobs for other Negroes

Chapter Five

or produce substantial revenue. Negro insurance companies, banks, and publishing companies are important symbolically as evidence of Negro achievement, but they account for very little wealth or employment."[10]

The erosion of Black economic development has had a significant decline as integration has spread. Since the 1960's Chattanooga and other cities has seen traditional Black businesses disappear. When Ralph grew up in Bushtown during 1940 and 1950 Jews were the people outside the Black community who operated businesses that catered to Black people. There were also a variety of Black businesses in Black neighborhoods. These businesses consisted of barber and beauty shops to drugstores and dry-cleaning establishments. etc. People foreign to the Black community have always invaded our communities and sold us goods and services. Historically these businesses replaced Black businesses. Eventually new foreigners only replaced other people that are foreign to the Black community.

Presently the most impacting aspect of this ongoing destruction and deterioration of Black businesses is the attack on the last independent Black businesses left in the Black community. Beauty-shops and barber shops that cater to "Black people are noted throughout Black America. These shops are owned and operated by Blacks.

Creative and capitalistic Koreans are making progress to control this industry. Koreans have already locked down the nail and manicure business in the Black community thus dominating this market and running many Blacks out of the business. Meanwhile, these very industrious, eager Korean merchants have been allowed to set up nail businesses inside many Black beauty shops.

So while they securely corner the nail business they are quietly learning how to do Black folks hair. Koreans have established businesses in the nail and hair care products industry. Meanwhile, Koreans have already established interest in a few Black beauty shops.

The manufacture of cosmetics and hair care products for Blacks at once was controlled by Black manufactures. Tragically since the civil rights era Blacks have lost considerable influence in manufacturing and in the distribution of Black hair care products. The evidence of Korean hair care shops throughout the Black community clearly reveals that these people have a virtual monopoly on Black hair care products.

We need a monopoly on rice. It is impossible for Blacks to have a monopoly on rice. So how did Asians come by monopolizing products that we spend billions on yearly?

Black funeral homes are also traditional Black businesses. Blacks have always buried their own and Black morticians have always been an established and respected business entity in our communities. Since the 1960's once again there has been an ongoing attack on this bastion of Black businesses.

While the Asians seek to wipe out our ownership in the hair care industry, white corporations seek to takeover our undertaking needs. Throughout America large white corporations are buying the largest and most prestigious Black funeral homes. The biggest and the best are not the only targets because the strategy is to buy all the funeral homes in the Black community if possible. The business strategy is to undersell the other small Black funeral homes thus running them out of business. The saddest side to this story is the Black owners of these establishments that sell out. Black people were bought and sold on slave auction blocks and are still up for sale a century and a half later.

So as the Black community is held in a dependent position many factors contribute to our inability to enter the American system of free enterprise. Many Blacks also suffer from enormous inferiority complexes. Thus some scholars of the Black experience argue that these Blacks are unwilling to compete in an integrated society.

"As the U.S. Commission on Civil Rights concluded sadly in 1961, a principle reason for continued Negro poverty is "the lack of motivation on the part of many Negroes to improve their educational and occupational status." [11]

Apathy and more explicitly self-hatred is the leading cause for the conclusions of Black inferiority. The demeaning legacy of slavery has caused many Black people to hate themselves. Since they hate themselves so much they try to be like white people. This confusing love/hate relationship causes this confused Negro to attempt to lose his identity and take on the culture of another race of people.

Chapter Five

Since many confused Blacks have accepted the notion of inferiority by their actions, their subservient status has been justified by white racists. Here slavery and segregation have been justified.

The contemporary intellectual racist makes a strong argument regarding Black inferiority by referring to IQ scores. They have also established a measuring stick of Blackness. This measuring stick compares skin color and hair texture of Blacks to that of white people.

"Liberals have countered the racist argument, moreover, by calling it a stereotype, as if labeling the argument disposed of it. It does not: on the contrary, the stereotype is at least partly a description of reality. That is to say, Negroes do display less ambition than whites; as we have seen, apathy (with the self-hatred that produces it) is the worst disease of the Negro slum. Negroes do have "looser morals": there is no belying the promiscuity of the Negro slum dweller or the high and apparently growing rate of illegitimacy. The Negro crime rate is substantially higher than the white. Negroes do "care less for family"; the rate of separation is six times greater among Negro families than among the white. Negroes score lower on IQ tests than whites of comparable socioeconomic status, and Negro children do poorer work in school." [12]

The previous statement by Silberman has some merit. Like so many Negro, white liberal and Jewish liberal writers, Silberman exaggerates. For example Blacks do have a high rate of illegitimacy but to say Blacks have "looser morals" is an exaggeration. Once we weed out the exaggerations in Silberman's statement we can place it in perspective. For the record Silberman concludes his argument on Black stereotypes with a statement that for the most part is accurate.

" To acknowledge these unpleasant facts, however, does not imply that they are inherent characteristics or that they reflect intrinsic Negro inferiority. On the contrary, every one of them can be explained by the facts of Negro history in the U.S. In denying the existence of these traits white and Black liberals merely betrayed their uneasy suspicion that perhaps the racists are right after all. They obviously are afraid that to admit the existence of unflattering traits of character or performance would be to admit that Negroes are inferior." [13]

Big Ralph

The truth of the matter is that many Blacks have been born and breed in an environment of inferiority. In this instance these Blacks exhibit many characteristics that reflect Black inferiority. Thus, the soldiers of the rebellion have been limited. Meanwhile, the struggle and confusion continue. As early as 1905 there was a clear cleavage between accommodation and integration. Lerone Bennett states "the Negro rebellion began not in Montgomery in 1955, not in Greensboro in 1960, not in Birmingham in 1963, but in Boston in 1905. William Monroe Trotter who started it all, was the last abolitionist and the first modern rebel. With a commitment to integration and revolt, Trotter was the advance man of a new breed of Black rebels who flushed out the renaissance of the Negro soul.

"Trotter was haunted by the creeping misery of the Negro masses and the surging tide of accommodation. With scarcely a backward glance, Trotter repudiated the elite and became an activist. Aided by George Forbes, another well-educated member of the Boston elite, Trotter founded the Boston Guardian in 1901 and dedicated his life to the destruction of Booker T. Washington and the ideas he represented." [14]

During Trotter's day and time his integrationist viewpoints were considered militant and radical. Unfortunately early integrationist like Trotter did not visualize the negative aspects of integration. No doubt Trotter and his supporters confused integration with equal rights for Blacks.

This period, like the contemporary period, has recognized accommodationist, integrationist and Black Nationalist theories and ideas. I would argue that the period of slavery held only two motivations for slaves. There were the house slaves who mostly were accommodationist. Then there was the field slave who often would run to freedom and to rebellion.

Accommodation and Uncle Tom Negroes are loved by white America. No doubt from the turn of the century until the modern civil rights era accommodation and integration stifled Black Nationalism. Black Nationalism would have a rebirth at the height of the modern civil rights era.

The birth of the civil rights movement "came December 1, 1955

Chapter Five

when Rosa Parks boarded the Cleveland Avenue bus in Montgomery, Alabama. And the Negro revolt is properly dated from the moment Mrs. Parks said "no" to the bus driver's demand that she get up and let a white man have her seat." [15]

Mrs. Parks was a product of the times in which she lived. Black people were hopeful for some changes regarding equal rights since the end of WWII. Jim Crow and segregation was a thorn in the side of southern Blacks and they were tired. Rosa Parks exemplified the attitude of many Blacks who had gotten fed up with the restrictions placed on them by Jim Crow laws and customs.

The white response to Blacks disobeying Jim Crow laws was to arrest and punish the individual. For all practical purposes southern custom allowed Blacks to be beaten or lynched for getting out of place. By 1955 white Americans moved by racism had gotten more civilized and seldom openly beat Blacks or lynched them publicly.

Nonetheless Mrs. Parks was arrested for refusing to give her seat to a white man. Black leaders in Montgomery, fed up with abuse and the slave time attitude of the white power structure in Montgomery, planned a boycott of the city buses.

Martin Luther King, a young minister accepted the job of distributing flyers announcing the boycott to the Black community. A few days later an organization was formed and named the Montgomery Improvement Association and Martin Luther King was chosen as the leader.

The Montgomery Improvement Association did not ask for the end to segregation in Montgomery. They instead noted three concerns:

"1. Negro bus riders be given courteous treatment.

2. All bus riders be seated on a first-come, first-served basis; that Negroes would sit from the back toward the front; the white passengers from the front toward the rear.

3. Negro drivers be hired on routes that served predominantly Negro sections." [16]

The NAACP did not support the efforts of this new organization because they did not ask for the end of segregated seating. Meanwhile, the white backlash escalated into acts of violence against Blacks. Also, King and other leaders of the movement were jailed on various trumped

Big Ralph

up charges.

The white backlash and the callous resistance by white racist caused the Montgomery bus boycott to eventually attack segregation. With the direct attack on segregation the NAACP brought in their support. On May 11, 1956 the legal counsel for the NAACP argued the case before the federal district court.

Robert Carter, legal counsel for the NAACP was successful and the court ruled against segregated seating on city buses. By October the Supreme Court upheld the decision by the lower court.

The success of the Montgomery bus boycott was a great inspiration for Blacks throughout the south. The Montgomery Improvement Association became the Southern Christian Leadership Conference (SCLC). As a national organization based in Atlanta the SCLC made segregated bus conditions the focus of their civil rights efforts.

But, how deeply rooted is segregation and Jim Crow in the south? Consider the following statement by Lomax.

"Six years later King leaves Montgomery. The buses are integrated but the schools are not; neither are the parks, playgrounds nor any other pubic facilities. And one of the questions now plaguing social scientists is why such a deep-rooted movement as the Montgomery boycott resulted in nothing more than the integration of the buses. " [17]

King and his followers had nonetheless taken the vanguard in the struggle for equality. In so doing King brought to the table a distinct philosophy and strategy. This philosophy was Ghandism.

"Ghandism was not an entirely new development in the ghetto. In the early twenties, when Ghandi began his nonviolent resistance campaign in India, hearts picked up and men said, why not here? E. Franklin Frazier, an angry young man of the day, examined the matter at some length in the Crisis and counseled against Ghandism.

"All in all, Frazier concluded, nonviolence was neither practical nor expedient. He did not believe in "wholesale violence," but he was convinced that violent defense in local and specific instances has made white men hesitate to make wanton attacks upon Negroes." [18]

Frazier no doubt saw nonviolence much different from Ghandi and

Chapter Five

Martin Luther King. Most likely Frazier felt arkward praying for a racist, who does not believe in God. Frazier also realized that no man respects another man that begs on his knees. Thus Frazier and others have concluded nonviolence brought disrespect to the Black man, woman and child.

Martin Luther King was the champion of the contemporary nonviolent movement in America. His philosophy of nonviolence propelled the civil rights movement and became the lesser of three evils. Similar to Booker T. Washington, King became the chosen Black leader with a wide degree of acceptance by white people.

Again the American Black experience produced:

1. Integrationist philosophy driven by the tenets of nonviolence. This cadre of leadership and followers essentially felt begging the white man for equal rights would be best for Black people.

2. Separatist philosophy driven by Black Nationalism and if you attack me I will attack you in return. This cadre of leadership and followers refused to beg the white man for anything. Thus, they were insulted by the attempts of other Blacks to lick the backside of the white man.

3. Militant philosophy that was also driven by Black Nationalism and the critique of capitalism. This cadre of leadership and followers refused to allow the continuation of blatant violence in their communities, committed by the police or any white people. They also demanded respect from whites and would die before they would get on their knees and beg the white man for anything.

To understand clearly what King meant by nonviolence you must examine five basic aspects of the nonviolent philosophy for Blacks struggling for equal rights in America:

"First, it must be emphasized that nonviolent resistance is not a method for cowards; it does resist. If one uses this method because he is afraid or merely because he lacks the instruments of violence, he is not truly nonviolent. " [19]

Regarding human behavior and human response it can be argued that there are only two responses to violence. One logically is of course

Big Ralph

meeting violence with violence to halt it or gain relief. The second logical response is to do nothing to defend yourself against violence, except shield your body or run away.

Ghandism and the nonviolent philosophy developed by King developed another response to violence. In their view nonviolence meant accepting any verbal or physical abuse from, for example, white merchants when attempting to desegregate a lunch counter. Meanwhile you prayed that your attacker would come to love you as you loved him. But King did not see this philosophy as a method of stagnant passivity.

"The phrase "passive resistance" often gives the false impression that this is a sort of "do-nothing method" in which the resister quietly and passively accepts evil."[20]

The nonviolent resister is passive in that he is not physically aggressive toward his opponent. But King argues that his mind and body, his emotions are constantly working to convince his opponent that he is wrong. So instead of being active physically the nonviolent resister becomes active spiritually.

The masses from time immemorial have had a bout with ignorance. Thus, throughout our various leadership ranks, certain philosophies have defied all sense and logic but have been a driving force for many who chose that leader.

What if we didn't have those brave but foolish souls called passive resisters? White America most likely should give King some honors because King headed off a bloody and ugly confrontation between white racism and Black pride.

"A second fact that characterizes nonviolence is that it does not seek to defeat or humiliate the opponent, but to win his friendship and understanding."[21]

So while protesting through boycotts, the nonviolent protester seeks to bring to life the sense of moral shame in his opponent. Thus, the nonviolent resister seeks redemption and reconciliation. They further conclude that the result of violence is bitterness while the result of nonviolence is love.

"A third characteristic of this method is that the attack is directed

Chapter Five

against forces of evil rather than against persons who happen to be doing the evil.

"A fourth point that characterizes nonviolent resistance is a willingness to accept suffering without retaliation, to accept blows from the opponent without striking back. "Rivers of blood may have to flow before we gain our freedom, but it must be our blood," Ghandi said to his fellow citizens. The nonviolent resister is willing to accept violence if necessary, but never to inflict it. He does seek to dodge jail. If going to jail is necessary, he enters it "as a bridegroom enters the bride's chambers.

"A fifth point concerning nonviolent resistance is that it avoids not only external physical violence but also internal violence of spirit. The nonviolent resister not only refuses to shoot his opponent but he also refuses to hate him. At the center of nonviolence stands the principle of love. "

The nonviolent philosophy was a cornerstone for theories on integration. Many integrationist felt for sure that they could transport love to the white man. Therefore, they could achieve integration. Segregation did come to an end in many instances throughout the south. But the love of white people by Blacks and the love of Blacks by white people is difficult to measure.

The 50's had by now passed to the turbulent 60's. Catherine and Ralph had gone on to college. College campuses would soon become the launching pad for the student civil rights movement.

Big Ralph

Part III The Civil Rights Movement

Chapter 6

College Experiences: Blacks Challenge Discrimination

Young impatient, restless, energetic and eager troops assemble, old troops sit, weary but still misinformed, they carry messages of mercenary charm to young and old.

By the time Ralph and Catherine had gotten settled at Lane College the south was a land of protest. They had graduated in the Howard High School class of 1956. They met soon after they both arrived on campus. There was a transition from the 1950's to the 1960's. This transition reflected the mounting growth of the civil rights movement.

Lane College is located in Jackson, Tennessee. Jackson Tennessee is about 250 miles west of Chattanooga and Jackson is about 50 miles east of Memphis, Tennessee. Lane College is a Christiam Methodist Episcopal college. In the Methodist Church the Christian Methodist Episcopal denomination is known as C.M.E.

This was a fun year for Ralph and Catherine. Catherine recalls that this was one of the happiest periods in her life. She got involved in

Big Ralph

various campus organizations and enjoyed college and the challenge of academics to the utmost. The social atmosphere at Lane was cordial. For example in Chattanooga at Howard School Catherine recalled that there were many cliques. Therefore if your parents were not of a certain social status or if they did not have a so-called professional job you were not allowed or welcomed in certain social circles.

Ralph did not love Lane College like Catherine. He was busy playing basketball, and he loved his travel experiences with the team. As an athlete Ralph had a super appetite, but like so many other young men in college the cafeteria food was not up too par. This was a constant source of displeasure for Ralph and Catherine remembers this very clearly. Ruby Iverson was a close friend whose father was a C.M.E. minister in New York. Catherine had been raised up in a C.M.E. Church. Phillips Temple C.M.E. Church was located on Grove Street when Catherine lived in College Hill Courts. This remained her home church for many years until she changed her membership to her husband's church Orchard Knob Baptist.

At Lane, Catherine achieved academically and spiritually. Her strong religious beliefs became a strong element that kept her family intact and gave her the strength to support her husband at all times. She enjoyed the fact that while at Lane she could walk to church every Sunday. She enjoyed teaching Sunday school and relished that she did not have to ride the bus to church like she had to do in Chattanooga.

Ralph and Catherine were dating so they readily had mutual friends. Dorthy Anderson was Catherine's room mate. Dorthy married a young man from Chattanooga named Melvin Brooks. They remained close friends over the years and visited Ralph and Catherine when they lived in Little Rock.

The years 1954 and 1955 caused a significant impact on civil rights. The year 1954 the world witnessed the U.S. Supreme Court outlawing segregated schools. The following year (December 1, 1955) the Montgomery bus boycott also launched what some social thinkers called the beginning of the civil rights movement. Five years later the battle for desegregated schools was still raging because white America

Chapter Six

attempted to defy the law of the land. Also, by 1960 the challenge to segregation extended to all fronts.

The battle over desegregating the schools was waged by the NAACP. This struggle took place in the courts. Chattanooga was typical of most southern cities as the city fathers attempted to defy the constitution, and the Supreme Court by manipulating the law.

Four years after the Supreme Court ruling Chattanooga segregationist were saying, along with the Board of Education, that the community is not ready for integration. Mixing of Blacks and whites in the same school was thought to be a clear road to violence. It is for sure that the term mixing was a clear way that white people sought to keep the race question in perspective.

Most white people expressed a displeasure with the mixing of the races. This displeasure resulted from their fear that they would lose their racial purity. Therefore, the ultimate mixing of Blacks and whites meant the mating of males and females. On the other hand the Black integrationist was favorable toward the mixing of the races.

Thus, the integrationist felt that his children would learn more seated next to white children in the classroom. For the most part the Black integrationist was favorable toward interracial copulation because, too many Blacks, mulatto children were more attractive.

So in 1958 the Board's program was:

"1. To elucidate, or to make clear, to the citizens all aspects of the problem.

2. To assess, or evaluate, public opinion in an effort to determine when an integration program would be acceptable.

3. To develop a plan for integration." [1]

By 1960 Black parents, led by NAACP president James Mapp, were threatening to file suit in federal court over the Board's failure to desegregate the schools in Chattanooga. Meanwhile Black parents and Black children were threatened with lynchings, bombings and being run out of town. Because of over crowded school conditions, Black parents attempted to enroll four Black pupils at Glenwood School. "The school population in 1960 was 15,740 white pupils and 10,369 Negroes, Negroes made up 39.7%. " [2]

Big Ralph

By April three Black parents sued to order the city of Chattanooga to desegregate the school system. The suit was filed on behalf of all children and parents in Chattanooga affected by segregated schools. R. H. Craig, a local attorney, filed the suit. The NAACP's legal team of Thurgood Marshall and Constance Baker Motley of New York were also involved along with Avon Williams and Z. Alexander Looby of Nashville.

"The suit sought the following relief:

1. A decree enjoining the city "from operating a compulsory biracial school system in Chattanooga."

2. A decree enjoining the city from "continuing to maintain a dual scheme or pattern of school zone lines based upon race and color."

3. A decree enjoining the city from "Assigning pupils to the schools . . . on the basis of the race and color of the pupils."

4. A decree enjoining the city "from assigning teachers, principals and other school personnel to the schools based on race and color.

5. A decree enjoining the city from "approving budgets, making available funds approving employment and construction contracts and approving policies, curricula and programs that are designed to perpetuate or maintain or support a school system operating on a racially segregated basis. "[3]

Also, involved in the language of the lawsuit was an alternate plank. This plan sought to reorganize the entire school system. The measures of this plan noted the following:

"1. The city operates a primary system of schools for whites.

2. The city operates a secondary school system for colored or Negro children.

3. There are also two distinct school zone lines based on race and color. These lines overlap where Negro and white children reside in the same residential area.

4. It was also charged that the system is predicated on the theory that Negroes are inherently inferior to white persons and consequently, may not attend the same public schools attended by white children who are superior.

Chapter Six

5. There was also the theory that Black teachers and administrators were also inferior to whites and may not teach white children." [4]

No doubt that ever since Blacks were first brought to America as slaves the European has had a superior attitude. So, for white parents to take this position as late as 1960 is not surprising. But ironically Black integrationist also would soon take this position to justify desegregation. Thus, inferior Black schools produced inferior Black students. Therefore Black children suffered discrimination when not allowed to remove their inferiority by attending white schools.

So as the Black integrationist philosophy took root the battle over school desegregation continued. The Board of Education had been preparing for a lawsuit since the court decree handed down in 1954. By now most of the school zones in Chattanooga had Black and white children. Thus the argument of strictly segregated housing patterns as a cause for all white schools was not a valid argument.

The following is a history of the actions of the school Board on the Supreme Court ruling:

"1. 22 July 1955 Board issues statement declaring that in time it would comply with the decision.

2. The Board proposed an advisory committee.

3. 9 September 1955 the original School Board statement was opposed.

4. 12 October 1955 Board stated that court had placed situation in our hands as long as we act in good faith.

5. 9 November 1955 the Advisory Committee was appointed, 23 white persons and 12 Negroes. The first meeting attended by 150 person's mostly segregationists, was broken up before any business could be conducted. The segregationist totally disrupted the meeting by releasing tear gas and shouting down the speakers.

6. 31 March 1956 Board issued statement saying integration could not be accomplished for at least five more years." [5]

So as the Board stalled the elements within the white community carried out threats of violence against the Black community. During 1960 the Chattanooga Times reported five bombings. July 16, August 11, August 12, August 17 and August 21. By the end of the year "Blacks

Big Ralph

were organizing and raising reward money to identify the persons responsible for the bombings." [6]

Meanwhile the court challenges the lawsuit filed to integrate the schools mounted. The Board asks for an advisory jury in the school integration case. Then they filed five questions to be answered if the jury is authorized. These five questions reflect the continued stalling tactics of the Board:

1. Has the Board ever discriminated against Blacks in the public schools in Chattanooga?

2. Has the Board honestly moved to assess and educate the community toward desegregation?

3. Has the Board assessed the attitudes of the community toward desegregation?

4. Is there danger or injury to citizens if immediate integration is ordered?

5. What is reasonable time for the Board to carry out plans of desegregation?

Evidently the Chattanooga School Board had a great fear of desegregating the public schools. "They admit they have pursued a policy, custom, practice and usage of operating a biracial school system. This system was established nearly a century ago under the concept "separate but equal." The Board also noted that in the past 60 days riotous conduct, bloodshed and almost open revolt broke out as Negroes tried to integrate downtown lunch counters. " [7]

So while white people had this great fear of integration the Black community continued to address the court. Meanwhile, the Black plaintiffs asked for a summary judgment in the case.

"The plaintiffs contend that there are no material issues of fact to be decided and that they are entitled to a judgment. They ask for an injunction to restrain the officials of Chattanooga schools from operating a biracial school system or for the board to submit a plan for complete integration." [8]

The Federal Judge hearing, the case was judge Leslie Darr. Judge Darr issued his ruling based on the two motions. The plaintiffs asked for

Chapter Six

a summary judgment since the defendants admit they are operating a biracial public school system.

On the other hand the School Board filed a motion for a summary judgment based on:

1. The facts in the case do not warrant a class action.

2. The plaintiffs have not exhausted their remedy under the Tenn. Pupil Assignment Law.

3. Board did not abuse it's authority by denying plaintiffs admission to Glenwood School.

The Judge eventually ruled: "A motion for a summary judgment is determinative if there is no issue of fact. There are not issues of fact in this case. The schools of the city of Chattanooga are biracially operated and the defendants continue to decline to desegregate them, gradually or completely." [9]

The School Board at this juncture continued to challenge the court ruling. They first instructed their counsel to prepare written statements of appeal of the decision by Judge Darr. They also instructed the staff of the Board to prepare alternate plans for desegregation.

Meanwhile (November 3) Judge Darr denied a summary judgment by the School Board. But, the Judge granted a summary judgment to Black parents who had applied for admission to a white school. Also the Judge ordered the Board to submit a plan for desegregation on 20 December and set 9 January 1961 as a date for a hearing on the plan.

There was a dispute among the city attorneys over the legality of an appeal. "Attorney Raymond Witt submitted a legal opinion forming an appeal. City attorney Joe Anderson and assistant city attorney Ellis Meacham submitted an opinion opposing an appeal.

Anderson and Meacham noted that there is nothing to appeal from. Also by appealing the Board runs the danger of having the appellate Court issue an order for complete integration with no regard to the Board's plans. Also it is undisputed that the Board is operating a biracial school system." [10]

Chattanooga may not have an exclusive hold on frivolous appeals and legal challenges but they have their share. The exact wording of the alleged appeal by attorney Witt clearly is evidence of the defiance of racist to the law of the land and the U.S. Constitution. The appeal by attorney Witt was based on two grounds:

"1. The substance of the district court: memorandum opinion is that the Chattanooga Board is in violation of the U.S. Supreme Court's decision in the Brown case. The Board denies the existence of any such violation, insisting that it has followed the directives of the Supreme Court to the best of its ability.

2. The Board believes the Pupil Assignment law became operative by its specific terms without any affirmative action upon the part of local school Boards, and, therefore the exhaustion of administrative remedies under such law was necessary prior to a suit in federal court." [11]

The School Board followed through with an appeal of Judge Darr's ruling. Although there was no physical school integration Witt and the Board felt they have not violated the law. The threat of violence again motivates the segregationist. "A community spirit that is overwhelmingly determined to head off rioting will make the police department's job comparatively easy." [12]

The absurdity of the appeal of the desegregation suit is noted by a Black minister and community leader. Rev. M. Jones, speaking for the Interdenominational Ministerial Alliance and the Pioneer Business League, noted that the Board is risking the good will of the community and evidently one can question the sincerity of the Board.

"First it is incredible that the School Board would want to appeal after spending so many years trying to educate the public to a point of compliance. Secondly it is hard to see why the School Board would want to appeal since the city counsel countered that there is no point of law upon which the Board can appeal. Thirdly, it is hard to understand why the Board would appeal when there is so much support for law enforcement and a peaceful achievement of the law.

It seems hard to believe that a School Board would go into a Federal Court having made no visible signs of compliance, to argue that it had complied to a degree simply because it had fixed on the word "elucidation" to the utter neglect of the admonition with all deliberate speed." [13]

Chapter Six

The confusion of racism in Chattanooga extended far beyond the ridiculous arguments the Board was making to stall desegregation. Any Black person that petitioned for equal rights was a threat to white society during the 60's. Even Dr. Martin Luther King as a moderate passive advocate of non-violence was seen by racist white America as a threat. In Chattanooga the "city School Board upheld Supt. Bennie Carmichael in refusing to permit the Howard School auditorium to be used for an address by Dr. King. Dr. Carmichael said that Dr. King is a controversial person and said that his appearance might threaten the safety of the school." [14]

It had been a long year of wrangling over desegregating the public schools. The Board in response to Judge Darr's mandatory injunction submitted a plank by the 20th of December. "The plan proposed to desegregate the first three grades of the city schools, beginning with the 1962-63 school term, and a grade a year thereafter. Under the Board's plan, desegregation would reach the Junior High grades at the beginning of the 1966 term and the senior high schools by the term starting in 1969 and in all grades by the beginning of the 1971-72 term." [15]

The confusion between integration and equal rights paints a sad irony of the American experience. How does a basic and logically human pursuit of equal rights get trapped in a battle over desegregation? Segregationist developed their philosophy that defies logic. The integrationist also developed an illogical philosophy.

The segregationist also reacted at times in a logical fashion. Since he did not want his children to attend school with Blacks he sent them to private schools. White people that professed to be Jews claimed the side of integrationist usually. But Jews already had established private schools and never were threatened by Blacks or Gentiles ever attending their schools.

So while Blacks pushed for integration of the schools, white people silently set up an underground system of private schools. In eight or nine years after 1954 the schools in the south were still segregated. Lomax makes the following statement:

"By 1961 only 7% of Blacks in the south were attending integrated schools. Black organizations have spent millions of dollars on lawsuits.

Big Ralph

Black families have been disrupted, many forced to leave their homes, others subjected to economic reprisals and physical abuse. "[16]

Lomax continues to make positive statements regarding the struggle for equal rights. An analysis of what he has said regarding the mood of Blacks concerning our question is important.

Lomax argues that the battle to end desegregation killed Black people's faith in the white power structure. Also the Black masses were angry, but Lomax, as a Black journalist, noted that the Black masses were informed. The Black press had kept Blacks informed about all forms of racial injustice.

Thus, Blacks were not moved to contentment by token integration. Discrimination and hopelessness were evident to every Black man in America. He suffered humiliation on his job and then saw his children humiliated by rocks when they tried to integrate a white school.

The African independence movement also caused the Black American to make certain assumptions. First there were distinct parallels between colonialism and segregation. Also, there were distinct differences. What greatly troubled Black Americans was that the White House went to great lengths too not discriminate against Africans.

If Blacks had not been so involved in the integration syndrome they may have been more observant. Clearly the African has always maintained his identity. Instead of the Black American accepting the reality of his ethnicity, he has tried to be white and tried to be African. Both missions are impossible.

As Lomax roamed through the south he talked with domestic workers, blue collar workers and a vast cross section of the Black masses. Lomax concludes that these Blacks voiced painful disappointment. Those in service capacities said they no longer trust, respect nor love white people.

Evidently these Blacks were what is known as niggers who were virtually traitors and Uncle Toms. It is clearly illogical for a people to love, trust and respect someone who despises you. Surely this was not the sentiment of the Black masses but only the wish of a few who conspired against their own people.

Chapter Six

How does one conjure up love, trust and respect in view of the oppressive circumstances of the 60's? For example:

'The school desegregation decision said nothing about the right of a Negro laborer to become plant supervisor. Negro homes were searched without warrants; the victim's heads were bloodied and their jobs were threatened if they dared protest. Negroes darted in and out of department stores where they dared not sit down; they were denied access to the polls; and if they received a just day in court it was usually when all parties concerned were Negroes." [17]

The court battle over desegregating the schools was at the center of the civil rights movement. The movement began to include other institutions when Blacks had been refused admittance. Again Black people confused integration with equal rights. Though if one had to integrate to gain equal rights he was to keep in mind his objective was to gain equality and not just integrate with white people.

The sit-in demonstrations started in February of 1960. The sit-in movement had spread throughout the south. It is for sure that this movement with students in the vanguard was a significant challenge to segregation. The movement had it's birth in Greensboro, North Carolina. On 1 February 1960 four freshmen from North Carolina A&T College began the sit-in demonstrations that spread like wild fire. By May they were also occurring in Chattanooga. Catherine and Ralph like a few other Black young adults were in College. They looked through a big picture window in a sense and witnessed the escalating civil rights movement. The Chattanooga Times continues to report news concerning sit-in demonstrations and acts of civil disobedience. [18]

Obviously the sit-in demonstrations had confused equal access with integration. By this time Black leadership had formed strict integrationist guidelines that governed the civil rights struggle.

By August Black students were being served at downtown lunch counters. "Negro students were served at seven downtown lunch counters at 4:00 Friday by prearranged plan." [19]

This movement, when compared to the Montgomery bus boycott, was said to be a revolt against segregation and the established leadership

Big Ralph

in the Black community. No doubt the main fault with established Black leadership was the fact that they were not independent. All of the established Black civil rights organizations depended on the government or some other white institution for funds. Eventually the student movement would do the same thing.

Meanwhile the student movement in Greensboro, in its infancy, contacted the NAACP for help. Eventually three national civil rights organizations came to help the students. The primary interest of CORE was to teach the students the science of nonviolent protest.

Thus soon after the student movement was established, it became influenced by the NAACP, SCLC and CORE. All three of these organizations were essentially controlled by white people and financed by whites. The potential of the movement was astronomical as it spread throughout the south and enlisted more people than any other civil rights movement in the history of the Republic.

The movement had a significant impact because by October of 1961 the sit-in case had reached the Supreme Court. By November the Supreme Court had voted in favor of the sit-in demonstrations and desegregated lunch counters throughout the south.

Throughout Black America and within the ranks of the white liberal supporters new tactics began to materialize. These new tactics were also realized by those in the power structure that were manipulating the civil rights movement. These new tactics resulted in a new conviction toward direct civil disobedience as a route to desegregation.

The new era that was unfolding is reflected in the following passage by Lomax. "Sentiment unfolds, "father forgive them, for they know not what they do." This new gospel of the American Negro is rooted in the theology of desegregation; its missionaries are several thousand Negro students. They are braving great dangers and using new techniques to spread the faith. It is not an easy faith, for it names the conservative Negro leadership class as sinners along with the segregationists." [20]

On the surface the new, student movement tried to exert some independence. But, they were quickly coopted by the controlled established Black leadership, by the same tactics money. If the student

Chapter Six

movement was able to see that established Black leadership was conservative, they should have been able to see the main ingredient that made them conservative and lackeys.

The student movement did not mark the end to established Black leadership. Young leadership emerged that was more aggressive but this cadre of leadership was also coopted as they turned to white people for financial support. A measure of independence did emerge as the students formed their own organization. This organization became known as the Student Nonviolent Coordinating Committee.

Previously the white power structure has financed the student movement through the lackeys in the NAACP, CORE and SCLC. By 1961 the students with their own organization now competed with the old time Black leadership for funds from the white man.

The new student organization had made a significant impact and the white power structure began calling them in for consultation instead of old established Black leaders. The economic boycott was a tactic that grew out of the student movement. Thus, the students were in line to negotiate and settle with the power structure in a given city.

The nonviolent protests at lunch counters had proved successful. Was there another way to gain equal access and equal rights? First when the crusade for equal rights is confused with a crusade for integration there is a problem. So what is a protest that is nonviolent? In this case nonviolent means a protester who will not defend himself against verbal and physical abuse.

How could student demonstrators during the sit-in movement achieve equal access by resisting attacks? Could the tactic of nonviolence be also based on the theory that I am only nonviolent if I am not attacked? Finally did this subservient posture of nonviolence reinforce white and Black attitudes of Black inferiority?

Mostly the nightmare of Black America continued. The nonviolent movement was entrenched and Black civil rights leaders preached that this was the only way to achieve integration and equality. Thus, to defend yourself against the physical attacks of white racism would prove counterproductive to the cause and result in a wide race war. In this

Big Ralph

visionary race war Blacks would be eliminated and the streets of America would run free with blood. In this case the best option would be to beg white America to allow Blacks to integrate with them. Begging for equal access was one thing but begging to integrate with white people that mostly despised you was quite foolish.

Meanwhile, the nonviolent protest movement continued. In the process these brave misinformed Black warriors paid the price. Black protesters were beaten, bitten by dogs, soaked with urine, smeared with defecation, sprayed by high powered water hoses, jailed and subjected to any inhumane abuse known to man.

The movement of protest and civil disobedience spread to discrimination on interstate buses. James Farmer became the chief of the freedom riders. Farmer had been a part of the Blacks and whites that organized CORE in 1942. Thus, by 1947 Farmer participated in the first freedom ride to challenge discrimination on interstate trains.

In 1960 Farmer was the Program Director for the NAACP. "February 1, 1961, 40 year old James Farmer became national director of the Congress of Racial Equality. 13 March, CORE announced that it would conduct freedom rides through the south to test racial discrimination in interstate train terminals." [21]

As the cadre of leadership trained the participants for the freedom rides the White House was also contacted. John F. Kennedy was the president and because of circumstances and the tradition of Black exploitation Kennedy became the major power broker in the civil rights movement. The initial contact made to the White House was for federal protection for the freedom riders.

The first group of riders left Washington, D.C. May 4,1961. By now the freedom rides just like the sit-in movement had caught national attention. The freedom rides were interracial while the sit-in movement was made up of only Black students.

By "17 May there were four organizations involved in the rides: CORE, the Nashville Student Movement, the Student Nonviolent Coordinating Committee and SCLC. " [22]

CORE has always been an interracial group and from its inception it was a hotbed of white liberalism. Evidently the particular history of

Chapter Six

CORE accounted for the interracial flavor of the freedom rides. Also, since the significant sit-in movement, radical northern white students and other liberal whites flocked to join the cause of social integration.

The term social integration is used at this juncture to clearly note that no one in the leadership structure emphasized economic parity for the poor, oppressed, so-called Negro. Meanwhile CORE along with James Farmer became nationally known. The distinction of mass protest expressed by CORE set them apart from established civil rights groups like the NAACP and the Urban League.

Racial demonstrations and the move to civil disobedience had a great impact on the morale of Black people. Many Blacks stood at the big picture window watching, waiting and sometimes thinking. So many of these Black watchers had various thoughts. Some did not believe in nonviolence but supported any human beings right too equal access.

Writers that even suggest that the mere fact that a small segment of the Black population that demonstrated for equal rights/integration would somehow cure apathy and the multitude of problems in the Black community are misinformed. For example "by 1963, most Negroes in Montgomery had returned to the old custom of riding in the back of the bus." [23]

Although the civil rights movement and the Montgomery bus boycott in particular gave Blacks pride, most Blacks still felt they were inferior to whites. The confusion over what Black people were really fighting for was a product of Black leadership and those in the power structure who manipulated the movement.

Martin Luther King was instrumental in establishing the theories and philosophy of nonviolence. We previously noted the essence of King's philosophy in his 1963 letter from the Birmingham Jail entitled "The Negro Is Your Brother."

The "Negro Is Your Brother" can be taken to a level of confusion, if you are directing this statement to those who sought to physically harm Blacks during this period. Some believe that King was a God sent man. Did God only send passive seekers of freedom, justice and equality?

Are those Black leaders not in the passive ranks also God sent men? Why have the passive resisters so confused equal rights with

Big Ralph

integration? Did the passive resisters attempt to pay homage to white people when they should have reserved this exclusively for God?

Since King's thinking had such an impact on the movement, let's go back to his letter and hopefully gain some clarity on points of interest. Concerning a nonviolent campaign, King believes there are four basic steps: collection of the facts to determine whether injustices are alive, negotiation, self purification, and direct action.

The following point is quoted verbatim to gain further insight into this deceptive and often confusing philosophy. "We know through painful experience that freedom is never voluntarily given by the oppressor, it must be demanded by the oppressed. " [24]

You can do very little demanding from a human being on your knees. In prayer to Almighty God you do not demand, you ask for blessings. I do not believe that God meant for those that seek equal rights as human beings to pray for their attacker instead of defending themselves. Surely your enemy should be prayed for but not in public. Somehow the advocates of passive resistance also confused themselves, and the people they sought to lead with a prophet. Furthermore this prophet was confused with Jesus who is the son of God. Mere mortal men cannot hope to capture the divine attributes of Jesus. If man can capture a reflection of the attributes of Jesus he has served himself well.

There is a great difference in Jesus humbling himself to render salvation to his brother than passive resisters humbling themselves to those that seek their ill will. The direct action of nonviolence also caused civil disobedience. Civil disobedience meant breaking laws. So how could peaceful, nonviolent demonstrators advocate breaking laws? King argues that there are just laws and there are unjust laws. The distinction between just and unjust laws has to do with morality and God. Therefore, a just law follows moral law and the law of God. On the other hand an unjust law is out of touch with moral law.

Further, when laws are made to discriminate against certain citizens and deny them their constitutional rights the law is unjust. King notes that early Christians engaged in civil disobedience and so did the great philosopher Socrates.

Chapter Six

King in his letter from the Birmingham jail also notes the frustrations he has experienced from other so-called Christians. He calls this group moderate white people. He reveals that there are some bigger stumbling blocks to freedom than white supremacist like the KKK. We know that King had the mindset of love for all people. Unfortunately King also thought these people or most of them loved him in return. It is more accurate that the white moderate was expressing his honest opinion and that opinion was steeped in racism.

King concludes his letter by relating that from his analysis there are two opposing forces in the Black community. These forces obstruct the road to freedom and equality in his judgment. The first force is filled with complacency and apathy. These people have adjusted to segregation and accept an attitude of inferiority for Blacks as a way of life. Then King notes that there is a lesser number of middle class Blacks who are also in this category. They are motivated by a degree of academic and economic security and King believes that in some way they profit from segregation. Therefore, they are not sensitive to the problems of the masses.

The other force King notes is the rhetoric coming from Black Nationalist groups. King claims these groups advocate violence, bitterness and hate. He also notes that the Nation of Islam led by Elijah Muhammad is the main advocate of hate. In conclusion King states:

"I stand between these two forces. There is a more excellent way, of love and nonviolent protest. I'm grateful to God that, through the Negro church, the dimension of nonviolence entered our struggle. " [25]

King no doubt was a visionary and an idealistic philosopher. There is evidence to support the likelihood that King was duped in Christian philosophy used to control and manipulate Black people. This Christian philosophy had its origins on slave plantations where few if any Blacks could read including the slave preacher who was acting at the slave masters direction.

Also I would argue that there were basically three opposing forces instead of the two noted by King. The complacent and integrationist Blacks made up a force that was passive and posed a minimal threat to white society. Islam, motivated by Black Nationalism, self-pride and respect, was another force. Thirdly was the militant and radical rhetoric of groups like the Black Panther Party.

None of these significant groups, however, advocated violence against white America. They only logically concluded that if white people, or anybody regardless of race, attacked them they would defend themselves. No doubt these people would be highly insulted if anyone suggested they do otherwise.

So while the opposing forces challenged discrimination the chosen force of accommodation continued the grand challenge of school integration. Black children from the ghetto would not automatically get a better education merely by being placed in a classroom with middle-class white children. Poverty and a background without academic achievement put Black children at a disadvantage with forced integration.

In any case Black integrationist and white liberals are disgruntled at anything other than full integration of the schools. "The thesis that Negro students cannot receive an adequate education in an all- Negro school needs to be carefully examined. Research by Kenneth and Mamie Clark notes that Blacks in the north attending integrated schools had more self hatred than Blacks in the south attending segregated schools." [26]

The realization of self-hatred is a crucial yardstick in an analysis of Black complacency and apathy. King talked about this complacency but his orientation would not allow him to deal with certain concrete factors that would offset complacency. It is interesting that even Silberman notes that Blacks must first develop pride in self as a prerequisite to understanding other cultures.

Thus, we see the reality of the following quotation: "Indeed the fervor with which some integrationists insist that equal education is impossible in an all Negro school sounds suspiciously like self-hatred on their part." [27]

Integration continues to be confused with equal rights by a group of passive resisters who feel inferior to white people. This accounts for the begging and pleading and the lost sense of reality. The reality is that

Chapter Six

sensible Blacks only want quality education for their children and not the so-called privilege of being close to white people.

Meanwhile, in Chattanooga the debate over desegregating the public schools continued. At the end of 1960 the Federal Court ruled that the Chattanooga Board of Education set a timetable in which integration would take place. At the beginning of the year 1961 the same stalling tactics were being used by the School Board.

The plan proposed by the School Board to desegregate the schools was objected to by the NAACP's lawyers who were representing the Black community. Meanwhile, the Board filed an appeal on the decision by Judge Leslie R. Darr to grant a summary judgment in desegregating the schools.

"The decision appealed by the Board of Education involved three matters:

1. The denial by Judge Darr of a summary judgment in favor of the Board.

2. Granting a summary judgment sought by the four Negro children who seek to desegregate the schools.

3. The mandatory injunction ordering the Board to submit a plan to desegregate the schools on or before 20 December." [28]

So while the Board continued to stall and impede the process of desegregation Black integrationists became even more confused. Judge Darr flatly refused the plan submitted by the Board and noted that desegregation of the schools meant physically desegregating the schools. [29]

A statement by a group of 50 clergymen of all faiths pleaded with the Board of education to comply with the law. They noted that the School Board was under a federal mandate. Thus, the School Board has a direct responsibility to help promote a favorable climate for peaceful transition to a desegregated school system. But, the Board only pushed for an illegal appeal.

"Judgement against the appeal noted that in view of the divergence of opinion on this question, a decision of the U.S. Supreme Court will be necessary to resolve it.

Big Ralph

"The sixth circuit, however granted the appeal and overruled a motion to dismiss it. Attorneys for the Negro children countered there was not a finality in the litigation in the district court, therefore the case was not yet subject to appeal." [30]

Black parents began to protest the zoning regulations and started making attempts to enroll their children at all-white schools. The county schools also came under fire as a Black parent attempted to enroll his two children at Lookout Elementary. [31]

By September the Board declared that school desegregation would take place during the 1962/1963 school year. Nine white schools and seven Black schools would be affected by the plan. This plan would allow 83 Blacks and 189 white children to attend previously segregated schools.

A Board member on a local TV show noted the intense and ongoing confusion and debate over school desegregation. "George Hudson School Board member said his TV appearance was the 397th meeting discussing the desegregation plan. As officials have met 396 times since the Supreme Court ordered formulation of desegregation plans in 1954." [32]

In the midst of all this rhetoric hopefully there is some clarity on the issue of desegregation. Raymond Witt vice-chairman of School Board and a typical segregationist gives us some clarity in a speech he made before the local Jaycees, and reported in the Chattanooga Times.

Witt said, "there has been an interchanging of the words desegregation and integration. Where as the meaning of the two are quite different.

1. Desegregation, he said involves the legal requirement of elimination of race as a basis for separating students in the schools.

2. Integration, which is not required by the legal decision, involves a change of attitude, an acceptance positively of those of the opposite race in the classroom as a right and desirable condition.

3. Integration, he said, can be achieved only gradually, over a period of time. But, he added integration must eventually be achieved if there is to be quality education, because equal education is not possible in the classroom where there are hostilities, where Negroes are not accepted

Chapter Six

by the white children or the teacher or both."

It is really ironic that a white racist like Witt attempted to unclutter the confusion over desegregation, integration and equal rights. But evidently the Black integrationists were not listening. But Witt was ill informed on the inevitable nature of integration. Respect for another human being does not require integration.

I would argue that one can gain equal access without so-called integration. Integration means mixing and eventually becoming one. This evidently frightens the hell out of white people who fashion themselves as a superior race. But Black integrationists continue to feel that the road to equality is paved with integration.

The NAACP in Chattanooga, with support from the NAACP Legal Defense Team continued to oppose the efforts of the segregationists. The NAACP opposes a plan by the Board and stands by their original petition that asked for immediate and total integration.

Also, the city-wide Black PTA issued a statement urging immediate and total compliance with the Supreme Court decision. "They said in some instances students are traveling 12 to 16 miles, passing schools of the opposite race, on the way to segregated schools. They cited surveys that show that the Negro has a lower economic level because of a lower education level and indicated that segregated schools contribute to the lower education level." [34]

The day after Christmas an article in the Times noted that "integration of Chattanooga schools during 1961-62 school term became a remote possibility Thursday when the 6th U.S. Circuit Court of Appeals denied a motion to advance the appeal from the district court here on its calendar." [35]

Big Ralph

CHAPTER 7

Civil Rights Organizations And Leadership

**Institutions often planned organized and controlled,
by those, with other agendas than those, who seek
freedom here told,
Captains, bought and sold, comfort, status, prestige is in vogue.**

    Little Rock Air Force Base was a much different place than the small college campus of Lane College. Ralph and Catherine had attended Lane for about three semesters. They left school for various reasons but at the center of their decision was financial resources. The year was 1958. Ralph took a job at the local Black YMCA. The Henry Branch YMCA had a swimming program for boys 7-15 years old and Ralph taught swimming to these young men. Meanwhile Catherine took a job in New York as a live in house keeper. Catherine later returned to Chattanooga and took a job as a nurse's aid at Carver Memorial Hospital (Carver Memorial Hospital was an all Black hospital that was located on west 9th Street). She had thought about nursing as a career and from this experience she determined that nursing was a good career choice.

    Ralph and Catherine first met at Lane College in 1957. They began to date and actually had their first date back in Chattanooga. The first date took place at the Liberty theater on east 9th Street on Christmas day December 25, 1957. After leaving school and working briefly at various

Big Ralph

jobs Ralph and Catherine became engaged on May 22, 1960. As a way of announcing their engagement Ralph and Catherine visited Catherine's aunt Ida Sanderfur and they also visited Calvin and Betty Murray.

Ralph and Catherine were married August 20, 1960, at Phillips Temple C.M.E. Church. Ralph had joined the Air force and was on leave. Catherine was working at Carver Hospital and had plans to return to Lane College. In 1960 the world was a changing place. Gary Powers the U2 pilot was shot down over the Soviet Union and the Cold War between the U.S. and Russia was intensified. Meanwhile, the Republican White House was praising their stand on civil rights.

Women in 1960 were wearing pointed toed shoes and ballon dresses. The men who called themselves stylish were sporting the Continental look. New inventions came on the scene. Record players now had more sound because something called high fidelity came into existence. Self defrosting refrigerators were now available and sewing machines now could cut button holes. Catherine decided to stay in Chattanooga when Ralph returned to duty as an Airman.

By November 1960 John F. Kennedy was elected president and the United States was no doubt entering a new era. This new era would note this great upheaval over the human and God given rights of Black citizens. Catherine was lonely and had visited Little Rock to see Ralph in October. She decided that she would like Little Rock but she lost her job while she was away. Ralph continued to write letters and she enjoyed every letter she received.

In June when Ralph returned to his duty station in Little Rock, he thought of his lovely young wife back in Chattanooga. The following letter reveals his deepest sentiments:

Dear Catherine,
Today is one of those days when I miss you very much, there is no one here but myself. Everyone else has gone to town and I am alone with all the wonderful memories of you. The fellows have all gone to town looking for girl friends and female companionship. With me this

Chapter Seven

can never be. My love for you is so great until there can never be anyone else or a day of sin, for to me you are the loveliest, sweetest, and most tender young lady that the world has to offer. It seems that the coming of August is becoming almost unbearable, truly being with you is the only time that I can live, the rest of the time I am completely in a trance thinking of the next hour of our meeting, this my love is all that keeps me going. It is very difficult for me to put in writing the way I feel whenever I come near you. So perhaps I will simply say that my heart pounds and skips beats as though someone was using it as a piano. If it was possible for humans to fly whenever they were happy then I would be with the highest birds of the skies, and my feet would never touch the ground again. Catherine all these words come entirely from my heart and I am saying all this to state simply that I love you very deeply. I hope that August comes as quickly as a sound night of sleep.

"Love Always"
   Ralph [1]

Ralph had been injured in a car accident in September. Catherine was worried but during her visit she noted that he was doing well. Ralph was released from the doctor's care in November. He resumed playing basketball for the post team and they continued to correspond. Catherine would soon be joining Ralph but meanwhile they wrote letters of love and loneliness.

Dearest Catherine,
I received your letter as usual I was very happy to hear from you, I am doing quite well now, except being broke. However I could not ask for a better feeling than in knowing that I have but two more weeks of loneliness left for the year. I am now playing basketball and the team has climbed to second place that will give us a berth for the tournament. I have also been picked to play with the L.R.A.F.B. all star team and the base team. Now that I am writing I may answer some letters I have been getting. By the way Marianne answered my letter while I was in the

Big Ralph

hospital. I have also received a letter from Roy and Leon, also one from mother. I will definitely be looking for you on the morning of the 17th o.k

    With All My Love,
    Ralph [2]

Back in Chattanooga Catherine counted the days. Soon after the first of the year she planned to join Ralph in Little Rock and set up housekeeping. Meanwhile back in Little Rock Ralph also counted the days and anxiously waited the month out. This letter also written in December speaks of his anticipation.

Dearest Love,
Your last letter is the one that I have longed for since the day we were married. Darling I can think of nothing else in this world that I would much rather have than for you to be with me. This truly will bring an enormous light into my life. So once again I am looking forward to being with you, and this time there will be no definite deadline.
I hope you are not too angry with the delay in this letter. This is the last week we will be apart for a while at least I will promise it will not happen again. Here's hoping that this week will past as quickly as possible without any complications.

With All My Love,
Ralph [3]

When John Fitzgerald Kennedy and Jacqueline Bouvier Kennedy entered the White House in January 1961 Catherine had joined Ralph in Little Rock. Catherine looked forward to being a wife and a mother. While Ralph settled in as an Airman, Catherine attended nursing school. At first Ralph and Catherine roomed in at least two different homes. The most pleasant home was with a minister and his wife. Rev. Torrence was a country preacher and a very pleasant man. Ralph

Chapter Seven

developed a love for country churches that would last for the rest of his life. They began to raise a family and their first son was born. In 1961 on December 20 their first child Stephen Raoul Cothran was born in Little Rock, Arkansas.

The heat in Arkansas was something you had to get accustomed to. It got hot in Chattanooga but not as hot as Little Rock. Most days in the summer were well over 100 degrees. Milk would spoil and this was a problem because the baby needed milk. It was so hot that you had to put corn starch on the children to protect them from the heat. Since they could not afford an air conditioner they would place a block of ice in front of a fan and try to get some relief. During those days Ralph vowed to get an air conditioner as soon as he was able.

By now Ralph had moved his family to a more permanent home. Hemlock Courts was a public housing project in North Little Rock. Ralph and Catherine settled into a two-bedroom unit. Stephen was born in December and Cyzanne the second child was born May 9, 1963. Catherine continued her nursing training and took care of her children.

Ralph and Catherine made lasting friendships during this period. Ralph being an Airman had found great friendships with: Wilbert "Lip" Adams, Tommy Pierce, Timothy Raines and David Eugene Gayles. Meanwhile Catherine recalls that she developed some lasting relationships at her workplace and at nursing school. When Catherine attended Little Rock Vocational School, it was segregated. (The school is now known as Pulaski Technical School). Ms. Osmond, Ms. Hinson, Joyce Downs and Ms. Houston were some teachers that taught her. These instructors made a lasting impression on her life. Catherine also remembers two good friends at The University Arkansas Medical Center. Betty Jones and Norris Cross became close friends when Catherine worked at the Medical Center while completing her nursing training.

Ralph had to come back to Chattanooga to take care of some family business during the summer of 1962. Again he missed his family very much. The following letter is very interesting because Ralph writes about so many things including politics.

Big Ralph

Dear Catherine,

I arrived here Wednesday morning about 3:30 in the morning safely. Everybody here is fine, all healthy and working. I have not seen Baby Brother's wife. Grace Lee has a little boy about three weeks old. Vincient is running all over the place. Barbara and Vanessa have not changed a bit.

Carl Allen is a little more settled and serious minded and does not act as silly as he use to. Gerald is as studious as always. By the way all those classes that he said he was going to take were for the whole three years, and not for one as we thought. They have a white man that comes over and teaches the Russian class. He teaches at all the high schools and Carl Allen says that Howard is one of the outstanding schools. By the way before I forget Grace and Buddy have an apartment of their own. Honey you should see your church it is the most beautiful church I have seen in a long time. I have not seen the inside yet but from the outside it is terrific. Gerald says that it is air conditioned and has all the qualities of a school such as the new Orchard Knob and I believe him too. Honey do you know a Mrs. Phoebe Collier? She is Dr. Collier's wife, well she is running for state Legislature in fact she is the only Negro running for this particular slot so all the Negroes are getting ready to try to put her in office and if the white folk split their vote among the other white candidates she will get it to. Also Frank Clement is running for governor again, Ellington can't run and get a load of this will you, mayor Oligiati of Chattanooga is running for governor also. The campaign is a little more refined here than in Arkansas. Carl Allen is going to come back with me and stay a while at least until school starts. Vanessa just walked in and said Hi to you. Everybody wants to see Stephen. I guess we will get Mom or somebody to come and get him for a couple of weeks before he gets too old. Barbara just walked in and said hello to you she said she has been promoted to the 5th grade. Mom, Gerald, Carl, Barbara and myself were up until 3:30 in the morning can you think of me talking until that hour in the morning? Your Daddy is fine and doing well. However, my Daddy is not doing so well. He cannot work now, he is

Chapter Seven

suffering from rheumatism. This is all the paper I have so I have to close.

Love Always,
Your loving husband [4]

    Catherine has three sisters and three brothers plus a half brother who lived with the family for a brief period. Ollie who is Catherine's father's child was born before he and her mother were married, he lived with the family for about seven years. Ollie was at least 18 when he came from Alabama to live with the family. Ollie was called Moon Dog when he lived in Chattanooga. He is now known as Pat Patrick Patton and has traveled extensively and has only visited Chattanooga once since he left in the early 60's. Carl who was the fourth child with a younger brother and two younger sisters under him was Ralph's favorite. Catherine recalls that Ralph saw some potential in Carl and wanted them to be involved in developing this potential. Ralph also considered Carl his little brother. Ralph had no brother and had only an older sister.
    Catherine had encouraged Carl to attend college when he was still quite young. Carl graduated from Howard High School in 1963. Ralph and Catherine urged Carl to come and live with them in Little Rock and attend one of the local colleges. Carl took them up on their offer and enrolled in Shorter Junior College in North little Rock during the fall of 1963.
    Ralph worked at the base market as the produce manager. When Catherine shopped on the base, she always got the best produce available. Her neighbors would always wonder how she managed to always get such fresh produce. This was one of the few perks of being a serviceman's wife. Any time a family member is in the Armed Services there is always the potential for them to be assigned to an undesirable duty station. Catherine dreaded these thoughts especially a duty station for example in Greenland or some other God forsaken place.
    Catherine really loved Little Rock, she had adapted well to her nursing training and loved her training. She later found out that the standards were higher for nursing in Arkansas and she could have had a

Big Ralph

more solid career in nursing had they remained in Little Rock. Ralph, thought otherwise, after completing his tour of duty, he was set on returning to Chattanooga. Catherine felt it should be his decision so she left it up to him. So in 1964 they left Carl to make it on his own and returned to Chattanooga. Carl got a job at the Marion Hotel, the largest convention hotel in the state. He also found a rooming house with a vacancy a few blocks from the campus. He had one good semester under his belt and he had gotten adjusted to college life. So Ralph, Catherine, Stephen and Cyzanne headed back to Chattanooga.

Like thousands of other Black people they looked through the window of the Black experience. They saw, and they began to think and form opinions. The south and America in particular, is a vast area of Black people cast in the mold of subservience. As Black people became conditioned to accept a second-class role, this idea also became a part of Black leadership and organizations.

How can Black people receive salvation, freedom, justice and equality with leaders that beg for the left overs from a table of plenty? How can a human being who acts like a dog get up and lead anybody anywhere? Unfortunately the selected leadership of Black America had been an exclusive realm of misdirection. For all practical purposes they were sent (by those who benefit from Black exploitation) on a precise and manipulated journey to continue the initial priority of Black economic exploitation.

Thus unselected Black leadership that was independent was under attack. Frequently this leadership was defeated and attacked by bourgeois elements of the Black intelligentsia. How can Black people come to realize the reality of planned exploitation? This question is answered when we see that Black leadership and organizations are controlled by people outside our communities who have a profit motive agenda.

How does one become exposed to knowledge? Black colleges and universities have been controlled by the same exploitative interests since their inception. The independent Black scholars in these institutions are just as rare as independent Black scholars in predominately white universities.

Chapter Seven

Material motivations and a calculated scheme of brainwashing have caused many of the greatest scholars in the Black community to share the exploitative sentiments of the former slavemaster. So the independent Black scholar in the circumstances of North America must be as elusive and durable as a great running back.

Many people outside the Black community resent any effort by Blacks to be independent. Although these groups may even be composed of liberals from various church groups they still react adversely when Blacks attempt to control their own destiny.

The interest in Black independence, I would argue, is deeply imbedded in the civil rights movement. I do not agree with writers like Charles E. Silberman who thought the civil rights movement had been dominated by whites up to the 60's. For all practical purposes the civil rights movement is still dominated, controlled by white people. The simple way this control is sponsored is by money. Civil rights organizations rely on white financial support. In the process most of the civil rights leadership is more interested in getting paid than the rights of their brother and sisters.

Ralph Bunche in 1942 prepared a statement on Black organizations and leadership for Gunnar Myrdal. In this statement Bunche is critical of the white influence in the NAACP.

"The interracial makeup of the NAACP is an undoubted source of organizational weakness. There can be no doubt that the Negro leaders in the organization have always kept a watchful eye on the reactions of their prominent and influential white sponsors." [5]

Ralph Bunche's statement makes it clear that Black people have not all been duped by the white influences in Black civil rights organizations. Why has the influence of white sponsors continued to dominate the major civil rights organizations? What was the impact of the documented statements on white involvement in Black organizations?

For example members of the Atlanta Project who were members of SNCC released a clear and precise statement on the need for Black people to control their own organizations. They began their statement and/or discussion by saying the answers to the following questions leads

Big Ralph

us to believe that the form of white participation, as practiced in the past, is now obsolete:

"The inability of whites to relate to the cultural aspects of Black society; attitudes that whites, consciously or unconsciously, bring to Black communities about themselves (western superiority) and about Black people (paternalism); inability to shatter white-sponsored community myths of Black inferiority and self-negation, inability to combat the views of the Black community that white organizers, being "white," control Black organizers as puppets; insensitivity of both Black and white workers towards the hostility of the Black community on the issue of interracial "relationships" (sex); the unwillingness of whites to deal with the roots of racism that lie within the white community; whites though individually "liberal" are symbols of oppression to the Black community--due to the collective power that whites have over Black lives." [6]

The students go on to say that because of these reasons they have had to view America through the eyes of victims. Thus they advocated for a change in the role of white people that will promote self-sufficiency of Black people. Also the students make an effort to note that this position is not derived from racism or hatred of white people.

They assert further that Blacks have never been allowed to organize because of the ongoing white interference. Thus stereotypes have been established that Blacks can't organize themselves and whites have come to believe that they have to watch Blacks. Meanwhile Blacks feel threatened by the power white people have.

"It must be offered that white people who want change in this country must go where that problem (of racism) is most manifest. The problem is not in the Black community. The white people should go into white communities where the whites have created power for the express purpose of denying Blacks human dignity and self-determination.

"If we are to proceed towards true liberation, we must cut ourselves off from white people... we must form our own institutions, credit unions, co-ops, political parties, write our own histories. One interesting example is the SNCC "Freedom Primer." Blacks cannot

Chapter Seven

relate to that book psychologically because white people wrote it and therefore it presents a white point of view." [7]

The students, disgust with white liberals is further noted when it comes to the question of organizing. In this instance the students note that no matter how liberal whites are, they should not be involved in organizing Blacks. The students reached this position because white people cannot dispel the myths of western superiority.

Therefore the students note that SNCC should be staffed by Blacks, Black controlled and Black financed. The position paper by the students concludes with documenting that the white liberal establishment has used Black people. For example they assert that these same liberals have a great fear of Black Nationalism and a gross misunderstanding of the basic aspects of Nationalism.

Part of this misunderstanding is the link between racism and Black supremacy in Black Nationalism and Black self-sufficiency. In a final statement the students, give an excellent brief assessment of integration.

"If one looks at "integration" as progress then one is really perpetuating the myth of white supremacy. It is saying that Blacks have nothing to contribute, and should be willing to assimilate into the mainstream of the great white civilization, i.e., the west." [8]

It is for sure that the students of the Atlanta movement made the correct analysis of white liberals in Black organizations. So how did SNCC just like the traditional civil rights organizations become controlled by white power brokers?

Robert Allen gives us some answers to this question. Allen argues that two events occurred during the summer of 1966 that had a great impact on the Black liberation movement. First was the Meredith march against fear across the state of Mississippi when William "Papa" Ricks, originally from Bushtown in Chattanooga, Tennessee, and Stokley Carmichael coined the phrase "Black Power."

The second event was when "McGeorge Bundy, president of the multimillion dollar Ford Foundation addressed the annual banquet of the National Urban League in Philadelphia. Bundy told the Urban League that the Ford Foundation had decided to help in the task of achieving

Big Ralph

"full domestic equality for all American Negroes.

"What the Urban League delegates and the American public did not know was that the gigantic Ford Foundation, which already had fashioned for itself a vanguard role in the neocolonial penetration of the Third World, was on the eve of attempting a similar penetration of the Black militant movement."[9]

Simply what this meant was that the Ford Foundation would now start doling out large sums of money to the major civil rights organizations. When one concern financially supports another concern, a degree of control also comes along. Thus, you can see a calculated direction of traditional civil rights organizations. Here the integrationists felt that full civil rights and/or integrating with white people will solve all of their problems.

For example the NAACP has never pushed for Black economic development of the Black community. Ironically Booker T. Washington talked about Black economic development but he placed his idea in a subservient context. Washington's position as an accommodationist and Uncle Tom during a time of a nationwide attack on Black people is appalling. The nation wide attack principally on the Black male poses a serious contradiction in the philosophy of Booker T. Washington if for some reason you think he was a Black leader and not a Negro leading us for white people.

In the wake of the wholesale murder of Black people the NAACP was formed. The Black Holocaust had been a reality since the landing of the first slave ship. For all practical purposes it continues even as I write. The following statement notes the reality of the ongoing Black Holocaust in North America.

"In the decade preceding the Springfield riots of 1908--the event that precipitated formation of the NAACP -- an average of two Negroes a week had been lynched, and terror had become a principle means of forcing southern Negroes back into their servile place."[10]

The opposition to inhumanity against other human beings has always stirred the souls of men and caused debate. In North America, the question of how to continue to use the ex-slaves was an everyday reality.

Chapter Seven

Eventually national organizations were formed to help control the natural urge for freedom.

Unfortunately in the midst of alleged movements for equality the initial interest in economic exploitation continued. It is for sure that the Black masses of America need not be slaves to suffer economic exploitation. A brief history of the NAACP gives greater clarity to our discussion on Black organizations and leadership.

Lomax notes that the history of the NAACP "begins in the north when men had some basic freedoms. At the turn of the century another sort of migration came to the north, Negro workers in search of work and hundreds of Negro intellectuals in search of a platform to work for the betterment of the race." [11]

W.E.B. DuBois became the most significant Black person involved in the formation of the NAACP. DuBois was clearly on a different page than the selected Black leader of the time who was in the person of Booker T. Washington. It is for sure that the ongoing Black Holocaust and the Uncle Tom antics of Booker T. Washington were great incentives for DuBois and his colleagues to organize Black people.

DuBois and his friends first met in Niagara Falls, Canada in June 1905. This meeting resulted in the formation of an organization called The Niagara Movement. The following year they adopted a platform at Harpers Ferry. For about two years the Niagara Movement met and gained a small amount of support from Blacks and a few whites who were described as militants. To a large degree, the Booker T. Washington thinking Blacks at this time felt DuBois was a radical. This attitude was also reflected in the white community because undoubtedly they manipulated their selected leaders and Uncle Toms to criticize DuBois and the Niagara Movement.

So while the Niagara Movement floundered, the Black Holocaust continued. Even in these dire circumstances the covert actions of white power brokers defeated legitimate and independent Black organizing. Springfield, Illinois first gained notoriety in 1904 with a bloody race riot. By 1908 a bloody and brutal race riot in Springfield allegedly shocked many white people who were described as liberals.

Big Ralph

I imagine these liberals were not angry that Blacks only wanted to be treated as human beings. Often though Black equality is equated with being equal to whites and/or a challenge to race superiority. In any case white and Jewish northern liberals like Arthur B. Spingarn, John Dewey, Jane Adams and William Dean Howells publicized plans to establish an organization. This organization was called the National Association for the Advancement of Colored People.

So white people and Jews initially were the founders of the NAACP. The Niagara Movement was of very little impact. In this drama a precedent was clearly set. Black organizations could not exist without white support, leadership, membership etc. Thus the white influence in the NAACP gave it credibility and secured it's formation.

The progressive white liberals who formed the NAACP were well aware of DuBois and the group of intellectuals who had formed the Niagara Movement. The white liberals also knew that an organization formed to help with equal rights for Blacks needed Black members and a semblance of Black leadership. Thus, they contacted DuBois. In so doing DuBois and his cadre of followers were invited to join with the white liberals. Monroe Trotter, although a hard line integrationist, refused to join claiming, he did not trust white people, even white liberals and Jews. By 1910 the Niagara Movement was non existent and DuBois joined the white liberal sponsors and the NAACP was formed with DuBois as the only Black in the leadership ranks.

The year 1910 was only 45 years since the end of the Civil War and slavery in the south. Thus, any idea of equality and constitutional rights to Blacks were frowned upon by most whites. This is why white people were so fond of a selected Black leader like Booker T. Washington accepting a servant and slave like role for Black people. This inferior status of a slave and the superior status of master was the most comfortable and accepted position of the white man of this day.

So when the white and Black radicals of the NAACP presented their program white America was shocked. Their program or goals were:

1. Abolition of enforced segregation.
2. Equal education advantage for colored and white.

Chapter Seven

3. Enfranchisement for the Negro.
4. Enforcement of the fourteenth and fifteenth amendments to the U.S. Constitution.

The group of philanthropist that awarded money to Black institutions were appalled. These white benefactors were accustomed to giving money too people like Booker T. Washington and the Tuskegee Institute. In this case the white man was assured he was giving to a cause that supported a leader that honored the white man as his slave master.

Now you had Blacks talking about equal rights. Surely Blacks did not think they were equal to the white man, so how could they expect equal rights. The slave mentality thinking whites also got their Black lackeys to speak out against the NAACP and their efforts to speak for Black equality. Meanwhile, the NAACP began to solidify an organizational thrust to equality through the courts.

"The NAACP received three important court victories the first 15 years of its life:

1. 1915 Supreme Court ruled against the grandfather clause that kept Negroes from voting in several states.
2. 1917 Court struck down a municipal ordinance requiring Negroes to live in a certain section of town.
3. 1923 courts over turned a murder conviction against a Negro because among other things Blacks had been excluded from the jury that convicted him." [12]

Meanwhile, with the additional thrust of mass migration of Blacks to the north, the NAACP grew in membership. Blacks had a history as the labor force in America. With the end of slavery and the Industrial Revolution countless white people were also in the ranks of laborers. These white laborers had formed labor unions but they did not accept Blacks. The NAACP had not included equality in labor unions as part of their agenda for Black equality.

With the total exclusion from the established white unions Black laborers began in 1920 to organize their own locals. In five years the Black labor union movement was firmly established when A. Philip Randolph organized the Pullman Porters and Maids, but not without white support. By 1937 Randolph had gained bargaining power and the

Big Ralph

support of the NAACP and the Urban League.

So A. Philip Randolph's "Brotherhood of Sleeping Car Porters," Walter Whites' NAACP and Lester Granger's Urban League were the three prominent civil rights organizations. The NAACP continued to grow and was the dominant Black organization up to the 1950's. This growth was a direct result of the successful legal campaign to dismantle segregation throughout the south. From 1910 to 1939 the NAACP was one organization. In 1939 the NAACP was one organization and the Legal Defense and Education Fund originally headed by Thurgood Marshall became a separate organization.

Thurgood Marshall spearheaded great legal victories for the NAACP. The highlight of the Marshall era was the Supreme Court victory over segregated schools in 1954. Some students of the Black experience claim the question of dignity and respect remained unanswered. Also, the victories of the NAACP only affected a small amount of the Black population.

One reason the NAACP began to be criticized was their focus on school desegregation. Thurgood Marshall and the NAACP Legal Defense team won the case against school desegregation. Although the battle to desegregate the public schools in America is a never ending struggle, the struggle continues. Even during the present time few school districts are truly freely integrated.

Roy Wilkins took over the helm of the NAACP after the tenure of Walter White. Wilkins believed that the end of segregated schools would win the day for the Black community.

While speaking at Spelman College in Atlanta, Georgia, Wilkins said that "everything is tied to the school desegregation fight. The principle task before any community; Wilkins added, is the abolition of the segregated school. The inadequate and unequal education our children are receiving under this system is literally placing them in leg irons to run the race of life." [13]

School desegregation as the focal point of the NAACP'S civil rights policy is absurd. Realistically the NAACP failed to attract mass support throughout the Black community. Criticism reached a new height in the

Chapter Seven

aftermath of the sit-in and freedom ride demonstrations. The old tactics were questioned and direct mass action was seen as a tool for advancing the cause of civil rights.

The NAACP never believed in direct mass action although the national office claimed to have supported this as a tactic. The defeat of direct action is just one example of the undemocratic character of the NAACP. Critics note that the elected delegates to the NAACP Convention should be allowed the right to make basic organizational policy on the floor of the convention. Also the delegates should have the right to nominate or elect the people who will lead the organization. The reality is that the executive secretary and the national president are appointed by the board.

Therefore, many critics within the ranks of the NAACP want more freedom. This freedom would allow them some control over the leadership and the ability to get directly involved in mass action. A good example of the NAACP failing to respond to the interest of the Black community can be noted with a review of the convention of 1959.

The constitution of the NAACP does not allow delegates to fix policy. Thus delegates can introduce resolutions but the governing board of 48 members only have authority to act on the resolutions. During this convention many critical delegates planned to attack this undemocratic structure of the NAACP's constitution.

A more radical cause resulted, in the name of Robert Williams. Williams was the president of a local branch in Monroe, North Carolina. Williams released a statement at a press conference urging southern Blacks to take up arms to protect their persons and property. Williams was dismissed by the national leadership. Also the support for Williams at the convention was defeated and so was the cause for mass action.

Unfortunately the class structure of the NAACP that reflects white liberals, Jews and bourgeois Blacks in leadership has never represented the true interest of Black America. This conservative posture has stifled the organization and one has to seriously question a Black organization established and dominated by white people and Jews.

The impact of the NAACP is further illustrated with an examination of the NAACP Legal Defense and Educational Fund. As noted earlier this separate entity under the NAACP umbrella came into existence in 1939. Thurgood Marshall as the director of the new organization would soon reexamine the strategy taken by the NAACP regarding school desegregation.

Before 1940 the NAACP sought to deal with the principle "separate but equal." In other words, in reference to public schools, they petitioned the courts to provide equality within the school districts. In this instance they hoped that the southern segregationists would voluntarily integrate the schools.

"In 1945 Marshall, Walter White, W. H. Hastie and others met in New York and decided that it was time for a frontal attack on segregation. This decision was one of the most important in the history of race relations. This was a fundamental turning point in the Negro protest movement, for the shift from attacks on the inequality of separate facilities to open demands for integrated facilities involved a shift not only in strategy but in orientation." [14]

The shift by the NAACP was motivated by several decisions by the Supreme Court that noted a move from the fictional phrase of "separate but equal." The segregationists in the south also were prepared for any suit that challenged the "separate but equal" clause. Marshall further concluded that a suit that advocated integration received immediate action by the white south.

So from a legal point of view the confusion of desegregation, integration and equal access becomes ingrained in the philosophical thrust of the movement. Unknowingly Marshall and his staff clearly established the philosophy of integration as they pursued the doctrine of integration of public schools. To give this point more clarity we will move to the realm of questions.

What do Blacks want? They want quality education. How do they receive quality education? They can receive quality education from schools that are adequately equipped with the proper staff and materials. Fact one, white America in the south refused to adequately equip the schools assigned to Black citizens. Fact two, Black civil rights activists

Chapter Seven

(NAACP) petitioned the court to allow them to attend white schools that were adequately equipped.

Meanwhile this legitimate action got lost on the road to freedom and got bogged down in a spite game, the rules of which were: So (despite my initial and legitimate interest in quality education now I am only motivated by making you angry by badgering the courts to force my Black child in your suburban school).

Marshall began his challenge of segregation with an attack on the segregated law school at the University of Texas. The Supreme Court ruled on the validity of segregation and to the delight of Marshall and his team of lawyers the court accepted the notion that equality involved more than physical facilities.

Well, what did this mean, equality is more than physical facilities? Does this mean that equality also means the equality of human beings? The expert testimony Marshall used from sociologists, psychologists and anthropologists concluded that it was impossible for Blacks to receive an equal education in segregated schools. This most likely also meant that no matter what you did to provide this school with adequate supplies, teachers, physical facilities etc. the school would be discriminatory because it excluded whites. Thus, Black children took on inferiority complexes in segregated environments. Thus, they only would find relief to this dilemma in an integrated school.

Meanwhile the United States foreign policy was suffering because of the undemocratic aspects of Jim Crow and segregation. By December 1952 secretary of State Dean Acaheson submitted a statement to the Supreme Court.

"The continuation of racial discrimination in the U.S. remains a source of constant embarrassment to this government in the day-to-day conduct of its foreign relations; and it jeopardizes the effective maintenance of our moral leadership of the free and democratic nations of the world." [15]

Finally, what does the court decision of 1954 really mean? "Does segregation of children in pubic schools solely on the basis of race, even though the physical facilities and other tangible factors may be equal,

Big Ralph

deprive the children of the minority group of educational opportunities?"

"We believe it does we cannot turn the clock back to 1868 when the 14th amendment was adopted, or even to 1896, when Pleesy v. Ferguson was written . . . We conclude that in the field of public education the doctrine of "separate but equal" has no place. " [16]

Again what is the court saying? Does this decision also mean that Blacks are inferior and they can only gain a sense of equality by being with those whom they vision as superior beings?

The Urban League was formed in 1912 two years after the NAACP. Like the NAACP the Urban League was also established by white people and receives economic support from white power brokers. The Urban League is clearly a bastion of white capitalism. Here the Urban League has become a job center with national corporations and local business concerns are a part of the organizational structure.

Lomax notes that the League became a job center for two kinds of Black people:

"1. The Negro masses, at least those who knew about the League, went in search of menial jobs and factory work.

2. Breakthrough Negroes, those who were being let into certain job classifications for the first time, found that the League was their best ally." [17]

The Urban League is a mere illusion regarding the challenge to discrimination. The token and selected Black leadership are conservative Blacks who draw distinct class lines. The Urban League clearly represents the "Big Lie" because it represents the interests of corporate America under the guise of civil rights.

I won't use the devil here to keep down the confusion. But, I will advocate for the poor Black man, woman and child somewhere in the woodshed or lost in the woods. How could Whitney Young the most widely known director of the Urban League be so knowledgeable about the Black experience and be associated with the Urban League. Whitney Young most likely is a classic example of a Black intellectual who has sold his mind, completely to white racism and the continued economic

Chapter Seven

exploitation of the Black community.

On the other hand the following statements by Young may not be construed as knowledge. "The Negro masses are certified as an underdeveloped people, and that they are given special, accelerated treatment in order for them to assume full responsibilities in American society. This is going to make a lot of Negroes mad for they will assume Young is saying they are inferior." [18]

Furthermore Young argues that the background of the Black masses is inferior. Does this also mean that the person is inferior? I see a difference in inferior housing and the ethnic inferiority of a people. One of the most disturbing things Young wrote, is an essay on Black Power and Integration. In this instance Young seems to understand Black Power but the confusion of the Black integrationists creeps in.

"Black Power is less a cry of violence than a cry of desperation. What it says is: I am somebody. I want to be acknowledged as a human being. I have roots. I have pride I have made a contribution. I want to participate in the affairs of my destiny and my children's destiny. I want to mobilize my strength and resources to reward my friends and punish my enemies as all other groups have done." [19]

The evident confusion over integration is noted in the following statements by Young. The statements are even more absurd because they represent the thinking in part of Blacks that says "We have to have white people involved in everything we do."

"When I took over the Urban League (seven years ago) only 1% of our staff was white and I had to go through this special effort to attract, to recruit, to give special training to the whites because they didn't really meet our standards. We did these things because we were anxious to integrate and take advantage of the many skills these people could bring. Now 30 percent of our staff is white." [20]

The Southern Christian Leadership Conference was quite different from the NAACP and the token job opportunities embraced by the Urban League. Also SCLC was a contemporary civil rights organization that grew out of the Montgomery bus boycott of 1955.

The initial organized effort was called the Montgomery

Improvement Association. This organization was eventually named the Southern Christian Leadership Conference and Martin Luther King became the executive Director. Thus, King and SCLC became prominent players in the civil rights movement. King also became a significant intellectual and philosopher who dictated the definitive qualities of the driving force behind his social protest movement. This driving force was undoubtedly nonviolence.

The Southern Christian Leadership Conference came into existence with the coming together of the clergy. Throughout various southern cities clergymen joined with civil rights as a goal through a national organization. Soon after the inception of SCLC lines were drawn. Local chapters wanted to get all the glory for any civil rights victory.

King and his aides were able to deal with the "who gets the credit" problem and continued their campaigns of direct action. These campaigns consisted of "Voter registration, nonviolent action, student liaison and citizenship training.[21]

Direct action and mass protest were effective and so was legalism championed by the NAACP. The mood of the masses questioned Black leadership and Black organization. The organizations held up for review by the masses were the traditional civil rights groups. This also included SNCC, which by now had been co-opted by white power brokers. Lomax argues that the decline in Black leadership organizations is reflected in three factors:

"1. Negro leadership organizations, dominated, as they most are, by middle-class Negroes and white liberals, lost touch with the mood of the Negro masses. The result was a concentrated attack on segregation that reflected "class" rather than "mass" concerns.

2. Even after it became apparent that legalism and "class" concerns could not accomplish the swift change demanded by both the temper of our times and the mood of the Negro people, these organizations persisted in their basic philosophical approach to the problem of segregation; more, they interpreted any desire to debate the question as an attack upon the organizations and the individuals who head them.

Chapter Seven

3. These organizations failed to make room for the younger educated Negroes who were coming to power in the Negro communities." [22]

So when these factors are taken into consideration we see a breakdown in communication. This communication problem is between the local and national offices of civil rights groups. Thus, many social scientists argue that the traditional groups have failed. As Black people questioned the efforts of King, Roy Wilkins and nonviolent direct action, there were some available alternatives. The alternatives to the traditional civil rights groups were an exercise in independence. Unfortunately most Blacks felt helpless without white involvement in civil rights organizations. Thus, white liberals were so involved as civil rights activists that they were certain that they had every right to lead Blacks.

The critical nature of Black leadership organizations is further illustrated in the competitive nature of the organizations. So, while the traditional civil rights organizations compete to impress white people, they also overlap. It is for sure that selected leadership and manipulated Black organizations are conditioned to compete with their counterparts, as a tactic of disunity.

So as traditional Black civil rights organizations and leaders directed a social movement of integration they qualified a new phenomenon called "Black Power." Roy Wilkins is a typical example of the selected and programmed Black leadership. Wilkins argues that "Black Power" means anti white power. He further draws a parallel between white supremacy and "Black Power." The following statements gives additional clarity as to how Wilkins and the NAACP conceived "Black Power."

"In the Black, white relationship, it has to mean that every other ethnic power is the rival and the antagonist of "Black Power." It has to mean "going it alone." It has to mean separatism. Ideologically "Black Power" up with Black and down with white. It is a reverse Mississippi, a reverse Hitler, a reverse KKK. It can only mean in the end Black death." [23]

Big Ralph

Catherine Patton Cothran Tennessee Licensed Practical Nurses Association Convention Knoxville, Tenn. 1968. Front row second from left

Ralph and Catherine at wedding August 20, 1960.

Chapter Seven

Ralph and Catherine at wedding from left sister Grace Lee Patton and best man Arless Holloway.

Hilda's children left to right Ricky, Sunserray, Renee', Robert and Roger.

Big Ralph

Chattanooga District Ushers Association at Orchard Knob Missionary Baptist Church 1958.

Basketball team Little Rock Air Force Base, Ralph back row 4th from Left.

Chapter Seven

Ida Jean Keith, Ralph's first cousin

Air Force buddies, left Wilbert (Lip) Adams, right Timothy (Tim) Raines.

Big Ralph

Chapter 8

DOES CIVIL RIGHTS MEAN INTEGRATION?

**Pray tell those who march, cry out for mixture,
to merge and mingle, has freedoms parity lost?
Tis freedom the loud cry, hence the natural order
of life will set the tone of consolidation.**

Ralph and Catherine, just like most Blacks, had formed some ideas about integration. A particular incident happened when Catherine attended Roosevelt University for six months during the 56-57 school term. This was before she and Ralph attended Lane College during the 57-58 school term. While at Roosevelt University Catherine recalls a everlasting example of discrimination. She like so many other Black students were struggling financially. So she applied for financial aid but, she never received any word on the status of her claim. Meanwhile the country was being invaded by Hungarian refugees. Many of these immigrants enrolled at Roosevelt University, Catherine noticed that these new refugees received all the benefits available to students. Even though her ancestors slave labor had helped to build the United States she could not get any assistance. But people from another country could, only because they were not of the Black race.

Big Ralph

Ralph pursued various job possibilities and career choices when they returned to Chattanooga in 1964. Catherine on the other hand was hired immediately at Erlanger Hospital in the emergency room. Ralph expressed his feelings that were typical of that day and time after Catherine told him of an incident in the dining room at Erlanger. Catherine worked with a number of white nurses in the emergency room. Although when it came time to eat lunch she had to go to a small undesirable area designated for Blacks. Meanwhile, her white counterparts went into a modern well lighted clean dining room. One particular day Catherine decided to eat in the dining room with her white co-workers. She felt no sense of inferiority and felt she just as much right to eat in the dining room as any body else.

When Catherine told Ralph about the incident, he said "girl what is wrong with you, you going over there sitting down." This was the time of the sit-ins and mass protest by Blacks, but nothing developed from the incident. In some respects' Catherine felt that Ralph's statement was comical but this was the attitude of Black people at this time. They had been conditioned to think a certain way and to stay in their place, and this was the ultimate result of Jim Crow.

The school desegregation issue was a very hot issue during this time. Catherine recalls that although white people had no objection in most instances to working with Blacks the school issue was a different matter. One day one of her white co-workers who claimed to be a Christian boldly said she did not want her children going to school with Black children. Ralph and Catherine like most all other Blacks in America who lived either north, south, east or west were confronted with some aspect of racism.

Ralph had also worked at a hospital when he was quite young. Charles Caldwell a family friend got Ralph a job as an orderly at Memorial Hospital when he was in high school. Ralph had dreams of becoming an orthopedic surgeon, as he was fascinated with the human bone structure. Bonnie Edwards was also a good friend of Ralph during his early years. The Henderson family, Joseph and Cecil were also special friends that Ralph cared for throughout his life. Just like Ralph his friends also witnessed the changing times and the move toward equality.

Chapter Eight

So the picture window continued to unfold the struggle between Black and white, the haves and the have-nots. Black people had been conditioned to accept what those who had been assigned leadership status said about civil rights. Thus, most Blacks, during the height of the civil rights movement in the 60's, believed that integration was the way to achieve equal rights.

This leads us to the question. Does civil rights mean integration? Well it's according to whom you talk to. The integrationist believed that the only way, for example, for Blacks to have an equal education was to integrate the schools. Thus, one can clearly see that evidently civil rights must mean integration because if one can integrate he has acquired civil rights.

On the other hand it is also possible to achieve civil rights without integrating. In this instance civil rights means equal access and parity that should be assigned to all American citizens. This question is not complex; but it has been lost in confusion, just like most of the questions concerning integration.

A good framework of analysis can be found in how Blacks have interacted with the federal government over time. This framework exposes the different priorities of Black people that they feel would render them freedom.

With the passage of the 13th, 14th and 15th amendments newly freed Blacks established faith in Congress. With the passing of Reconstruction the Southern hatemongers were reborn in the U.S. Senate and Congress.

By the 1880's the Supreme Court established the "separate but equal" doctrine. Blacks now believed the Supreme Court was their friend and would render fair treatment. But, the implementation of court decisions always depends on the chief executive. It is also very important how constitutional guarantees are first interpreted by the courts and by the president.

No doubt then the American presidency, from the turn of the century up to the civil rights era, has had a great impact on our question. Black people had been conditioned to accept Booker T. Washington as their leader. Washington, as an ally of the white power brokers who wanted

Big Ralph

to keep Blacks on the plantation, was invited to the White House. In 1901 Theodore Roosevelt invited Booker T. Washington to the White House for dinner. This gesture impressed Blacks and they concluded that Roosevelt was their friend.

Independent Black thinking so soon after slavery was rare. Very few Blacks realized that Washington worked for the white power brokers against his own people, Black people. Thus, the gesture by Roosevelt was about the business of directing a so-called Black leader toward the continued economic exploitation of his people.

Meanwhile Roosevelt made a few Black appointments. Roosevelt tried to cater to Blacks, but William Howard Taft did very little to appease Blacks. So as Blacks continued to be lynched and murdered, Booker T. was hailed by white America as a savior of Black and white relationships.

The disenchantment with the Republicans grew and Blacks began to look at the Democratic party for help. Woodrow Wilson, a skillful politician, wooed Black voters and won the election. In so doing the largest amount of anti-Black legislation ever introduced in an American Congress resulted. For example, Wilson segregated most of the Black federal employees in the use of rest rooms and dining facilities.

By 1915 Booker T. Washington had died. Monroe Trotter, who was considered a radical, led a group of Blacks to the White House. President Wilson, a typical racist of his day was only interested in talking with Black Uncle Toms. Trotter did not have a Uncle Tom posture like Booker T. Washington, thus, he and his supporters were thrown out of the White House.

World War I was approaching. Blacks felt they could help fight for freedom abroad and win freedom at home. So by April 1917 Blacks joined the Armed Forces in droves. Victory in Europe did not spell victory over racism at home. Meanwhile the Republican administrations of Warren Harding and Calvin Coolidge listened to Black leaders but took very little action.

Chapter Eight

The history of Blacks as exclusive Republicans was ending. The old Republican party, as the party of Abe Lincoln, was now a party of big business. The interests of the poor and ex-slaves were not a priority. Also in 1928 the Republicans took Black support for granted and attempted to gain support from southern voters.

As the depression approached, Black people were hit harder because they had less in the first place. So by 1932 the Democratic party, with their social welfare programs, became a living reality for the Black masses. Lomax notes that there were two things that enhanced FDR's prestige with Black voters:

"1. It was public knowledge that both the president and his wife had Negroes as personal friends.

2. Roosevelt brought a number of "Negro specialists" to Washington as aides and advisors to major government departments known as the "Black Cabinet."[1]

Roosevelt thus far was considered by the Black masses as their greatest friend in the White House since Lincoln. By 1941 A. Philip Randolph threatened a march on Washington. Randolph and his Black supporters were protesting discrimination in federal contracts. Roosevelt issued an executive order that struck down discrimination in businesses with government contracts. The Fair Employment Practices Committee was later established because of this action.

Harry Truman made his mark by issuing an executive order to end segregation in the Armed Forces. This event occurred in 1948. World War II had ended and again Blacks thought that a victory for Democracy overseas would translate into Democracy for Blacks in the United States.

General Eisenhower succeeded Truman in the White House. Eisenhower was a Republican and challenged Truman when he moved to desegregate the Armed Forces. Led by the NAACP legal staff, the Black masses again looked to the Supreme Court. Then came the 1954 Supreme Court decision declaring segregated schools are unconstitutional.

Big Ralph

Now Blacks had a change in attitude. In 1952 very few Blacks voted for Eisenhower. The Black masses rallied to the democratic candidacy of Adlai Stevenson. In 1956 Blacks reconsidered and over 40% voted for Eisenhower. Finally after 60 years of non-action the Congress passed a civil rights bill in 1958.

The 1960's was one of the most significant periods in U.S. history. This period was especially significant for Black Americans. Also, a liberal Democrat entered the White House in the presence of John F. Kennedy. Kennedy was very rich, Catholic and from Massachusetts. The times were filled with a revolt by descendants of slaves for their constitutional rights denied because of their legacy as slaves. All human beings with humane principles realized the criminal abuse placed on these people. For the record these despised people are the people of God who accepted Jesus Christ as the Messiah. It was just a matter of time for significant changes to take place. Blacks had hopes that these changes would provide some semblance of mercy and justice to the descendants of slaves whose ancestors' labor power aided in the establishment of the United States as a world power.

Since the last days of Reconstruction the despised and downtrodden Black man and woman had been struggling for rights as citizens. Sixty years into the next century Black people were filled with a burning desire for respect and parity. This emotional upheaval was misdirected by unrealistic philosophies and frivolous elitist notions toward social mobility. Within this atmosphere appeared the Kennedy clan that coopted the civil rights movement.

As the traditional civil rights organizations acted like they were challenging Kennedy, the reality was quite different. The reality was that Kennedy knew the difference between Martin Luther King and Malcolm X. So all of the traditional civil rights organizations, including newly co-opted SNNC, were given large sums of money to operate.

Meanwhile Kennedy had a grand strategy. This strategy would, from JFK's assessment, give respect to the Black man in the south. Thus he instructed "his" civil rights organizations to sponsor voter registration drives throughout the south. One cannot discount the merits of Black

Chapter Eight

registered voters who use the vote as a tool for equal rights, but Kennedy most likely had other motives.

Sustained voter registration would take some energy away from Black direct action campaigns. Also Kennedy, as the white savior of Black America, would benefit from the Black vote come election time. This period would also witness some evidence of school desegregation.

In Chattanooga at the beginning of 1962 the local newspapers reported that city officials were preparing for a peaceful transition. [2] Meanwhile the city leaders were also attempting to delay the process by saying there would be violence.

"Mrs. Constance Baker Motley filed a brief citing the original desegregation ruling by the U.S. Supreme Court in 1954 and states that the high court in its 1955 opinion in that suit provided for "flexibility in school desegregation, not delay. " [3]

The Federal Court eventually insisted on a gradual plan of desegregation. This plan would start with the first three grades in 16 designated grammar schools by next fall. The completion of desegregation of all schools, elementary and high school was to be completed by September 1968. The following interesting reminder was noted in a Times article.

"The Chattanooga system has operated on a biracial system since it was organized in 1872. Chattanooga High School was established in 1874. Howard High was organized more than 40 years ago. Before it came into existence, Negro high school students attended the Lincoln High School operated by Hamilton County." [4]

The confusion over desegregation, integration and equal access is an on-going dilemma for Black people and America even today. The "freedom of choice" concept is one concept that has a relationship to the terms. By March of 1962 the Chattanooga Board of Education developed an admissions and transfer plan that would insure both Black and white parents "freedom of choice." This decision would allow the choice between two schools during the transition to a desegregated school system.

Big Ralph

In response to the "freedom of choice" ruling counsel for the Black children noted that this measure was violating the Supreme Court ruling. But Raymond Witt counsel for the School Board declared that "segregation in pubic schools is unconstitutional only when it results from the state acting in such a way as to deny admission to schools because of race alone." [5]

Mr. Witt was definitely one of the leading segregationists and racists of that era. But Mr. Witt and other racists helped form a particular segregationists' philosophy. This philosophy was at times a response to certain tactics of Black integrationists and their supporters. Here we credit racists with helping us better understand the confusion over segregation, integration and equal access.

The following reply by Mr. Witt in response to the Black counsel's request for total desegregation is profound:

"Some would have the federal courts believe the 14th amendment requires the states to take affirmative action in their public schools to make certain that each child is in a classroom composed of children of both races. They support their thesis by arguing that otherwise the Negro children are being deprived of an equal educational opportunity. Under this viewpoint, the desires of the Negro parents are irrelevant as are the desires of white parents." [6]

As the showdown approached the business community also got involved. The economic effects of the failure to maintain law and order were noted and so were the possible negative media reports. William Brock a business leader said "the answer to possible violence is community leadership."[7]

Finally, at the beginning of the 1962-63 school year, Black and white children enrolled at the same schools. Integration occurred at the city and county schools. "Forty Negro children were enrolled in six formerly all-white schools. Eleven Negro pupils were enrolled in an orderly manner in two formerly all-white elementary schools in Hamilton County." [8]

Civil rights laws were also passed that included public school desegregation. The civil rights law of 1964 struck down racial

Chapter Eight

discrimination in voting procedures, certain areas of public accommodation and public facilities, and in some places of employment.

There was also an analysis of the Black experience coming from those that understood the economic motives of racism. Robert Allen gives a different view of civil rights and the concept "Black Power" than the integrationist philosophers. Allen makes the following statement concerning civil rights laws:

"Civil rights laws became merely more testimony to the truism that American democracy is subservient to the economic and political interests of those who hold power." [9]

Ingrained in Allen's statement is the fact that the economic interests in America control the political arena. Civil rights laws and the civil rights movement were manipulated by the controlling economic interest in America. For example the civil rights movement was a middle class movement. These class lines held in check any real improvement for the Black masses.

So as the economic powers directed the political arena to control the civil rights movement there were token gains made by the Black middle-class. Allen argues that nonviolent demonstrations definitely presented a challenge to the morality of white America. Although the power brokers did not see the movement led by King as a threat to the entrenched distribution of power.

Meanwhile the Black (bourgeoisie) middle class is set with confusion. As integrationists, this group takes on white attitudes when at all possible. Since it is impossible for Black people to become white they suffer from a gross identity crisis. They legitimately relate to Black people, i.e., the Black middle-class and attempt to relate to white people.

This period also produced the so-called Black militants. The militants were advocates of "Black Power" and tried to make some sense of the confusion established by the "wannabe whites." So to some Black power advocates Blacks needed to be more involved in the political system. They sought to reform the social system.

"The militants were sophisticated enough to know that integration was not satisfactory because it did not change political relations and consequently could not affect the oppression suffered by most Blacks. Therefore it was logical to conclude that only the political integration of Black people as a group into American society could offer any real hope." [10]

One reason that militants were not a strong voice was the Ford Foundation. As noted earlier the Ford Foundation had made a move to control the traditional civil rights organizations. Before 1966 the Ford Foundation had only been involved in donating money to education and research projects in an effort to motivate Blacks to become middle-class wannabe whites. The Ford Foundation saw a grave need to manipulate and control the civil rights movement through its leadership and organizations. So the NAACP, Urban League, SCLC, CORE and SNCC became lackeys of racist white America. The Black Panther Party was not made up of middle-class Blacks. Their fate was different, because they refused to be controlled.

To gain the greatest clarity over the confusion of integration we need to closely examine what the Black Nationalists were saying. Thus the question is posed, should Blacks want integration? Then there are those that claim that there can be no solution to the problems of Black Americans without full integration into the mainstream of American life.

Separatism is another term that also causes confusion along with segregation, integration and equal access. Because proud conscious Blacks want, their own institutions do not mean they are a bunch of Black supremacist. So developing Black neighborhoods is not separatism and the continuation of segregation. The confused Black integrationist misdirected the civil rights movement when they declared that integration in essence is only fulfilled in a predominately white environment.

"The more important problem is a good deal subtler: What do Negroes really mean by integration? As C. Eric Lincoln asks the question, do Negroes want "true integration," or do they want what he terms "a conspicuous, superficial integration that relieves them of the self-hatred and insecurity that come from second-class citizenship." [11]

How can integration relieve Blacks that suffer from inferiority complexes? This is why there is so much confusion on this subject.

Chapter Eight

Unfortunately the Black integrationists are so filled with inferiority and self-hatred that they see integration as assimilation not only into the mainstream but to lose their lowly cultural identity.

My answer to this insane notion is that all Black institutions including schools are not necessarily inferior. It is for sure they are not inherently inferior because they are Black. These institutions logically may suffer inadequacies because of lack of funds to repair the physical structure of the building and lack of equipment. Again white people give us more clarity about these confusing concerns than Black civil rights advocates.

"The experience of the European ethnic groups suggests that integration need not mean assimilation, that integrating the Negro into the mainstream of American life does not depend, indeed, cannot depend, on making color irrelevant by making it disappear as a fact of consciousness."[12]

If white people know it is impossible for Blacks to disappear thorough assimilation, why don't Blacks conclude this also? Again we see the confusion over integration and equal access. This confusion is noted in the Black integrationist believing that mixing and not equal access will remove his self-hatred and provide freedom. No doubt these integrationists are very close to being insane because this is abnormal behavior.

Lerone Bennett argues that there is a white problem in America. There is also a Black problem in America. If white people have developed a particular mental attitude toward Blacks, so have Blacks developed an attitude toward whites. The reality is that white America, including those that are racist, largely have come to conclude that Blacks are inferior. So on the other hand Blacks and/or the integrationists have also come to conclude that they are inferior.

So Blacks have a responsibility to make the correct analysis about their predicament. This has been difficult, especially for the Black masses, because throughout the history of man the masses have been ignorant. However, in the case of the Black masses the efforts of exploitation have been a planned and calculated tactic of racism.

Big Ralph

It is for sure that just because many white people have come to believe their own lies and falsehoods it does not mean that I, as a Black person, should also believe in an untruth. So often the ignorant white racist sincerely believes that he is a part of a superior race and that all Blacks or nonwhites are inferior.

Bennett makes good sense when he defines racism in the context of economics. "We must come to see that racism in America is the poor man's way out and the powerful man's way in: A way in for the powerful who derive enormous profits from the divisions in our society." [13]

So a mental attitude of racism based on the dominate race as superior and the subservient as inferior developed. At the core of this premise is economic exploitation. Thus, those that were in the ignorant ranks, of the white community and those that took on the ways of the ignorant, in the Black community accepted this rule and lived by it.

"From 1619 to 1660, a period of primary importance in the history of America, America was not ruled by color. In the 1660's, men of power in the colonies decided that human slavery, based on skin color, was to be the linchpin of the new society. Having made this decision, they were forced to take another, more ominous step. Nature does not prepare men for the roles of master or racist. It requires rigid training." [14]

Regardless of a climate of hate, that is propelled by racism, many Blacks now want to integrate. These Blacks do not bring equal access into the equation but see integration as an idea of race mixing. To really capture the ideas of the integrationist let's look at some of the things Edward Brooke has to say about this subject. Edward Brooke was the first Black U.S. Senator of U.S. modern history. Brooke was also a Republican . If Senator Brooke was still around today, he would most likely join hands with J.C. Watts, Clarence Thomas and the few other clones of high-level Republican Uncle Tom's. Here is Brooke's statement on integration.

"The Negro wants to live in an integrated society with all that implies. He no longer is willing to live on the outside looking in. He wants his children to attend good schools. But he also wants them to attend integrated schools. He wants school busing as necessary but

Chapter Eight

temporary relief in the establishment of integrated schools. But he also wants the destruction of the Negro ghetto which among other benefits, will establish permanent school integration." [15]

This is the classic example of a people so mistreated that now they want to join the oppressor. Evidently the Black Holocaust has been the ultimate in degradation and oppression. I know some of you are thinking, well, with some prisoners of war they have joined those who have incarcerated them. But, is there any valid reason supporting the right of one group of human beings to enslave another human being, especially an act of slavery based solely on economic exploitation? Even after that particular economic system had become outdated and the slaves received freedom, the acts of economic exploitation continue.

No wonder Blacks have wanted to separate from white people. Some Blacks are so confused, that they want no part of the confused integrationist philosophy. It is interesting that Bayard Rustin places' Booker T. Washington in the ranks of the separatist. Historically most separatist have expressed some feelings of Nationalism. But this was not so for Booker T. Washington.

Unfortunately if we accept Rustin's claim, Booker T. Washington is the only separatist in our history who preached separatism of Blacks and whites based on Black inferiority. Washington openly says that Blacks are inferior and should take a subservient position to white people.

Booker T.Washington foolishly thought Blacks could gain dignity from, accepting a, slave mentality. I imagine Booker T. felt that even though Blacks were inferior to Europeans there was some dignity found among the race though they were not equal to whites. As an aside, contemporary integrationists led by Thurgood Marshall and the NAACP legal team came to believe that Blacks became inferior when whites would not allow them to integrate.

Rustin seeks to answer the dignity question with using three examples. Here he argues there are three ways Blacks can maintain dignity.

"1. By gradual advancement in the economic order.
2. By being a participating element of the democratic process.

Big Ralph

3. Through the sense of dignity that emerges from their struggle. Blacks gained dignity from King, and the successful Montgomery boycott and Selma." [16]

So now if Booker T. Washington is confused over the question of Black dignity in white racist America, what about Bayard Rustin. Surely all Black people did not proclaim that they received dignity from the King led boycotts and nonviolent campaigns.

Although many intellectuals in the Black community have been coopted by racist power brokers there is much to gain from education. Ignorance allows exploitation and oppression. What is the case when one is not ignorant? Well, there are different viewpoints. For example, some Blacks thought King was a savior and supported nonviolent demonstrations. Many other Blacks preached a conscious feeling of Black Nationalism and vowed to protect themselves, their family and community from offensive acts of violence by white America.

Usually it took more reasoning power to become a Black Nationalist than it did to blindly follow a civil rights leader in America. There, (as mentioned earlier) are also those that are intellectuals in the Black bourgeoisie of whom we just spoke. They knew both sides of the issue. Some sincerely believed in integration and some strongly believed in Ford Foundation money.

Education no doubt is a good way to examine our question does civil rights mean integration? To some, quality education for Black people can only be attained through integrated schools. Then there are those who believe that quality education for Blacks can only be obtained by Black controlled community schools.

The history of civil rights litigation for Black Americans can be placed in two different frameworks. These two different models both have merit and one cannot fully understand this phenomenon without realizing the essence of both models. First one can argue that leading up to Brown v. Board of Education in 1954 the court dealt with precedents. These precedents began with the Dred Scott decision of 1857 and gained more direction with the Plessey vs. Ferguson decision of 1896. This model supports the theory that the Brown decision was based on other major civil rights decisions made by the court in the past.

Chapter Eight

The second model suggests that the Brown decision be based on concerns regarding the social context of legalized segregation. The Supreme Court, most likely would not have declared that segregated schools were unconstitutional, if not for the contradiction to democracy, as viewed by the people throughout the world.

So with the social, historical and psychological testimony of the witnesses assembled by Thurgood Marshall the court concluded: (Seperate educational facilities are inherently unequal by virtue of being separate). Somewhere in this jargon was the lost reality that culturally disadvantaged does not mean inherent Black intellectual inferiority.

Since the idea of inherent inferiority was advanced to describe Black schools, the only way to quality education was in a white school. Thus all those Black children who were previously required to attend segregated schools took on feelings of inferiority.

Of course this was not true. For example I can personally admit that I did not feel inferior to white people or white children when I passed white schools on my way to a segregated Black school in Chattanooga, Tennessee. But I imagine, some Black children did. Regrettably our own leaders helped further entrench Black inferiorities in those who were probably already struggling with problems of self-esteem.

If Kenneth Clark is confused over the question of integration he is even more confused over Nationalism. Clark confuses Black Nationalism with racism. For example let's review the following statement by Clark:

"Perhaps the most ironic development since the 1954 Supreme Court handed down the Brown decision, however, has not been the continuation of white racism in the south, nor the acknowledgment of the more subtle white racism of the north, but the emergence and growth of Black racism." [17]

Clark incorrectly equates Nationalism with racism. The confusion of Black intellectuals like Kenneth Clark helped further the erroneous notion of the Black priority of desegregation and integration. This was a priority coming from civil rights leadership. In reality Black people should have wanted a desegregation that means equal access. Integration, if realized at all, is only a natural outgrowth of allowing Blacks equal access to institutions conveyances etc.

Big Ralph

So with this utter mass confusion rational Black people not duped by the selected leadership of civil rights organizations questioned integration. But those who questioned integration and the civil rights leadership were destroyed or labeled as negative.

For example people like Roy Wilkins called the cry for Black studies programs, Jim Crow studies. Wilkins states "that no Black history becomes significant and meaningful unless it is taught in the context of world and national history. In it's sealed off, Black Studies Centers, it will be simply another exercise in racial breast-beating." [18]

What Wilkins fails to realize is that the reason Black students demanded Black Studies Programs is because Black history had been left out of the college curriculums. Also, Black Studies was not an attempt to exclude white or European history but simply a valid academic request to include Black history. From an academic point of view one cannot adequately study U.S. history and exclude Black history. Previous racist college curriculums left students with only a superficial understanding of U.S. history.

Surely to come to know your own history is not criminal. Most integrationist felt they had no history and were so inferior to whites that they were willing to do anything to appease them. We have been very fortunate as a people that this insane thinking does not include most of the Black community.

In support of Black Studies Programs were out spoken activist like Nathan Hare Jr. The following brief quote places' the reactionary integrationist in perspective. "Appalling is the only word I know to describe the sneaky way in which critics like Roy Wilkins accuse us of separatism." [19]

Hare and others like him who supported Black Studies saw the Black perspective as a revolutionary idea. Thus, they view Black Studies Programs as revolutionary and nationalistic. The power brokers in America refuse to allow any Black move to independence. Since they control Black colleges and universities they coopted, established and infiltrated all Black Studies Programs.

Chapter Eight

I have come to conclude the following from my experiences in a Black Studies Program at Fisk University during 1971 to 1973. Black Studies Programs during the height of Black awareness were breeding grounds for young Black revolutionaries. The power brokers of America wanted to identify this group and take steps to monitor their activities. So they brought in spies of all types. Some were professors and some were students. By the 70's college campuses had spies of all types that reported on everything that took place.

Does academic freedom exist on Black college campuses? Yes, if you accept an accommodationist philosophy, no, if you aspire to be, an independent thinker. Here the United Negro College Fund is a means of financial control. Instead of wasting Black minds the power brokers, and their Black lackeys seek to brainwash young Black students.

While the power brokers of America sought to monitor and control all aspects of the Black experience we chased white people. As Jim Crow fell to the dust and as the courts forced school districts to integrate, white people fled to the suburbs. As they ran, we chased them and pleaded with the courts to allow us to integrate with them.

One important tactic used to force integration was to cut off federal funds to school districts that practiced segregation. Federal judges were not immune to racism and this tactic had limited success. Julian Bond a state legislator and activist was prompted to say? "America gave birth to the rhetoric of democracy while it breathed life into what became institutionalized racism."[20]

Does civil rights mean integration? The reality is no, but those who profess the philosophy of integration say yes. They believe that integration is a natural component of civil rights. In reality integration may result from civil rights but civil rights should be the major objective and not integration.

Big Ralph

Chapter 9

Some Results Of Integrationist Philosophy

*Youth, have now life to live, as the old fade and fold,
what preparations hast thou made,
As movement, turns into motion, the revolution of transition,
the elusive threshold, a vision the dream of reality.*

The battle over integration continued and school desegregation was at the center of the controversy. Ralph and Catherine had returned to Chattanooga and were still just trying to survive. Their first two children had been born in Little Rock. Stephen was almost three years old and Cyzanne was almost 15 months and not even a toddler. Catherine had attended nursing school and started a career in nursing while Ralph still pondered his next career move.

Chattanooga like most cities in America during this time noted the new opportunities that were available because of the human rights movement. The human rights struggle that was confused with civil rights and integration began to open up doors. Those that had ambition and applied themselves were able to latch onto these new opportunities in various areas of life.

Ralph was discharged from the Air Force at a time of Black Awareness. They would return to Chattanooga at a time of this century's greatest struggle and a climatic chapter in the everlasting Black Holocaust. The mood of change was in the air and the

Big Ralph

suffering Black masses were locked in America's heroic battle for freedom. Although many Black people confused freedom with integration, both seemed to elude the outstretched grasp of Catherine, Ralph and their kinsmen.

The year of 1963 was an eventful year in Chattanooga. School desegregation and/or integration would officially begin during September of 1963. I was completing the 12th grade at Howard High. My sister Catherine had encouraged me to attend college. She asked me to come live with her and Ralph and attend college in Little Rock. I would eventually live with Catherine and Ralph for the first semester of my first year in college.

It was a hot spring afternoon when the Commissioner of Education came out to Howard School, during my senior year at Howard. Commissioner Dean Peterson came to all Black Howard High to tell us about integration but he really came to tell us about segregation. He claimed he came out to tell us that old City High that was a white school would now be turned over to Blacks. He went on to say that the white kids would now attend a new school (which would be named City High out in the suburbs).

Integration of the first three grades in elementary school was to begin in the fall. Evidently integration/desegregation of the high schools was a long way off. Meanwhile, the Chattanooga School Board established zoning laws. Also, the NAACP continued to criticize the School Board. [1]

The NAACP and CORE led sit-ins at the downtown S&W cafeteria, the locally owned Krystals and the Rogers Theater. [2] So while Blacks were refused service at the S&W and Krystal, the local University (University of Chattanooga), which was private then, and not part of the state system, allowed Blacks to attend. This action by the University was keeping with the spirit of 1963 to desegregate/integrate educational facilities. The Times reported that: "Seven educators, and a postal worker were admitted for the summer session. This was the first time Blacks were admitted and it was accomplished without tension or confusion."[3]

The public schools were due to integrate/desegregate in the fall. The power structure speaking through the mayor and other city officials

Chapter Nine

pleaded for a peaceful transition. One particular concern that affected the desegregation/integration process was the zoning issue.

"Children are required to attend the schools in which they are zoned, except that transfers may be granted under special circumstances. Also the Supreme Court ruled that transfers may not be granted solely on race." [4]

As the 1963-1964 school year ended, Blacks were still pleading for integration of the schools. Meanwhile the Chattanooga School Board ignored the court order and claimed white children were not assigned without regard to race. [5]

The argument over segregated schools causing Black academic inferiority raged in Chattanooga and across the nation. Blacks began to argue that their children did poorly because they were not taught properly. Here white teachers, even the best in their teacher education classes, had difficulty teaching Blacks. As hopeless victims of prejudice they felt that Blacks inherently were intellectually inferior.

The Black teacher, when properly trained, was equipped to teach all youngsters. He or she was not burdened with the kind of race prejudice associated with their white counterparts. To best understand the debate over school segregation and academic inferiority for Black students one can review the court rulings.

Brown vs. Board of education in 1954 reversed the "separate but equal" doctrine of the Plessy vs. Ferguson decision in 1896. The court clearly based it's ruling on psychological and sociological data that the Black plaintiff's, attorneys' claimed caused Black inferiority.

The argument against segregation and the promotion of Black intellectual inferiority is succinctly elaborated on by Charles Silberman:

"The case against de facto segregation rests on more than just legal grounds. A great many argue that Negro children cannot receive an equal education in an all-Negro environment---that a segregated school, is inherently unequal, whatever the reasons underlying the segregation." [6]

The argument toward psychological and sociological factors as a prescription for Black inferiority continued to gain popularity. Nobody seemed to consider that despite one's circumstances, they

Big Ralph

have a responsibility to survive. Thus, it seems that to a large degree, many Blacks accepted the notion of inferiority. This acceptance grew into a cold reality bred by weak-minded men and women of the Black community.

Even outside the south many Blacks had an attitude of inferiority brought on by segregation. For example in the state of New York the commissioner of Education noted: "That the racial balance existing in a school in which the enrollment is wholly or predominantly Negro interferes with the achievement of equality of educational opportunity and must therefore be eliminated from the schools of New York state."

Dr. Allen (New York state commissioner of Education) went on to say that "modern psychological and sociological knowledge seems to show that in schools in which the enrollment is largely from a minority group of homogeneous ethnic origin, the personality of these minority group children may be damaged. There is a decrease in motivation and thus an impairment of ability to learn." [7]

The Black integrationist and the lackeys of white America were not the only voices heard during this time. Militant and radical voices loomed on the horizon. Shirley Chisholm was a teacher and a Member of Congress from the state of New York. Speaking on a topic called "Black Is An Attitude" she informed students and all of America of very different attitudes held by some Black people. For example she said:

"Black people have freed themselves from the dead weight of the albatross of Blackness that once hung about their neck. 'They have said "yes" to it and found that the skin that was once seen as symbolizing their shame is in reality their badge of honor." [8]

Ms. Chisholm goes on and gives us a closer look at what she calls a Black Attitude. First many people are judged in a superficial manner. But the "Black Attitude" is best seen in action. This action is a pledge to change social factors in one's environment even at the expense of loss of personal power and gain. In this instance Black people should be about causing a social revolution and joining elitist leaders who want an elitist revolution.

Chapter Nine

The Black Attitude also gives the masses' power and courage to challenge leadership that represents only the elite. This attitude also argues that a social revolution consisting of only Black Americans is unrealistic. Though we realize the special category of Blacks when we see a Black assistant personnel manager whose job is to make sure that no other Black people get jobs in his company.

So regardless of these circumstances, Congresswoman Chisholm argued that Blacks and whites should be moved into the economic mainstream of America. You cannot force poor whites who have a different badge of racism to join poor Blacks. Thus, the conclusion: "every revolution that has been attempted in the name of bettering life for the total society has produced only a new ruling class." [9]

James Forman made an incredible statement when he issued "The Black Manifesto." Forman demanded $500,000,000 to be spent to help the Black community. For example the manifesto called for the establishment of a southern land bank, establishment of four major publishing and printing industries, establishment of four advanced scientific and futuristic audiovisual networks, establishment of a research skills center to provide research on the problems of Black people, establish a training center to teach skills in community organization etc. Recognize the role of the national welfare rights organization, we call for $20,000,000 to establish a national Black Labor strike and Defense Fund, establishment of the International Black Appeal (IBA) to produce capital for cooperative businesses in Africa and the United States, we call for the establishment of a Black university and we demand that IFCO allocate all unused funds in the planning budget to implement the demands of this conference. [10]

James Forman was truly a so-called radical of his day. Within the ranks of the radicals and the militants there were various view points. Even the integrationist were, at most times, at odds as this was a time of controversy and confusion. Malulana Ron Karenga as an organizer and teacher offered his views on the Black community and the university.

Karenga offers three rules for white people and white universities: "nonintervention, foreign aid, and civilizing committees." [11] In defining

Big Ralph

these terms' Karenga states that the university is solely an educational institution, but is a political institution. Karenga concludes then that "the white university is not primarily an educational institution but a political one, and it seeks to maintain the power base of American society." [12]

If Karenga was a visionary cultural Nationalist Leroi Jones and the militant posture of the Panthers was revolutionary. To get an idea of what these new---style militants were saying let's look at some of their essays. Leroi Jones: "Advocates a nationalistic revolution leading to the destruction of America as it now is and to the creation of absolute political and economic power for Blacks." [13]

Huey Newton had come to Oakland with his family from Louisiana when he was three years old. He grew up in Oakland, California and attended Oakland public schools. As a student at Merritt Jr. College, in 1965 Huey Newton founded the Black Panther Party.

While in prison Newton wrote two essays that became theoretical tools for the Panther Party: "The essays relate to the evils of capitalism which profits from poverty. He views all oppressed people as prisoners who must come to realize that this society is corrupt, illegitimate, and thus in need of being overthrown." [14]

Bobby Seale was one of the cofounders of the Black Panther Party. His thinking, as was the thinking of Huey Newton, was a crucial aspect of Panther philosophy. "Seale calls for a revolutionary struggle that uses ethnic, political and class alliances against those who perpetuated tyranny, oppression, and poverty." [15]

Eldridge Cleaver was also an important leader in the Black Panther Party. Socialism was an alternative political system for the new young radicals in the Black Panther Party. In this case Eldridge Cleaver "called for the creation of new political machinery to carry out the revolution against capitalistic exploitation and racism." [16]

Stokley Carmichael was also one of the new young vocal radicals. Born in Trinidad, he came to the U.S. at an early age and attended the public schools of New York City. As a student at Howard University, Carmichael became active in the civil rights movement. When he

Chapter Nine

graduated from Howard in 1966, he was elected Chairman of SNNC. After leaving SNCC in 1967 he briefly joined the Black Panther Party. In his essays' Carmichael "urges Blacks to gain collective power as a goal. He implies that such power might be necessary to destroy certain aspects of the system." [17]

H. Rap Brown succeeded Stokley Carmichael as Chairman of SNCC in 1967. He first got involved with the movement in 1960 in his hometown of Baton Rouge, Louisiana. The following is a basic conclusion drawn from his book "Die Nigger Die." "Meaningful change can only come about through the destruction of the system. For him, revolution is the only cure for oppression and colonization." [18]

No doubt that revolutionaries like H. Rap Brown, Huey Newton, Bobby Seale and Stokley Carmichael set precedents for the Black struggle. Thus, the passive theories of nonviolence were now being challenged by a new militancy. There were more spokesmen for the new militancy, and there was one thing they all had in common. This common denominator was the belief in "Black Power." What is "Black Power?"

Dr. Nathan Hare was interviewed by U.S. News and World Report, May 1967. In this interview Dr. Hare was asked specific questions about the nature of "Black Power."

First Dr. Hare defines "Black Power." Here "Power" is noted as the ability to influence another person. This influence can come about even against the will of the person. Dr. Hare sees no need to define Black. Thus the influence of "Black Power" translates into a philosophy that will hopefully cause equality and opportunity for Black people.

"Black Power" addresses the tactics of the past. The assimilation philosophy of the integrationist has not worked. Thus, at this point we don't see integration as a means to an end.

Many critics also bring in the question of Black racism when Blacks cry for "Black Power." In answer to this question, Black Power advocates see enemies in these that obstruct justice not in race. Also "Black Power" is not an anti-white thing, it is more precisely an anti----anti-Black movement.

Big Ralph

Dr. Hare also, in defining the concepts of "Black Power, " notes that most Blacks do not hate white people. He believes that on the contrary most white people hate Blacks.

Violence is often associated with "Black Power." "Black Power" does not necessarily mean violence. "Black Power concerning violence says that Black people have a right to defend themselves when attacked. This right is in line with the laws in America and is a normal reaction to violence. Thus, the defense against violence should be misconstrued as unregulated random violence.

In conclusion Dr. Hare speaks on Black universities. He is responding to the question: "If Black universities became known as centers of Black Power, how long do you think Black universities will last? "

"I don't know. But the way they exist now, we want to give them to white folks, anyway. If they are going to continue as they have, as brainwashing factories, putting out freak persons with Black faces and white minds, then maybe they should be closed." [19]

Dr. Hare was talking about Black colleges and universities in the 60's. It is now 1996 and white people who attempt to control the destiny of Black people, like they are God, still control our schools. The United Negro College Fund is just a sham to continue the mis-education of the so-called Negro. Very few escape the strings of brainwashing thus most of the Black intellectuals are caught up in many postures. The most prominent crises are in respect to gender and racial identity.

With so much confusion going on there was surely a leadership void. Oh how hopeless is an oppressed people when the bulk of their leaders are all mis-educated and think they can be pseudo whites. The fantasy of being an honorary white is so characteristic of sports stars and celebrities.

Malcolm X was one of the great thinkers of the 1960's. Through his writings, speeches and interviews we get the truth about the dilemma of Black and white America. Malcolm X realized the historical importance of the relationship of Black Americans to the original people of Africa. Thus, Malcolm was a natural Pan-Africanist. Malcolm informed Black

Chapter Nine

Americans about European colonization of Africa. Thus he hailed the Bandung Conference of 1954 that brought all the Black nations of Africa together to deal with European colonization.

In his legendary "Message To The Grass Roots" Malcolm talks about the so-called Negro revolution. He surmised that "the only kind of revolution that is nonviolent is the Negro revolution, the only revolution in which the goal is loving your enemy is the Negro revolution." Malcolm was clear on the question of the relationship of land and revolution. "Revolution is based on land. Land is the basis of all independence. Land is the basis of freedom, justice and equality." [20]

In a series of interviews, Malcolm responds to some prominent questions. At a Harvard Law School Forum he notes the difference between white racism and Black racism. "Usually the Black racist has been produced by the white racist. Often when you see it, it is the reaction to white racism, and if you analyze it closely, it's not really Black racism. I think Black people have shown fewer racist tendencies than any people since the beginning of history." [21]

From another interview we find Malcolm saying some of the same things about the American educational system noted by Dr. Hare. He responds to the question who is responsible for race prejudice in the U.S.?

"Ignorance and greed. And a skillfully designed program of mis-education that goes right along with the American system of exploitation and oppression. So it takes education to eliminate it. And just because you have colleges and universities, don't mean you have education. The colleges and universities in the American educational system are skillfully used too mis-educate." [22]

Finally on a TV show in 1965 Malcolm responds to the question of integration and intermarriage. The fear of white America when first faced with integration was the even greater fear of intermarriage.

Malcolm is asked "while with the Nation you were for complete segregation and opposed to integration and intermarriage?"

"I don't think it should even be put upon a Black man, I don't think the burden to defend any position should even be put upon the Black

Big Ralph

man, because it is the white man collectively who has shown that he is hostile toward integration and toward intermarriage and toward these other strides toward oneness. So as a Black man and especially as a Black American, any stand that I formally took, I didn't think that I would have to defend it, because it's still a reaction to the society, and it's a reaction that was produced by the society and I think that it is the society that produced this that should be attacked, not the reaction that develops among the people who are the victims of that negative society."[23]

Malcolm X no doubt was one of the leading spokespersons for Black Americans during the 1960's. His theories and philosophy had an unprecedented impact on the Black conscious Black man. In turn this impact developed into Nationalism, revolutionary thinking, Black Power and an attitude that saw Black liberation through equal access and not necessarily through integration.

Malcolm was taught by an even greater legend. The Honorable Elijah Muhammad rose from the ghetto in the 1930's in Detroit to lead the Black man, woman and child out of the wilderness of racist America. With the disappearance of W.C. Fard Muhammad in 1934, Elijah Poole became the prophet and the leader of the Nation of Islam.

Elijah dropped the slave name of Poole and became Elijah Muhammad in 1934. The Honorable Elijah Muhammad had a great impact on the history of Black Americans. From my opinion he was one of the most significant Black men in North America during the century in which we live. I would argue for the great significance of Elijah Muhammad because he was independent and not a Black leader appointed and supported by white America. Also the thinking of Black pride that Elijah Muhammad established still exists and the Nation of Islam is still independent. There were other independent Black leaders during this century but they were short-lived. Often great leaders have great students. Malcolm X was the Honorable Elijah Muhammad's student and so is Minister Louis Farrakhan.

Seldom does the greatness of the student exceed that of his teacher. Malcolm X was in the words of Muhammad Ali one of greatest orators

Chapter Nine

of all times. So is Minister Farrakhan but the teacher, in the person of the Honorable Elijah Muhammad, brought the message.

The following excerpts from the Honorable Elijah Muhammad's, "Message To The Black Man sums up much of the sentiment of this great Black man.

"Since our being brought in chains to the shores of America, our brain power, labor, skills, talent and wealth have been taken, given and spent toward building and adding to the civilization of another people. It is time for you and me, the so-called Negroes, to start doing for ourselves.

As a people, we must become producers and not remain consumers and employees. We must be able to extract raw materials from the earth and manufacture them in something useful for ourselves. This would create jobs in production. We must remember that without land there is no production.

"It is a shame and disgrace to the intelligence of any people to lie at the feet and doorsteps of another nation, asking, praying to be cared for. Love and unity of self and kind is the key to our salvation." [24]

The philosophy of the Honorable Elijah Muhammad set the standards for Black Nationalism in America. This Nationalism also took on other variables as it sought to liberate it's people.

Roy Innis was the Director of CORE in 1965 when he wrote about separatist Economics. The following statements and quotes are some important points made by Roy Innis on the Black struggle.

One of the first things Innis deals with is the controversy over a reformist ideology or a revolutionary ideology. Innis sees revolutionary ideology as a romantic dream. Thus, liberation is the most logical and sensible step to take. To make this argument clear one need only to define the two terms and note the distinct differences.

There is also the question and/or the principle of self-determination. In this instance there are theories about the order to go about reaching the goal of self-determination. Thus should the order of politics, culture or economics come first?

"Capitalism like socialism, is an economic and political philosophy

Big Ralph

that describes the experience of Europeans and their descendants-Americans. Blacks must innovate, must create a new ideology. It may include elements of capitalism, elements of socialism, or elements of neither: that is immaterial. What matters is that it will be created to foot our needs." [25]

Roy Innis made crucial statements regarding the reality of the Black experience during the 60's. He concluded that Black people are aspiring Black capitalists but logically like other Americans need economic development. Integration, and not economic development, was the driving force for the civil rights leadership. We still need to further define integration because it continues to have an impact on leadership and the masses.

Stokley Carmichael joined with professor Charles V. Hamilton in the creation of a book titled "Black Power." The following excerpts and quotes will give us essential information toward a better understanding of the terms "Black Power" and integration.

The authors see integration as a term lost in a white definition. This white definition of integration implies "race-mixing" and Black men striving to have sex with white women. On the Black side of this definition we see something totally different. Blacks hope to improve their lives economically and politically through integration.

Before we further define integration and focus on 'Black Power," the authors also look at the names' Black people are called. The word Negro became unpopular during the 60's. Thus, during the 60's terms like African-American, Afro-American and Black became popular. The name controversy resulted in African-American and Black being the chosen terms to identify those of African descent in America.

So if one is to understand "Black Power" he must be clear on whom he is. He must also be clear on if he is a Black American or African-American. With the name question settled Black people can then go about understanding the history of Black people in North America.

They also can go about understanding the principles of "Black Power." "The concept of "Black Power" is a call for Black people to begin to define their own goals, to lead their own organizations and to

Chapter Nine

support those organizations. It is a call to reject the racist institutions and values of this society. The concept of "Black Power's rests on a fundamental promise: Before a group can enter the open society, it must first close ranks." [26]

The call for "Black Power" has been mired in controversy and misunderstanding. "Black Power" advocates are called racist and Black supremacist. Thus unity and group strength for Black people must be defended and when Blacks seek to keep white people out of their organizations they are called racist.

Carmichael and Hamilton make the following concluding statement about "Black Power." "In the end, we cannot and shall not offer any guarantees that "Black Power," if achieved, would be non-racist. No one can predict human behavior. Those of us who advocate "Black Power" are quite clear in our minds that a nonviolent approach to civil rights is an approach Black people cannot afford and a luxury white people do not deserve." [27]

It is clear then that the advocates of "Black Power" also define integration differently than the traditional civil rights advocates. Thus integration is viewed as social justice and a way to include Blacks into mainstream institutions from where they have been historically excluded.

The reality of integration is that it is directed by middle-class Blacks. This small group receives token concessions. Meanwhile, the Black masses suffer. This middle-class and Negro attitude of integration is revealed in the following quotation. "Integration as a goal today speaks to the problem of blackness not only in an unrealistic way but also in a despicable way. It is based on complete acceptance of the fact that to have a decent house of education, Black people must move into a white neighborhood or send their children to a white school." [28]

The previous statement is how the integrationists view integration. Those that aspire for equal access and/or "Black Power" see another goal in this process. Black children should not be taken outside their community. This should not be a goal. What could be a goal is the building of a strong Black community to fit the needs of the people.

Big Ralph

The concluding statements give further evidence of the conflict and cleavages between "Black Power" and Black integrationists. "Integration also means that Black people must give up their identity, deny their heritage. Integration, as traditionally articulated, would abolish the Black community. What must be abolished is not the Black community, but the dependent colonial status that has been inflicted upon it. No person can be healthy, complete and mature if he must deny a part of himself. This is what integration has required thus far. This is the essential difference between integration as it is currently practiced and the concept of "Black Power." [29]

The cleavage between "Black Power" and Black integrationists can also be described as conflict within the leadership ranks. The leadership ranks ran the spectrum, from nonviolent passive protesters to the Black urban revolutionary, Black institutions also played a key role in this challenge to democracy.

Black institutions thus have caused distinct cleavages within the Black community. One reason is that these institutions have been tied to the status quo. They also thrived and were given life in an oppressive segregated society. The Black college, Black press, Black politician and the Black church are all significant institutions within the Black community.

The integrationist view point is that these institutions were hindered without integration. The disagreement with the integrationist is not over the question of equal access. Moreover, the disagreement resides in the validity of Black institutions. The integration of these Black institutions to the point where they do not exist is not beneficial to either group, Black or white.

So while the Black integrationists vision is to no longer have any Black colleges, Black nationalist say we must establish and support our own institutions. So there is nothing wrong with all Black colleges and universities. The reality has been that Black colleges have been controlled either by the government and/or white philanthropists.

Booker T. Washington set the standard for the accommodating posture of Black college presidents. Thus there is the argument that all Black college presidents are chosen for their acceptance of the spirit of

Chapter Nine

manipulation and control. The apologists for the Black intellectuals and Black college presidents say it was necessary for these men to humble themselves to get white philanthropists to give funds to Black colleges.

The control of Black colleges became quite clear during the student movement of the 60's. The philanthropists and the state boards of education insisted that the college administrators demand that the Black students stop their demonstrations for equal rights.

Black college presidents were placed in a great dilemma. Generally most, Black people during the 60's felt that they had the right to eat at lunch counters and sit any where on vehicles that provided public transportation. Black college presidents were forced to side with racism or lose their jobs. They were told to expel the student leaders and any students actively involved in the student demonstrations. This was the second order, the first order was to tell the students to stop the demonstrations.

Of course the students refused to stop the demonstrations. Expelling the student leaders and student activists also did not stop the student demonstrations. Meanwhile, the dilemma of Black college presidents tells a sad story. For the administrations to support the student movement they would not only lose their jobs but they also feared that Black colleges would also be closed.

"Negro college presidents are faced with a choice between two goods: integration and education for the Negro. Their dilemma is that they must choose one over the other. If they support integration, they are in trouble with state officials; if they don't, they are in trouble with the students." [30]

Louis Lomax goes farther in assessing the dilemma of Black college presidents. " I do not envy (college presidents) these men. Only with reluctance do I; sing their praise. Yet praiseworthy they are. They fashioned us into the rebels we are. Perhaps the time has come for the Negro revolutionaries to pause and be gracious toward the Negro educators, men who served their time and served it well." [31]

The Black politician also is caught up in the dilemma of accommodation or nationalism. The integrationist vision is that Black

Big Ralph

politicians will one day be elected by Black and white voters. They dream that predominantly white districts will one day elect Black representatives. If this is, the case Black politicians should represent those that elected them to office. This does not mean that Black politicians should give up on their identity, because no matter how much Blacks act white they are never mistaken for a white person.

The manipulation and control of most Black politicians has existed since Blacks first gained the franchise. During Reconstruction the Republican Party used Black elected officials to spite white southern democrats. Thus, often Black elected officials were tools of resentment used against the rebel south.

The impact of Black elected officials after Reconstruction was limited. In the south the phenomenon of Blacks elected to office became virtually nonexistent. However, the second reconstruction came with the civil rights upheaval of the 60's. Blacks were again elevated to office and sadly, for the most part, they were ineffective.

It was illogical for Black elected officials to harbor nationalist sentiments. For the most part they aspired to enter a white defined American mainstream. In so doing they professed an integrationist philosophy as a cure all for the Black dilemma.

The Black media is also an institution affected by the previous segregated society. Here again integration and the addiction toward integration has caused Black insanity. Black media, the Black church and Black colleges have distinct parallels when assessing their mood of nationalism or what can be described as the inherent aspects of Black Nationalism. Though often, they don't exist.

For example these institutions should for an eternity represent the culture of its people. Many Black politicians for whatever reason do not see the utility of representing the culture of Black people. He may also have to embrace certain aspects of other cultures if and when they come to represent people other than Blacks.

Black media is different. In view of the role of media and the historic circumstances of Black people, Black media has a responsibility to be an advocate for one's culture. Unfortunately, only a small percentage of

Chapter Nine

Black media sources live up to their responsibility to the Black community.

The greatest impact of Black media has been in the Black press. As in all forms of media, advertising is the life blood of the Black press. Before we look at the role of advertising and the Black press we must consider the historic predicament of Blacks as an underclass. Clearly then, Black institutions like Black newspapers are not comparable generally with their white counterparts.

The circumstances of Black people being used as slaves in this country set precedents for the resistance to Blacks receiving information and knowledge. Slaves were not allowed to read or write. Slave masters also did not want anyone with information about the abolitionist movement to talk with the slaves. Thus anti-slavery publications were outlawed and censorship was at the highest level in the history of the Republic.

The limited freedom granted to Blacks after slavery did not automatically remove the resistance to Blacks receiving information and knowledge. The dominant and ruling class in America has always been aware of the power of media and the written word. So historically there has been a very serious interest in the control of Black media sources. Therefore, independent Black newspapers have been few and short-lived.

Now let's look at the role of advertising. When we say "advertising," we are talking about money. The dominant class in America has the most money. Since releasing Blacks from the prison camps of slave plantations, they have sought to control Blacks with money. No doubt money is a needed and sought after commodity. One should not put money before God. Are Black people some of the most God fearing people on earth? Yes, and no, because the interest in this commodity called, money has been the driving force in the manipulation and exploitation of Black people over time. In this case many Black traitors have taken money and helped white racists exploit their own people, Black people. So as not to cause confusion the interest in money has also promoted the dominant class to limit information and knowledge to the Black community.

Big Ralph

Advertisers spend money on ads in newspapers. This money is in turn used to operate the paper, pay wages etc. Since most Black newspapers are given away, there is no motivation by Black publishers to gain revenues from the sell of the paper. Here they look for ads as the source of revenues to operate the papers.

Some apologists for Black newspapers note that Blacks own very few businesses so the Black press must depend on white businesses for advertising revenues. If this is, true Black publishers do not want to print anything that will offend their white advertisers. So for the most part Black publishers have a lack of commitments for Black causes.

Black publishers are guaranteed a certain amount of ads and in turn they consent to never publish anything negative about their advertisers. With this attitude, the Black press becomes revenue inspired institution. Thus, the Black press usually is not an instrument of information to the Black community. Many Black social scientists argue that the Black press becomes a tool of oppression and not a useful tool of information for Black people.

Thus, very little valuable information is rendered to the Black community. In an environment in which a group of people has a long history of oppression, discrimination and abuse, the Black press has a distinct responsibility. This responsibility is simply to inform the Black community of news and information from a genuine Black perspective. For the most part, this perspective is a white perspective written by mainstream Black journalist who have assimilated into white society and are employed by the dominant white press. Meanwhile, Black journalists at Black newspapers, are instructed by their publishers to not be critical and to appease their advertisers.

Most short sighted, ungodly Black publishers do not believe that Black newspapers can exist without dollars from big white advertisers. Thus, selling out to white advertisers is good business to them. This makes good sense to this breed of charlatans because they only pay lip service to the logical responsibility of the Black press. In other words one can say the role of Black media as a business enterprise should be twofold.

Chapter Nine

First is the interest in informing the Black community who is deprived of information and knowledge by the ruling class. Secondly there should be the interest in making money, showing profits etc. But they should go hand in hand. Most Black publishers have no principles and no interest in being responsible toward the Black community. For all practical purposes they are only coldhearted hustlers in the newspaper business selling ads to the highest bidders.

Thus they do not look for innovative ways in which to operate without selling out to big white advertisers. For example the Black community will support a relevant Black newspaper that will stand up for their rights and be independent. (For example Muhammad Speaks was a independent newspaper that was supported by Black people during the days of Malcom X. The Final Call is presently the Nation of Isalm newspaper and it is also independent and supported by the Black community). This support involves the sale of the paper. A relevant and independent Black newspaper can be sold in the Black community. Therefore any Black newspaper that is independent and stands up for the rights of Black people has the potential to circulate throughout a given Black community. The sale of the paper can defray up to 50% of the cost to operate the newspaper. The second source of income is from ads.

There are still many small Black businesses. They do not have the resources of large white businesses but the money adds up. Black beauty shops, barber shops, Black restaurants, clubs, funeral homes etc. Thus, ads from the various small Black businesses have the potential to defray the balance of the operational cost for a Black weekly or daily newspaper.

This theory seems to suggest that the sale of the paper and advertising revenue from the various small Black businesses in a given community will only pay to operate the newspaper. So what about salaries and other cost related factors. The sale of the Black newspaper and the steady increase in circulation will cause white advertisers to abandon their conspiracy to control the Black newspaper. Therefore white advertisers will just seek to sell their product in the marketplace with a well-circulated newspaper that happens to be Black.

Big Ralph

The Black church is another institution in the Black community that is set in confusion because of integration. Again, is the integrationist philosophy folly? Also is assimilation a fantasy that causes some Blacks to think that Black churches are obsolete?

Some confused integrationists think that Black institutions like the Black church are challenged by the move from ethnic to general institutions. In this case they no longer see the utility of a Black church. No one is saying that white people should not be allowed to worship at the Black church. We are not saying close down the Black church and beg to be admitted to an all-white church. Integrationists feel that all Black or predominately Black is not good and all integrated situations are inherently better.

Ralph had been stationed at Little Rock Air Force Base, Jacksonville, Arkansas for four years. He had decided not to re-enlist and was homesick for his hometown. Ralph felt like he could probably get a better job in Chattanooga rather than remaining in Little Rock or opting to move to another city.

Catherine was just the opposite from Ralph, she would have preferred moving to another city or staying in Little Rock rather than returning to Chattanooga. However, when Ralph asked Catherine whether she thought he should re-enlist or return home, Catherine felt it was only fair for it to be his own decision, and so he made it.

Catherine had gotten a job at University of Arkansas Medical Center. She had been assigned to work in research and development even before she had completed her training. Catherine looked forward to an exciting career in nursing.

Catherine had completed LPN training in Little Rock and had taken the State Board tests, but she had not gotten the results before they left for Chattanooga. She received the letter with the passing score after they had arrived back in Chattanooga. Her father William (Billy) Patton was very proud that she had a nursing license, although he wanted her to be a teacher instead of a nurse.

May of 1964 Catherine was hired to work in the emergency room at Erlanger Hospital. At that time Ralph was unemployed. He was job

Chapter Nine

searching. He applied at TVA and several foundries. Ralph told a funny story about going to Crane Company to apply for a job. Catherine's father worked at Crane Company and had told Ralph to apply for a job there. Ralph said "when he got inside a worker said to him come on in young-blood, I'll show you how to knock the "W" out of work. Ralph said that all he could see was white's of the man's eyes, amid the hot flames of fire. He said he started running and did not stop until he jumped over a fence and was out of there."

One day Catherine's father asked Ralph how he would like to become a police officer. Before Ralph could answer, Catherine began to say, no, no. On the other hand, Ralph seemed impressed with the idea. In those days the police department was largely politically controlled. William Patton, who was active in the Republican party used the influence he had to help Ralph. In so doing, he encouraged Ralph to apply with the police department. He was hired in September 1964. So in the fall of 1964 Ralph H. Cothran began his life as a Chattanooga police officer.

Catherine initially had a feeling of fear about Ralph becoming a police officer. After she thought about the situation, she became proud and supportive. She recalled that she was very concerned and would check Ralph from head to toe when he came home at night. Her nursing training prepared her for much of the trauma of being a policeman's wife.

Ralph also came into the emergency room on many occasions in the line of duty. This made Catherine proud and Ralph eventually established on-going rapport with most the emergency room staff. Dr. Paul Hawkins was Ralph's favorite doctor in the emergency room. Dr. Hawkins had a pleasant personality and was well liked by Catherine and all the nurses in the emergency room. Catherine realized later that there was truly a positive side of law enforcement.

Big Ralph

Part IV Crime In America

Chapter 10

Chattanooga Police Department 1964
The Mood Of Black Youth

**Institutions of public good that offer security,
that if not, confusion, the Kaos of man would take place,
hold in time,
Money sponsors most crime so does the yearn
for politics and crime.**

Ralph Cothran's early years, as a police officer were very outstanding. He was constantly in the news because he was vigorously fighting crime, arresting criminals and closing down places of ill repute. He was colorful, because he had a way of describing some of the criminal scenes with a sense of humor.

Officer Cothran was very progressive, he worked very diligently, and was doing sergeant's work as a patrol officer. With progressive and dedicated work ethics he bypassed sergeant's rank. His courtroom demeanor was excellent. Officer Cothran gained a well known reputation for his skill in presenting his cases. Officer Cothran began to realize that life as a police officer was often depressing. Especially depressing was the volume of crime and the deplorable living conditions he observed on calls to crime scenes.

Big Ralph

Ralph joined the force during the civil rights era." The City Commission Tuesday approved on the recommendation of Commissioner Turner the employment of 17 persons in the fire and police department, including seven Negroes as police officers. The Negro police patrolmen are Sully Batts, Ralph H. Cothran, Maodis Hugley, Frank Newson, Jimmie Wells III, James M. Wilkes and Napoleon Williams." [1] This was a time when city governments throughout the south sought to legitimately include and employ Blacks as bonafide police officers.

This was not true when Blacks were first allowed to join the force. The first Black officers were installed in 1948. The seven officers were: Thaddeus Arnold, Singer Askins, Bill Bauldridge, Charles Black, Morris Glenn, Arthur Heard and Tommy Patterson. In those days Black officers could not ride in cars with white officers and they could not arrest white offenders.

The Black officers also had trouble with Black people. Many Black people did not respect the Black officers because Jim Crow restricted their authority. Also many Black officers were more abusive toward Black people most likely because of the frustrations of Jim Crow.

An article printed in the Chattanooga Times in 1931 gives us some idea of the atmosphere of Chattanooga toward Blacks. Ingrained in the article is a subhuman portrayal of Black people by a city detective. The title of the article is "Intimate Knowledge of Negro Characters Has Been Big Help to Detective Gillespie."

"Detective Gillespie called, Tom is one of the most lovable men in the entire department. Patrolman Thomas A Gillespie became city Detective Gillespie on Nov. 11, 1918. Gillespie is proud of his spotless record over 17 years. But Gillespie is no "pussyfooter." His reputation among fellow officers and those he is sometimes forced to put in jail is that he is strict and stern. He tolerates no foolishness.

Gillespie's knowledge of the Negro criminal is of immense importance to the department. It is not that he knows so many Negro lawbreakers, which he most certainly does, but that he has made a life long study of the Negro.

Chapter Ten

You know, Detective Gillespie commented one day, a Negro is a funny thing. It's just as natural for him to run when he is guilty as it is for anybody to drink water, and a lot of them run when they're not guilty. And they will lie like nobody's business. Even when you've got a closed and shut case against em they'll figure out the dogonest alibi you ever heard of." [2]

So while white people viewed Blacks as a simple inferior species of humans in 1931, what did Blacks think. By 1947 there was talk of including Blacks on the police force. H. W. Newell a Black precinct leader declined to comment on the question of Black officers but he did comment on various other civil right concerns to the local newspapers. For example Newell said.

"The intelligent Negroes of the south do not want to do away with segregation at this time. You can't force things on people, he said, they will have to be educated before they can accept most of the recommendations of President Truman's civil rights committee. What we really need among both colored and white people is education-- not in the same schools, but the same standard of education." [3]

Apparently the openly racist News Free Press was thrilled to death with Newell's statements. The next day he was interviewed again. The best thing that can be said about Newell's attitude is that he was a classic Uncle Tom that got paid by racist white people.

"H.W. Newell president of the Willing Workers Club passed a resolution stating the Negro is not ready for the sweeping social changes recommended by Truman's committee on civil rights. Newell disagreed with the Truman committee on complete abolition of segregation in the south. He said this may be very good in the future."

Newell continued to make statements and further degrade Black people "He said Negroes are not treated better in the north. The truth is that racial equality in the north is a cruel hoax. The Negro is told up there he is equal. Under the law he has all the privileges that white men have-- until he tries to exercise them. Then he finds to his disillusionment and dismay that all the northern talk about equality is meaningless."

The article further noted "that Newell's attitude is one that inspires

Big Ralph

good will and appeals to the southern white man's national inclination to help the Negro---and, no matter what the politicians and busybodies in the north may do, the southern Negro will have to have this good will and help in order to make real progress." [4]

The local chapter of the NAACP condemned the views of Newell. In so doing the Chattanooga Chapter of the NAACP endorsed the report from the Truman committee on civil rights and supported the move to install uniformed Black police officers.

"Newell was quoted as saying in a recent newspaper story that Negroes were not ready for uniformed colored police officers here and not ready for enjoyment of their full civil rights." [5]

Despite what Newell thought the Chattanooga City Commission, in less than a year, installed seven Black police officers. It wasn't long before conflict arose regarding the limits of the Black officers authority.

"Officer Charles E. Black, a Negro officer was suspended for violation of a regulation forbidding colored police officers from arresting white persons on a misdemeanor charge. A colored delegation insisted that there would be no limitation placed on the authority of a colored officer to arrest persons violating the law; and that they should have as much authority to arrest a white violator of the law as they have to arrest a colored violator." [6]

In another article regarding the case of the Black officer arresting a white citizen the instructions given to the new Black officers are examined.

"The officers according to police department officials, were informed often that they must not arrest white persons for misdemeanors. In those instances they were to call the captain and squad car. They were instructed to arrest white persons whom they saw in the act of injuring physically any other person, who were breaking into stores or who were otherwise committing felonies." [7]

Things had changed quite a bit when Ralph Cothran was sworn in as a police officer in 1964. This was the height of the civil rights movement. The civil rights movement no doubt was the primary reason the number of Black officers was increased in Chattanooga.

The impact of the civil rights movement affected the American

Chapter Ten

landscape as a tremendous thunder storm that roared day and night. The white establishment though reluctant to change began to realize that change was inevitable. Even as Black and white people began to bear witness to this inevitable change there were those who tried to head off the inevitable as long as they could.

The Black and white communities were still in a showdown over school desegregation. Thus the NAACP since 1954 was still pleading for full desegregation when the white board of education stalled and held up the integration process. [8]

Yes, this was the time of marching and mass civil disobedience. Led by Rev. Martin Luther King of SCLC and the civil rights establishment Blacks petitioned throughout the south and the nation for civil and human rights.

Most of the new officers installed with Ralph would become life long friends and serve with him throughout his tenure. This was the first significant impact of Black police officers. For example Frank Newson and Napoleon (Doughnut) Williams along with Ralph would later make up the most dynamic vice team in the history of the department.

Morris Glenn, who was one of the first Black officers in 1948, now became the first Black staff officer. Glenn was promoted to lieutenant December 1965 by Commissioner Bookie Turner.

After five years as a patrol officer Ralph was promoted to the Narcotics' Division. Catherine noted that this was very dangerous work, because dealing with desperate addicts was risky and at times life threatening. Ralph was a compassionate person and the parents and families of many young men arrested or addicted to drugs would call Ralph seeking help. Catherine answered many of these calls and got a first hand look at the wretched side of those tragically affected by the monster of drug addiction.

Training is an integral part of police work. The Narcotics Division further exposed Ralph to additional training in the area of narcotics. The following letters note once again the trauma that resulted from Ralph being separated from his family. The training took place in Miami Beach, Florida.

Big Ralph

Hi Honey,
Happy anniversary I wish desperately that I was home with you. This is a very beautiful town, however, without you I could just as well be on a garbage dump. You never really know how much you need a person until you no longer are able to be near them then it all comes out. My love for you is a small portion of the loneliness, I feel the kids are also a portion of my sadness on this day in particular. I know that I will have no trouble passing the course. I will be leaving the minute I graduate for home for you and the kids. Kiss them for me and tell them I miss them very much.

Love Ralph
P..S. Did you get your flowers. [9]

    A few days later Ralph again writes about how much he missed his family. By all accounts' Ralph was a great family man. The dedication to his job took priority over some family experiences, but Ralph relished his family and the closeness of the family. Ralph did not come from a large family as you know he had only one sister. The closeness of his immediate family was very special and so was his closeness to his wife's family. Ralph was firm on the family staying together and being forever loyal to family needs and concerns.

    There are those that Ralph met in his life as a law enforcement officer that knew also of how much Ralph loved his family. If there were any attempts to disrupt his family after he passed away they failed. The confusion, lies and deceit of the ungodly will reap the wrath of Almighty God. First his wife Catherine is a strong spirit filled woman that knows she is filled with the spirit of Jesus, may God bless the Holy Spirit. It is hard to break the spirit of someone who truly loves God and obeys God. Those that do not know God can't understand what I am saying but those filled with the spirit of the Holy Ghost know what I am saying. There is no greater power and no one can capture the level of wisdom and knowledge of the Creator.

Chapter Ten

Dear Catherine,
Hi squaw I love you and miss you. I will never be away from you this long again. Kiss the kids for me and get me the address to their school. I would like to send the school two (2) live miniature Sea Horses for them. Here is a money order. Keep it I will send them because I do not need the money.

Love Ralph [10]

Working in the area of narcotics investigation, officer Cothran gained valuable knowledge that would prove invaluable later in his career. Big Ralph also had to deal with the potential for serious injury to himself or his fellow officers. During one investigation officer Sully Batts was seriously wounded in the head by gunshots. Ralph noted that he would have been on the scene instead of officer Batts but something else came up and officer Batts covered for him. At six foot seven inches and weighing over 250 pounds Big Ralph became a notorious door kicker for the narcotics' squad.

"The Big Three" was the name given to Big Ralph, Frank Newsom and Napoleon (Doughnut) Williams. This trio made up Chattanooga's infamous narcotics squad. The Big Three was infamous to those who were dealing in drugs. During the days when The Big Three rolled the streets of Chattanooga drug dealers suffered. The wrath of the Big Three, was quick and decisive and they had no mercy when it came to arresting criminals.

In those days, especially on the weekends, The Big Three arrested people all day and all night long. East 9th Street is a historic district that houses clubs and bars. East 9th Street has also been a favorite hang out for criminals. The Big Three also hung out on East 9th Street. In so doing, if you drove down east 9th Street day or night, you might see Big Ralph and his two sidekicks loading up five to six people in a paddy wagon at any given time. They made numerous arrests and were highly regarded by their superiors and the street criminals who ended in jail regularly. They made war on the heroin traffic in Chattanooga and drug

Big Ralph

addicts were hiding under any rock they could find. But "The Big Three" knew every rock and overturned them.

His life as a patrol officer had been typical and at times unique. Catherine his wife didn't know the kinds of problems a peace officer's wife would encounter. Nor did she realize that as Ralph rose in rank the problems of a peace officer would increase.

James (Bookie) Turner was the Fire and Police Commissioner when Ralph joined the force in 1964. Turner was elected the previous year along with Ralph Kelly, as mayor and Dean Petersen, George McInturff, and A. L. Bender filling the other Commissioners posts.

During the time Turner was Chattanooga's Fire and Police Commissioner illegal whiskey, gambling and all forms of vice were openly available. The newspapers began to report by 1967 that a federal investigation had been going on concerning corruption in the department for 18 months. [11]

A February 24, 1967 article in the News Free Press reported that Turner had been indicted and Chief Eugene McGovern stepped down from his post as Chief after his name appeared with three other police officers as coconspirators in the federal indictment of Commissioner Turner. [12]

Due to the indictment Turner was relieved of his duties. Meanwhile acting chief Jack Shasteen, who took over when Chief McGovern stepped down due to the federal probe was supposed to be in charge. But there was reason to believe that hard nosed Bookie Turner was still calling the shots. [13]

To maintain some semblance of integrity and to abide by the law, the city commission took action. The city commission passed a resolution May 16, 1967 giving the mayor and board of commissioners sole authority over the police department. But Turner still attempted to run the department. [14]

Turner went to trial in October and was acquitted. The charges centered on moonshine conspiracy. In other words Commissioner Turner was accused of operating the numerous illegal liquor houses throughout the city. Anyway it is conceivable that Turner furnished

Chapter Ten

liquor to the illegal Good--Time Houses and received further payoffs to allow them to operate.

Incidentally, these houses also had a political function. The people who operated these houses also had to support whomever Turner wanted them to, in any election, or face being shut down and thrown in jail.

The two-year investigation of Turner resulted in a 13-day trial. During the trial Black Minister Robert Richards became publicly known as a staunch supporter of Commissioner Turner who was most likely the most corrupt Fire and Police Commissioner in the history of Chattanooga City government. [15]

Evidently many people doubted that Turner was innocent of the charges. A local Law Commission was formed. They felt that there was corruption and inefficiency in the department. They further concluded that the probe be done on a non political basis and that the complete findings of the investigation be made public. [16]

Meanwhile Turner had established himself as a great friend of the Negro. Usually these Negroes benefited from their association with Turner. For example preachers like Rev. Robert Richards were paid to inform on the Black community. Also criminals who operated liquor and gambling houses argued that Turner loved Negroes because he allowed them to operate. They did not stop to think what would happen to their thriving illegal business if they bought whiskey from sources other than Turner.

As the civil rights movement escalated the city took action to upgrade the status of Black officers. By 1968 the city, in the wake of the riots and civil disturbances caused by the assassination of Dr. King, took direct action. Police cars on a limited basis would become integrated. Joseph Jackson was appointed acting sergeant. Three Blacks: Napoleon Williams, Joseph Parks and Oliver Collier were appointed acting detectives. Also, Morris Glenn became the first Black captain on the force. [17]

Ralph did not receive any promotions during this time which is unusual. Ralph had already established a reputation as a fair and honest peace officer. Bookie Turner thrived on dishonesty and greed and those

Big Ralph

that possessed these basic qualities were his close confidants and his greatest supporters.

Another interesting phenomena was also taking place. Police departments throughout the nation, in the wake of mass civil disorder by Blacks, knew the presence of Blacks in local law enforcement was essential. The presence was so needed that the city leaders and/or city governments across the nation began to place Blacks in high administrative posts within local police departments.

There was still fallout over the federal probe of Commissioner Turner. "The Hamilton County Grand Jury seeks a complete examination of the police department. The examination should include: the organization and administration of the department and it's sub units. Personnel Management and training practices, operational procedures. Evaluation of departments, facilities, equipment and resources. Recommendation and Grand Jury called for: More foot patrol officers. An expansion of tactical forces and squads, so as to produce a show of strength when as needed. Organization of a narcotic's unit and an intelligence unit."[18]

By 1969 the city commission became suspicious of monthly payments to two local Black ministers. The two ministers in question, Revs'. Robert Richards and J. Loyld Edwards denied that they were informers. They claimed that they were paid for special services and to help keep the peace between the Black and white communities.[19]

The move was still on to hire more Black police officers. While Commissioner Turner thrived on snitchers telling on the other Blacks, the International Association of Chiefs of Police advised the city to hire more Black officers.[20]

Commissioner Turner also relied on Black police officers to work for his slate of candidates during elections. Illegal whiskey and gambling houses had historically been used in Chattanooga as "Instruction Houses." Instruction in whom to vote for was their main function during elections. In the process these dens of sin that sponsored vice passed out free whiskey and at times barbecue pork as an incentive to vote for the people supported by Commissioner Turner.[21]

Ralph no doubt learned a good lesson in the ills of his department.

Chapter Ten

Ralph also learned a good lesson about the ills of society during this period. Bookie Turner was a grand example of corruption in every phase of law enforcement and he also brought corrupt politics to the forefront within the police department. Turner was so corrupt, that the white power structure finally said they had enough.

The school desegregation issue was still not resolved. While the white power structure sought to slow, stall and impede the process, the NAACP and their supporters sought immediate desegregation. [22]

Who is the man that would soon take an even more active part in the affairs of the city of Chattanooga. Big Ralph was a quiet man. Some excerpts from The Chattanooga Minority Business Directory of 1995 gives a concise insight into the man Ralph Henry Cothran.

"His hobbies are swimming and reading and his recommended reading is The Holy Bible. He says the people who most influenced him in his life were Mr. James Mapp and Mr. Arless Holloway. He says the priceless time he spent with Mr. James R. Map in the Boy Scouts of America program are his most memorable aspects of childhood. He says the word that best describes him is "introvert" and that if he could change anything about himself it would be to have devoted more time and attention to his studies in high school.

He recalled that one thing he's learned about life is that we all need to treat people the way we want to be treated and the words of wisdom that he lives by are the Ten Commandments. He says that every day in his job he sees Black on Black violence and that is what he considers the most important issue facing Black Chattanoogans. Helping everyone to be able to live with one another and be able to resolve any and all conflicts without violence is the one wish he would like to grant Black Chattanoogans if he could."

Big Ralph

Chapter 11

Moving Up In The Ranks: Protest And Violence

*Has freedom came without the turbulent protest of man,
at times the savage rage,
Does man react with anger, the assaulting fury,
when the oppressed petition for God given human rights?*

After six years on the force Ralph had gained considerable experience and knowledge. He always took his work seriously and had the ambition to excel in his work. This was a time of constant protest and dissension among many groups in society.

Ralph was a genius when it came to handling lunacy cases, riots and civil disturbances. For example Catherine recalls that when Ralph came in the emergency room with a patient that clearly had psychological problems he could always calm them down. Big Ralph often called the Gentle Giant had a calm disposition when dealing with unruly people. He could handle problematic psycho patients and never raise his voice. It seemed as if Big Ralph charmed them like the eastern snake charmer.

Big Ralph

Most officers had some reservations about approaching the lunacy patients/criminals. But Big Ralph had this uncanny ability to gently defuse any aggressive behavior they had. This ability to defuse potential violent situations was a gift from God. Big Ralph I think and to all that really knew him know that Big Ralph was Chattanooga's riot stopper. He could calm situations and bring people to dialogue.

Ralph had great faith in God. For example he would ask God to help him prevent a riot. He asked God to send rain to prevent a potential disturbance in Alton Park. Catherine remembers that Ralph told her "well God said it will not rain." In this case Ralph said "I guess I will have to handle the situation myself."

During the summer of 1980 Big Ralph was still a captain, but he was consistently called on during crisis situations. Alton Park is the home of the largest Black housing unit in the city. The following report in the Chattanooga Times relates a very dangerous situation.

"Despite announcements that redress for the Klan-related shotgun-wounding of four Black women will be sought through the federal courts, Chattanooga experienced another tense night of racial unrest Wednesday.

There was a potentially dangerous confrontation in Alton Park between angry Blacks and riot-equipped police. During one incident the Blacks chanted "we want rednecks." Captain Cothran and several other police officials talked to the group, finally convincing them to go back down 38th Street."[1]

Black people were in the vanguard of the protest movement. Civil rights issues loomed throughout Chattanooga and the nation. These particular civil rights issues and the school desegregation decision would impact greatly on Ralph who was still a young officer.

Therefore, a particular philosophy began to take shape. This philosophy was not superficial, or baseless. The philosophy of segregation had been a part of the American dilemma since the end of slavery. Slavery officially ended at the close of the Civil War. Southern segregationists quickly established their philosophy. This philosophy was clearly seen through the rationale for Jim Crow laws and the

Chapter Eleven

separation of the races throughout the south. Segregationist philosophy had as its major premise the notion of the inferiority of Black people. It is ironic that the integrationist philosophy that was developed leading up to the 1954 Brown v. Board of Education decision also had a major premise of Black inferiority.

Integrationist philosophy had been impacted by an on-going analysis of civil rights and school desegregation. It is for sure that integration and segregation theories eventually began to affect law enforcement. Here we see the conflict of crime and civil rights.

Two years before Ralph joined the force, the civil rights movement's leadership was having an impact on Chattanooga. "The annual board meeting of the SCLC was held in Chattanooga. Martin Luther King applauds city for grappling honestly with a serious problem." [2]

The controversy over school desegregation was an on-going cause of concern. Raymond Witt had served as the Chairman of the School Board since the Supreme Court had handed down the decision to desegregate the schools. Mr. Witt was also an attorney and had headed the legal efforts to stall the integration process. Thus many Blacks and the NAACP felt Witt was not a friend of Blacks and resented his being honored at the local Black high school.

"James Mapp president of the NAACP protested the ceremony to honor Raymond Witt, Chairman of the Chattanooga School Board. C.C. Bond the principal of Howard disagrees. Also NAACP members were not in the majority as many attended." [3]

By 1967 Mayor Ralph Kelly was making optimistic statements about Chattanooga race relations. "Mayor Kelly attending a workshop on Urban Leadership as a prelude to the National League of Cities Convention, said Chattanooga will continue to be a leader in race relations. Because in Chattanooga there, is good communication between white and Negro people." [4]

More issues regarding civil rights were being raised, In so doing more people got involved. Along the way some got side tracked and used a just cause for personal gain. [5]

The campaign, no matter how confused, continued. "Adoption of a

Big Ralph

proposed city ordinance to end discrimination in all public accommodations was urged by the NAACP, Human Relations Council and the city's biracial committee."[6]

The Black militant movement had been on the rise well before the death of King in 1968. Now militants began to organize in Chattanooga. In the process they attempted to form a coalition with Rev. Wright who had entered the civil rights struggle. Rev. Wright soon began to have problems.

"Rev. H. H. Wright has two fires--threatened since he allowed Black militants to speak in his church. Wright, president of the Action Coordinating Council, sponsored a meeting where militants from Los Angeles allegedly advocated the killing of white savages."[7]

Ralph continued moving up in the ranks and his impressions as a young officer were still growing. The protest movement was sweeping the nation and Chattanooga was no exception. Ralph continued his educational training as he surmised the dilemma of civil rights, human rights, civil disobedience and mass protest.

Ralph had attended Lane College before joining the Air Force. At that time he had no interest in police work. But now a degree in Criminal Justice was well suited for his career. Ralph enrolled at Cleveland State Community College, located 30 miles north of Chattanooga in Cleveland, Tennessee. Ralph attacked his course work with vigor as he knew this academic expertise would better prepare him for a career in law enforcement.

Ralph noted that one of the most exciting things about studying Criminal Justice was the exchange between students and instructors. The instructors were not trained police officers but they were well versed in theory. In this instance officers who had first hand experiences with various aspects of police work had taken the limited theory they had and placed it into practice. As they combined theory and practice, they were able to see the reality of theory and how it can be best used. On the other hand the instructors were able to discuss the theory they had in a more realistic fashion. Ralph relished this sincere mutual exchange and benefited greatly from the classes.

Chapter Eleven

Meanwhile racial tensions and boycotting continued in Chattanooga.[8] By 1970 the Commission on Human Development came under scrutiny for their efforts to achieve equal rights for all citizens in the state. "The state Planning Commission reports that the Tennessee Commission of Human Development has failed in getting equal rights for all Tennesseans. In this case they failed to enact effective equal opportunity legislation. Also, they did not provide enforcement power to The Human Development Commission to carry out existing federal laws."[9]

The next year the racial climate in Chattanooga was even more tense. Ralph was now a lieutenant and in this capacity he viewed the tense and explosive racial landscape of Chattanooga. The media continued to report the challenges to the American Democratic system. The militant voice of the protest movement was still being heard. Thus, the power structure began to react. The Black Panther Party was well organized and well known in 1971.

"William K. Brown, Panther recruiter claims Chattanooga civil strife will continue until white people decide to allow Black people to have equal opportunity."[10]

Less than a month after the Black Panthers began organizing, several mainstream organizations began making appeals for human-rights. Among these groups were: The League of Women Voters, Southeastern Tenn. Chapter of the National Association of Social Workers and the Unity Group.

"The League noted and called for, the following:
1. Equality of opportunity in education, employment and housing.
The Social Workers Called For:
1. Adequate health care, education, employment.
The Unity Group had 14 Demands the most prominent were:
1. Open Housing
2. Apology from mayor and city commission for police abuse of innocent citizens during recent disturbances.
3. Creation of Human Relations Committee.
4. That ticket money left over when Wilson Pickett refused to

Big Ralph

perform go to the family of Leon Anderson who died of gunshot wounds by police."[11]

No doubt there were appeals coming from all directions concerning the racial conflict in Chattanooga. There were very few legitimate efforts to answer these appeals. On the surface it looked as if the different Human Rights Boards and Commissions were beneficial to those that had been historically discriminated against and abused. But that was not the case. Even the appointment of Blacks to Boards and other positions was not just to place mere tokens, but, a planned tactic to control and continue the manipulation and exploitation of Black people.

What is most tragic are the Blacks who accepted these positions of lackeys and accepted the role as a Judas against their own people. "Roy Noel is appointed Assistant to mayor for Community Relations. Noel has been city Youth Coordinator since 1968."[12]

Clearly an unbiased review of the facts notes that the greatest effort by those in power was to continue the manipulation and control of the so-called despised Black minority. Another clear example of this ungodly deception was the school desegregation fiasco. Whites were not totally responsible for this confusion but they, by far, had the greatest authority and power to diffuse the situation. Meanwhile the media continued to update the arrogance and often ignorance of the city school board and their sponsors.[13]

The year 1971 was a crucial year for the desegregation issue. The conflicting testimony on this question adds fuel to our later discussions on protest and violence. I have chosen to place most of this information in the footnote section to not exclude what may be monotonous or unimportant to some but is crucial data to others.[14]

For a good overview of this issue the Times printed the following historical development of the school desegregation issue.

"1. May 17, 1954

U.S. Supreme Court ruling--racially separated schools unequal.

2. July 22, 1955

Chattanooga Board announces it will comply with the law.

Chapter Eleven

3. August 5, 1965

U.S. District Court orders completion of desegregation in 1966 instead of 1968.

4. April 12, 1967

Board says no faculty assignments will be based on race--except to assist desegregation.

5. June 16, 1971

Board submits plan for desegregation.

6. April 6, 1960

James Mapp files suit saying city operating a compulsory biracial school system.

7. September 5, 1962

1st day desegregated classes begin.

8. April 20, 1971

U.S. Supreme Court rules all vestiges of segregation must be removed from a school system and busing would be the means to accomplish desegregation.

9. May 19, 1971

U.S. District Court orders Chattanooga to submit plan that will remove all vestiges of state imposed segregation in Chattanooga schools.

10. July 26, 1971

U.S. District Court approves city's desegregation plan for elementary and junior high and gives tentative approval for high school plan." [15]

Gene Roberts was elected police Commissioner in 1971. During that same year Patricia Underwood became the first female officer taking full police training and the first woman sworn in--in the history of the Chattanooga police department. [16]

The City Commission approved a measure to encourage police to go to school. "City Commission passed amendment to budget ordinance that will provide incentive pay for education for police officers beyond high school." [17]

This measure not only encouraged Ralph to continue his education but also led him to the FBI Academy. In 1973 Ralph Cothran became the

Big Ralph

first Black officer in the history of the Chattanooga Police Department to attend the FBI Academy.

The FBI Academy has very rigorous training requirements. The Academy also has tough admissions requirements. The Academy would prove to be one of the greatest challenges of his career in law enforcement. Big Ralph would be away from his family for over a year. During this time he wrote several letters to his wife Catherine. During his first month at the Academy he writes:

Dear Honey,
 There is not too much to tell you about this place yet. We are still going through orientation and I do not know how rough the courses will be yet. Graduation is a big thing and there is no limitations so lets try and get ready so you and the kids can come down to see me graduate (Hopefully I will). My first class is at 8 am and breakfast is from 6:30 to eight. Our last class is over at five and there is a 12 o'clock curfew no exceptions. I miss and love you and the kids very much and this little time that I have already been away let me know just how much a fool I have really been not to have spent more time with my family. So when I get back count on a fellow that will not let any of you down again O.K. that is more than a promise it is the righteous truth.
Tell Stephen and Cyzanne I said hello and I miss them very much.

Love Always,
Your Husband (Honey)
Ralph[18]

Catherine recalls that this was a critical time in their lives. Ralph was away and she had the sole responsibility to raise their two children. Ralph was also going through a great physical and mental challenge. She was supportive like a dutiful wife and thrived on the letters she received
No doubt the FBI training was very demanding. It is for sure that in

Chapter Eleven

Ralph's letters we can get a good idea of what the training involved. Big Ralph's gut feelings come across in the letters not only about the FBI but also about his family. The following letter talks about his classes and grades. Ralph also talks about mutual friends and acquaintances.

Dear Catherine,

How are you and the kids doing? I am fine. However, the physical training has made my knee very sore and I can hardly walk. We had to write an abstract from a magazine in our communication class and I made an A on that one. This evening I am taking an exam in Forensic Science (blood and body fluids, hair and fibers, chemistry). I will not complete this letter until I come back from that class, so I can tell you how I made out in that class. Reuben Strickland's wife's brother is here. He is from Lincoln, Nebraska. Also there are several guys that know Chief Davis in class. Tell Stephen that the guy from Lincoln, Nebraska played on the same high school team with Oscar Robertson, they both were guards. We have a basketball team in which he plays guard and I will play center if my knees hold up. My partner Al Makey who played with Oscar in high school graduated from the University of Nebraska.

The food here is terrible and I cannot hold it in my stomach. I am going to the bathroom on the average of 5 times a day or at least after each meal. I have not lost an ounce of weight nor have I gained any. I will tell you one thing when I do get back home and finish this Academy you want have to worry about me going to any more out of town schools. I cannot stand being away from home for so long. I also miss Princess very much tell Cyzanne to give her a extra plate of food for me.

I miss you all very much,

Love Always
Ralph[19]

Dear Catherine,

I have finished the exams in Forensic Science. There were 10 questions on it and I feel fairly sure that I passed it. I will let you know the score in my next letter. Saturday I went to Kennedy's grave site, he is buried

Big Ralph

with his two children on each side of him. One was only a few days old and the other a little longer. The Tomb of the Unknown Soldier, however, is the thing to see. The changing of the guard at that tomb is unbelievable. Kiss the kids for me

Love Always
Ralph[20]

    Since Catherine had the sole responsibility of taking care of the kids she needed money. Catherine recalls that she will always appreciate the dependability of Ralph's friend and fellow officer, Robert Elsea. While Ralph was away at the Academy he asked Officer Robert Elsea to pick up his payroll check each pay period and bring it to Catherine. Catherine remembers that officer Elsea was never late not even once and always delivered the check on time.
    In the following letter Ralph gives a detailed description of his grades. The classes no doubt kept him very busy. His good grades gave him added confidence, and Catherine felt proud.

Dear Catherine,
It is Friday evening now and I have just finished taking a test in education. My score for the exam was 91 which was a letter grade of B, so for this particular course I have made two A's and one B. This marks the half way point for the course and now I can truthfully say for this class I have no doubts about passing the course. Here is a detail report on my scores to this point Education = A, A, B (one more test due) Management = B (test due next week) Foresenic Science = A (Test next week). Behavioral Science = B (test next week) Law = no test yet. As you can see Education is the only midterm test I have had. The rest are next week after that I will know what to expect from all the courses, no problem I will pass them and that's a promise. The courses just mentioned are taken for college credit. But by no means are they all of my courses. The rest includes: Firearms Training (Pistol Shooting) Raid Concerns (Narcotics and Vice) Physical Training (Exercise) Swimming (Advanced). I am brushing up the instructors, hope

Chapter Eleven

to make a training film to show future students exactly how to do the different strokes using me, if we can get the necessary underwater equipment before we leave. The above courses are no mental thing, however, they are quite demanding physically. How are my babies getting along tell them I miss them very much and love them. I hope to see all of you soon. I love you very much Honey and miss you terribly.

Love Always,
Honey [21]

Ralph gained the respect of the FBI swimming instructors. He was an excellent swimmer and the FBI Academy wanted Ralph to stay on and join the staff as a swimming instructor. Ralph loved Chattanooga and could not wait to get back home. He turned the Academy down.

The year before Ralph attended the FBI Academy there had been no peace as racial disharmony still loomed like the clouds over the Tennessee valley. "There were fights between Black and white students at Kirkman High School. Black Commissioner John P. Franklin listens to demands, concerns of Black students." [22]

Most likely the most serious concern for the city in 1972 were the organizing efforts of the Black Panther Party. The Panther Party, in an effort to solicit support from merchants who catered to an almost exclusive Black clientele, was accused of extortion plots. It began with Pruett's Food Town, a family owned grocery chain. The store in question is located on East Third Street. Pruett's initially agreed to make a small contribution to the Panther Party to help support their community projects. They were evidently pressured by the local economic/political power structure to remove their support and a boycott resulted.

"Pruett's refusal to comply with a previous agreement to contribute $15 weekly to support the Black Panther Party programs--resulted in an effective boycott. The store reconsidered in two days." [23]

A war now erupted against the Black Panther Party. The following news accounts show how the establishment sought to destroy the

Big Ralph

Panther Party. "Attorney General Edward E. Davis advised area merchants that threats of damage or harm cannot be used to coerce contributions from unwilling businesses under Tennessee law." [24]

A few days later the News Free Press reported. "A spokesperson for the Tri-State Citizens Council told the City Commission his organization deplores and condemns coercive acts against certain local merchants and business people by gangs of Blacks in attempts to extort money." [25]

In response to these charges the Panther Party spoke to the media. They said that "the Pruett's Food Town boycott was done by the community. Panthers say no threats were made against the business community who refused to donate money to Black survival programs. The Panthers sponsor a breakfast program for school age kids, transport families to prisons to see relatives, sponsor a free food and clothing program and test Black people for sickle cell anemia." [26]

Race relations was still the hottest topic in town as Ralph began to adjust to the rigid requirements of the FBI Academy. His military experience paid off and the strict discipline in the Academy was similar to his previous military experience. Thus, the Academy exposed Ralph to a broad knowledge of law enforcement by trained professionals. Also impacting was how the bureau operated on a national level to solve crimes. Ralph would take this information and create a formula within his department by which the FBI and his department could work together as professionals.

During 1973 the local Black Panther leader went on trial. "Ralph Moore the leader of the Black Panther Party was given two years. The jury made a unanimous recommendation for clemency, but the judge ignored the clemency recommendation." [27]

In 1974 Ralph was promoted to captain. [28] No doubt Ralph was now considered one of the leaders in the Chattanooga Police Department. He had prepared himself for the job. As a Black man with a sworn duty to uphold the law in a fair and impartial manner, the yoke of racism was a heavy burden to carry.

The year 1974 also had a bright moment, Ralph and Catherine were blessed with another son. David was born March 22, 1974. Little David would soon grow taller than his father. David like his brother Stephen

Chapter Eleven

would also play basketball like Big Ralph.

Racism existed not only in the department but throughout society. Even in 1974 organizations like the VFW refused to admit Blacks. Two marine recruiters one white and one Black were confronted with a dilemma at the local VFW Club. The white marine was admitted to the Club and the Black marine was not. The Club claims it is private and you must have a membership card." [29]

The yoke of racism still hung around the neck of Black people in Chattanooga. A coalition of Black organizations claimed that the gains of the past were eroding. The statement was signed by "James Mapp, NAACP, Rev. H.H. Wright, President Action Coordinating Committee, Rev. Paul McDaniel, President Unity Group, Ralph Moore, President Black Panther Party and Rev. Robert Richards, President Operation PUSH." [30]

Ralph Moore the local Black Panther leader who was active in the coalition against racism was still in trouble with the authorities.

"Ralph Moore Black Panther Party leaders' appeal on extortion charge is denied by state supreme court. Moore withdraws from city commission race and awaits transportation to state prison. Moore still seeks appeal and a Ralph Moore Defense Fund is started." [31]

In 1980 Big Ralph was appointed Assistant Chief of police. [32] (The promotion to Assistant Chief was a first in the department. Ralph received many letters of congratulations. See Appendix B Letters of Congratulations). It was very difficult to work for Chief McCutcheon because he was prejudice, Ralph recalled that Chief McCutcheon went out of his way to discriminate against Black officers and Black people. Eventually Big Ralph breathed a sigh of relief when Chief McCutcheon finally retired.

Captain Downing was a part of a group of officers that also gave Ralph and other Black officers a hard time. These officers were very prejudiced and they resented any Blacks serving on the Chattanooga Police Force. Ironically Catherine as a nurse at Erlanger Hospital ended up nursing Captain Downing later in his career when he was critically ill. As Ralph rose through the rank's Black officers usually received the worst beat

Big Ralph

assignments. Captain Downing and his cronies would always do everything possible to make the Black officers' job difficult. Fortunately Ralph usually could out think most of his fellow officers even his superiors, so he did not suffer as much as other Black officers. Also Big Ralph helped his situation by always excelling at whatever he did.

The protest movements had culminated during the 70's. Law enforcement agencies across the nation had been affected by this movement and so had America. Ralph saw a direct relationship between protest and crime.

The protest movements of the civil rights era, often, turned into political violence. Political violence has not been a recent occurrence in American political history. The native Americans were the first people in America to engage in this act of protest.

"Beginning early in the 17th century, American Indians engaged in a series of revolts aimed at securing their land and liberty against invasion by white settlers supported by colonial, state and federal governments. These were armed insurrections by domestic groups to which the U.S. had denied the privileges of citizenship as well as the perquisites of nationhood. The suppression of Indian revolts was the chief occupation of the U.S. army for more than a century after its creation." [33]

Political violence is a interesting phenomena. Initially political violence was seen in a group oppressed. This pattern is not consistent as we trace the historical development of political violence and view groups that advocate political violence in the 90's. So in this land that eventually became a democracy, the native American protested when his land was seized and he was slaughtered. Blacks protested their enslavement and the ongoing attempt to maintain neo-slavery in the U.S.

White people have always participated in this phenomenon. "Appalachian farmers living in the western regions of the eastern seaboard states participated in civil disorder from the 1740's, when Massachusetts farmers marched on Boston in support of a land bank law." [34]

Eventually the European settlers of North America revolted against the colonial masters of Great Britain.

Chapter Eleven

"American colonists gained their independence from Britain after a decade of civil strife and eight years of revolutionary war. The insurgents resorted to political violence and the authorities to repression. This pattern was repeated in American history.

In the years between 1820 and 1860, white Southerners became a conscious minority. This was the period in which Southerners committed themselves economically to an agricultural system based on slave-breeding and plantation farming, which led to a Civil War.

A guerrilla war resulted after the surrender at Appomattox by terrorist groups (KKK) supported by the mass of white Southerners. The purpose of this struggle was to prevent freed Negroes from voting or participating in politics to restore the substance of the prewar southern social and economic systems and drive carpet beggars and scalawags out of the south." [35]

Violence was also used against other Europeans who were felt to be inferior. "White, Anglo-Saxon, Protestant Americans (WASP) engaged in a long series of riots, lynchings, mob actions, and abuses of power in their effort to protest their political preeminence, and life-styles of the immigrant onslaught." [36]

"Beginning in the 1870's, working men attempting to organize for collective action, engaged in more than half a century of violent warfare with industrialists." [37]

Since the beginning of slavery Blacks have rebelled against the inherent oppression of human bondage. The end of slavery did not end Black oppression. The second coming of Christ most likely will be the only solution to the problem of oppression.

"Black Americans participated during the years of slavery in at least 250 abortive insurrections and were, after the end of the civil War, the victims of white attacks in dozens of cities ranging from Cincinnati (1866) to East St. Louis (1917). Blacks retaliated violently against white attacks in the Chicago and Washington, D.C. race riots of 1919 and in the Detroit riot of 1943." [38]

Women have also gotten involved in political violence. Females have a history of oppression by a male dominated society. The contemporary

Big Ralph

feminist movement has answered some of these problems. But feminism to a large degree has become a problem itself.

"Prior to the passage, in 1920, of the 19th Amendment granting female suffrage, women engaged in militant action to protest their exclusion from American politics." [39] So, what does political violence mean? What are the implications? Does this history of political violence in America mean anything for us in the 90's? In conclusion the following is what professor Skolnick says about political violence.

" The previous examples provide a historical background against which to test the most important implication of the myth of peaceful progress the idea that political violence in the United States is, and always has been, relatively rare, needless, without purpose, and irrational."[40]

"The proposition that domestic political violence has been unnecessary to achieve political goals is ambiguous, but it is historically fallacious no matter how one interprets it. It means that the established machinery has permitted major" outgroups" to move nonviolently up the political-economic ladder, it is demonstrably false. On the contrary, American institutions seem designed to facilitate the advancement of talented individuals rather than of oppressed groups. Groups engaging in mass violence have done so only after a long period of fruitless, relatively nonviolent struggle."[41]

Professor Skolnick has made a good succinct analysis of political violence and terms like protest and politics. The relation of protest to violence is an essential variable up for our review. In so doing Skolnick notes three critical points about protest and violence in America. First, instances of violence have been limited in contemporary group protest. Secondly, usually if violence occurs, it is difficult to find out where it came from. Thirdly, mass protest demonstrations, whether violent or not, must be analyzed in regard to crises in American institutions.

Here Skolnick argues that culture is not the sole means to make an analysis of protest and violence. Thus, mass protest is a necessary political phenomenon engaged in by normal people. Violence usually, when it does occur, is most likely a reaction to the authorities. Mass protesters do not plan violence, when violence does occur it is related to issues, rooted in fundamental oppression.

"The political character of the phenomena of violence and protest are noted in 5 reasons:

1. Violence is an ambiguous term whose meaning is established through political progress.

2. The concept of violence always refers to a disruption of some condition or order, but order, like violence, is politically defined.

3. Even as defined, violence is not always forbidden or unequivocally condemned in American society.

4. The decision to use or not use such violent tactics as deadly force in the control of protest is a political one.

5. Almost uniformly, the participants in mass protest today see their grievances as rooted in the existing arrangements of power and authority in contemporary society, and they view their own activity as political action-- on a direct or symbolic level--aimed at altering those arrangements." [42]

An important element in making an analysis of protest and the elements of violence and disobedience is types of protest. Civil rights protests were not the only type of protest. For example the antiwar movement was a product of the times.

The 1960's was a time that witnessed various attacks on the established authority. Not only did Blacks protest for civil rights and basic freedoms but white, free, young adults spoke out against the war in Vietnam. The war was unpopular, but it was not just a time of protest by Black Americans. Although the 60's was the day of Martin Luther King and equal access for Blacks, it was also a time of freedom of expression for young white adults.

This freedom of expression for young white people did not include war. Thus, the antiwar movement was at times called the Peace Movement. In this case dressing and wearing whatever type clothes you felt comfortable in was popular. Letting your hair grow as long as you wanted to, growing a beard, sexual freedoms and the free use of drugs and alcohol was most important. So a group of people with this

Big Ralph

mind set was not interested in going half way around the world and fighting people they had never seen. Nor did they view these people as their enemies.

"Most of the support for the Anti-War Protest Movement has been among white professionals, students and clergy. Much of what is called resistance has taken the form of nonviolent civil disobedience by individuals or groups whose purpose has been moral witness. Individual draft resisters have engaged in a form of opposition that has dramatized their outrage at the war but has not impeded it's implementation. And nearly all the violence that has occurred in mass demonstrations has resulted, not from the demonstrators conscious choice of tactics, but from the measures chosen by public authorities to disperse and punish them."[43]

"While there have been scattered acts of real violence committed by antiwar activists, by far the greater portion of physical harm has been done to demonstrators and movement workers, in the form of bombings of homes and offices, crowd-control measures used by police, physical attacks on demonstrators by American Nazi Party members, Hell's Angels and others."[44]

Skolnick argues that sometimes the police actively engage in violence against antiwar demonstrators. "When police are encouraged by public officials to regard free assembly as subversive, they do not need much provocation to attack even innocent bystanders. When, as at Chicago, it appears that police provocateurs mingle among the demonstrators and incite their fellow officers to violence by such acts as helping to lower the American flag, it is even less likely that the spirit of nonviolence will prevail."[45]

The student protest movement was also a particular source of protest during the era of protest movements. The student movements of the 60's and 70's were said to be totally different from the student generation of the 50's. Students of later years were better educated and more politically conscious. They also had been influenced by the civil rights movement. Student participation in the Peace Corp. also had an affect on their political conscious. Meanwhile, their involvement in university protest introduced them to direct action.

Chapter Eleven

The Vietnam war and the civil rights movement also caused college campuses to be focal points for the antiwar movement. Students also surmised that the university was a part of the problem. In this case the university complex was a part of the military/industrial complex that promoted war.

University administrations also answered to the established order and introduced law enforcement and domestic intelligence units on campuses. Domestic intelligence units consisted of professors and students. These undercover operatives infiltrated student organizations and are the cause of some people being harassed even into the 90's because they were perceived to be a radical student during the 60's or 70's.

"Those who believe that disorder and conflict are unique to the campuses of the 1960's are unacquainted with the history of American colleges. Dormitory life in 19th century America was marked by violence, rough and undisciplined actions, and outbreaks of protest against the rules and regulations through which faculties and administrations attempted to govern students." [46]

"Student activism during the 1960's appears, however, to have unprecedented qualities. Compared to earlier activism, that of the 1960's involves more students and engages them more continuously, is more widely distributed on campuses throughout the country, is more militant, is more hostile to established authority and institutions (including radical political organizations), and has been more sustained. Such activism seems better considered as part of a student movement, something largely unknown before in the U.S. rather than as a collection of similar but unconnected events." [47]

The student movement was in the vanguard of all protest movements during the era of protest. The civil disobedience that marked student protest would someday have a serious impact on the youth. Thus the positive aspects of direct action would some day be a nightmare for law enforcement and for analysts of the Black experience.

"February 1960 Negro students began to attack segregation in public facilities by 'sitting-in" at segregated southern dime-store lunch

Big Ralph

counters. Northern students supported these demands by picketing and boycotting northern branches of Woolworth's and Kresse's. The success of the southern sit-ins led to the formation of the SNCC. Northern white student groups formalized their organizations to support the southern movement.

By the late 1961, students consciously began to use the civil rights techniques of nonviolent direct action marches, vigils, and pickets-- to protest aspects of American foreign policy. Student concern for the nuclear arms race, nuclear testing, and civil defense prompted the first national student demonstration in several decades-- the Washington Peace March of February 1962." [48]

Clear examples of the strategy of civil disobedience are seen in what can be described as the politics of confrontation. "Resistance" and "Confrontation" refer to such forms of direct action as deliberate disruption of or interference with normal, routine operations of persons or institutions by large masses of persons deliberate violation of authoritative orders to disperse; forceful retaliation against police use of clubs, chemicals, or other force; the use of barricades or "mobile tactics" to prevent or delay police efforts to disperse a crowd; the use of ridicule, rudeness, obscenity, and other uncivil forms of speech and behavior to shock, embrass, or defy authorities; refusal to comply with orders or to accept authoritative commands or requests as legitimate." [49]

Skolnick also notes several tactics he argues that militant students described as confrontational tactics:

"1. Confrontation and militancy are methods of arousing moderates to action.

2. Confrontation and militancy can educate the public.

3. Confrontation, militancy and resistance are ways to prepare young radicals for the possibility of greater repression.

4. Combative behavior with respect to the police and other authorities, although possibly alienating "respectable" adults, has the opposite effect on the movement's relationships with nonstudent youth.

5. The experience of resistance and combat may have alliterating effect on young middle-class radicals.

6. The political potency of "backlash" is usually exaggerated." [50]

Chapter Eleven

Black students began the student movement and they also spearheaded the movement. Blacks were driven by a lust for freedom while white students advocated change for other reasons.

"Without a doubt, the most extensive challenge to the moral authority of the university has begun to emerge from nonwhite students. Until a few years ago, Black students tended to be individualistic, assimilationist, and politically indifferent; the drive for Black power, however, offered a clear opportunity for educated Blacks to give collective expression to their grievances and to identify with the Black community."[51]

Black students as they made a historical analysis of the Black experience took on different attitudes. They rejected integration and spoke out for independence. Black students also took a close look at nonviolence and replaced it with a self-defense ideology.

"Four factors influenced the transition of Black students:

1. The failure of the civil rights movement to improve significantly the social economic, and political position of most Negroes has led to doubts about the possibility of meaningful progress through law.

2. Urban riots in the 1960's, which symbolized this frustration, have been met with armed force, which in turn has mobilized militant sentiment within Black communities.

3. The world wide revolution against colonialism has induced a new sense of racial consciousness, pride, and affirmative identity.

4. The war in Vietnam has diverted resources away from pressing urban needs.

There has so far been relatively little violence by militant Blacks in this country--as compared to nonviolent Black protest--despite the popular impression conveyed by the emphasis of the news media or episodes of spectacular violence or threats of violence. This is true historically, and it is largely true for the contemporary situation. It must also be remembered that much of the violence involving Blacks has originated with militant whites in the case of the early race riots and the civil rights movement or from police and troops (in the case of ghetto riots)." [52]

For many people the civil rights movement was marred by the

militant philosophy of many Blacks in the protest movement. It is for sure though, that militancy is not a contemporary phenomenon. Therefore Booker T. Washington and his "Buckwheat" philosophy was not a product of the times, but a particular personality, evidently within the soul of Booker T. Washington. It is for sure then that Booker T. Washington could have existed during the contemporary period. In fact many clones of Booker T. do exist in today's Black community who pimp the civil rights movement for material gain.

The history of Black militancy in America is rooted, first in the slave rebellions and mutinies aboard the slave ships. No doubt rebellions continued throughout the period of slavery in America, when Black people were dehumanized as a fact of life.

"It is inaccurate, for example, to suggest that Black protests have moved from peaceful use of orderly political and legal processes to disorderly protests and, finally, to rejection of nonviolent means. Leaving aside the history of southern, slave insurrections, many Black writers before the civil war called for violent action.

David Walker, in his "An Appeal To The Coloured Citizens Of The World" (1892), called white Americans "our natural enemies" and exhorted Blacks to kill or get killed. The abolitionist Frederick Douglass, discussing the kidnaping of escaped slaves and their return to the south under the Fugitive Slave Act, argued that "the only way to make the Fugitive Slave Law a dead letter, is to make half a dozen or more dead kidnappers.

In supporting John Brown's armed raid at Harper's Ferry, Douglass advocated the use of any means to secure freedom. There is a similarity between the Douglass' statement and Malcolm X: our objective is complete freedom, complete justice, complete equality, by any means necessary."[53]

The civil rights protest movement was the centerpiece of all protest movements during this era. The antiwar movement, student movement and the cry of militancy all evolved from the civil rights movements. The Garvey movement ended in the 1920's, this also marked a turning point in the philosophies of protest. The mainstream

Chapter Eleven

philosophy that resulted had it's roots in the philosophy of Booker T. Washington. In this case white America chose particular leaders for Blacks and told them what to do.

Largely, Black leadership did not witness independence until the militant movement of the 60's, with the exception of the Nation of Islam. "The dominant thrust of Black protest was toward political, social, economic, and cultural inclusion into American institutions on a basis of full equality. Always a powerful theme in American Black militancy, these aims found their maximum expression in the civil rights movement of the 1950's and early 1960's. Some Black militants continued to pursue these goals but a transition began to take place. Several features of this transition stand out." [54]

"1. The civil rights movement was largely directed at the south, especially against state and local laws and practices, and, in general, it saw the federal government and courts as allies in the struggle for equality. The new movement for Black liberation, while nationwide in scope, is primarily centered in the Black communities of the north and west, and is generally antagonistic to both local and federal governments.

2. The civil rights movement was directed against explicit and customary forms of racism, as manifested in Jim Crow restrictions on the equal use of facilities of transportation, public accommodations, and the political process. The liberation movement focuses on deeper and more intractable sources of racism in the structure of American institutions, and stresses independence rather than integration.

3. The civil rights movement was largely middle-class and interracial. The liberation movement attempts to integrate middle-class and lower-class elements in rejection of white leadership.

4. The civil rights movement was guided by the concepts of nonviolence and passive resistance. The liberation movement stresses self-defense and freedom by any means necessary." [55]

Spearheading the early civil rights movement was the NAACP. Prior to the civil rights era the NAACP had sought legal reform. In this case they had many successful litigations. For example in Shelly v. Kramer the restrictive covenants in housing was struck down and of course the celebrated Brown v. Board of Education decision.

But, the Supreme Court was quite different from the southern courts. The southern courts and law enforcement continued to keep in place a system of Jim Crow that was honored in the south and was the southern way of life. There was also a gap between the common Black folk and the conservative middle-class values of the NAACP.

These old values are set in the ways of Booker T. Washington and bourgeois thinking produced a climate for new leadership. "By 1955 Dr. King came on the scene and with less publicity in the northern ghettos came Elijah Muhammad and the Nation of Islam." [56]

King came on the scene with a direct action approach to achieving civil rights. Ingrained also in King's philosophy was an assimilationist approach that equaled integration. Elijah Muhammad's approach to solving the Black man's problems in America was centered on the religion of Islam. But Muhammad's Islam took on theories of Black Nationalism and separatism.

None of these approaches were new to the Black experience in America. Both approaches had been adopted due to specific conditions that came about in the Black Holocaust in America.

"Direct action was used by the abolitionists before the civil war, by left-wing ghetto organizers in the 1930's, and by CORE in the early 1940's; it had been threatened by A. Philip Randolph in his march on Washington in 1941, but called off when FDR agreed to establish a federal Fair Employment Practices Commission. The roots of separatism are equally deep, beyond Marcus Garvey to Martin Delaney and the American Colonization Society in the 18th century." [57]

Direct action became the driving force of the civil rights protest movement in the south. Civil rights groups like King's SCLC were created because of the lack of broad results by organizations like the NAACP who only sought relief for Black oppression in the courts.

Social thinkers like professor Skolnick argue that racism was a disease. This disease only affected a segment of the population. The moral fiber of the American people was of good morals and principles

Chapter Eleven

and racism could be rooted out.

"Nowhere were these premises more explicit than in the thought and practice of Dr. King. Nonviolence was for him a philosophical issue rather than the tactical or strategic question it posed for many younger activists in SNCC and CORE." [58]

The questions that arose concerning King's strategy was a battle cry for the challenge to Ghandism. Also young students began to question the belief by King that racists were inherently Christians and moved by some moral authority. For example the following quotation depicts King's strategy in dealing with the white southern racists.

"The aim was to awaken a sense of moral shame in the opponent. Such a philosophy presumed that the opponent had moral shame to awaken, and that moral shame, if awakened, would suffice.

During the 60's many civil rights activists came to doubt the first and deny the second. The reasons for this did not lie primarily in white southern terrorism as manifested in the killing of NAACP leader Medgar Eavers, or three civil rights workers in Neshoba County, Mississippi, or four little girls in a dynamited church in Birmingham. To a large extent white southern violence was anticipated and expected. What was not expected was the absence of strong protection by the Federal government." [59]

Although the protest movement of the south expected violence from white racist they did not anticipate the level of southern violence. The tactics of direct action especially by SNNC and CORE met with greater resistance. Freedom riders were beaten senselessly. Mobs were allowed to terrorize the students and their supporters at bus terminals throughout the south. The police beat them with clubs, cattle prods, turned blood thirsty German Shepherd dogs on them and hosed them with high powered waterhoses.

Night riders of the days when Billie Holiday sung about "Strange Fruit" that hung from southern trees reappeared. The "Vale of Tears" was once again revisited in the south. All civil rights activists were victimized, Black or white.

Big Ralph

"It was not surprising, then, that student activists in the south became increasingly disillusioned with nonviolent tactics of resistance. Following the shotgun murder in 1966 of Sammy Younge, Jr., a Black civil rights activists at Tuskegee Institute, his fellow students organized a protest march." [60]

Despite the new found laws on civil rights, and the legality of the principles of integration the white south would not yield. The southern courts defied the federal law, and refused to abide by the Supreme Court decisions that had outlawed Jim Crow and segregation. The terror of post Reconstruction returned to the south, and the southern states officially took on the state's right attitude once again.

Thus, the legal authorities in the south openly suppressed the civil rights movement. In the mean time they made a mockery out of democracy and the American judicial system. The only time Blacks got relief from the federal government was if they were in Washington. The local FBI in Mississippi for example violated the law and treated Blacks just like the local authorities.

Meanwhile in northern ghettoes Blacks rebelled and caused massive civil disorder. These rebellions were also called riots and were challenged by armed police and the National Guard and U.S. military forces. While Blacks were shot down for looting and protesting, the white southern racist was protected by the same forces. Thus, in the south racists literally had a license to kill Blacks.

The militant wing of the protest movement in view of so many contradictions began to question former allies. Liberal institutions became suspect. Labor organizations, schools and civil services were questioned and liberal academic institutions came up for review.

"The increased criticism of liberals, academics, and federal bureaucracies was part of a broader turn to a renewed critique of the situation of Blacks in the north.

With the explosion of Harlem again--along with several other northern cities--in 1964, attention began shifting to the problem of institutional racism in the north, and this shift was accelerated by the Watts riot the following year. In a real sense, the riots surprised not only

Chapter Eleven

liberal and academic whites, but civil rights leaders as well. There was a wide spread sense that civil rights leaders either could not, or would not speak to the kinds of issues raised by the riots, and that a wide gulf separated those leaders--mostly of middle-class background--from the Black urban masses.

During the 1964 Harlem riots Bayard Rustin and other established civil rights leaders were booed and shouted down at rallies and in the streets, while crowds shouted for Malcolm X." [61]

One of the most crucial issues raised by the Black protest movement was the Vietnam issue. The Vietnam War, was very unpopular among those involved in a struggle for human rights in North America. Many Blacks saw a gross contradiction in the protection of people in Vietnam from communism and the abuse of Black people in America. Simply, Blacks felt that they were being oppressed by a racist government. This government also wanted them to go half away around the world to fight for the freedom of the South Vietnamese when they were not free in America.

"In 1965 the McComb branch of the Mississippi Freedom Democratic Party issued a leaflet:

1. No Mississippi Negroes should be fighting in Vietnam for the white man's freedom, until all the Negro people are free in Mississippi.

2. No one has the right to ask us to risk our lives and kill other colored people in the world. We know we have caught hell under this American Democracy." [62]

No doubt, by this time the protest movement had produced thinkers and people who seriously questioned the integrationist philosophy of the traditional civil rights organizations. These thinkers became known as radicals, militants and Black Nationalists. During the 60's not only were the civil rights and protest movements evident, but, on the world scene colonialism was falling. The decline of colonialism in Africa and Asia came to play a significant role in the theories of liberation of those who were described as Black radicals.

Some Black Nationalists compared the oppression of Blacks in America to colonialism. Here the question of culture came to the

Big Ralph

forefront. Culture defined in the context of Colonialism reveals that to colonize a people one must separate them from their culture. The other components of the colonial system are the political and economic systems that maintain the political and economic exploitation of the people.

Within the American landscape the integrationist and assimilationist theories of the civil rights leadership are tied in to the assimilationist theories of colonialism.[63] Here a dependency complex is revealed and all trappings of Black independence are destroyed. The destruction of all trappings of Black independence has been an integral part of the political and economic apparatus of the American system since Blacks were freed from slavery.

To understand the phenomenon one should digest Kwame Nkrumah's work on neocolonialism and see how it applies to the situation of Blacks in America. At this point, it is also useful to note that the downfall of colonialism throughout the world eventually brought up the question of "power." Is power described or achieved in numbers or population figures?

"Two-thirds of the human population today wrote Malcolm X is telling the one-third minority white man, get out. And the white man is leaving. As perhaps most significantly, the recognition that whites are an international minority necessarily changes the meaning for many Black militants of the national minority position. There were four African and three Asian nations in the UN in 1945; twenty years later their were 36 African and fifteen Asian countries represented."[64]

The new young radical also made an analysis of violence and riots in the colonial context. Colonial domination was/is rooted in violence as a control mechanism. Therefore, revolutionary violence against the colonial structure is logical, justifiable and necessary. For example white people staged such a revolution against other white people in north America. This revolution gave birth to the United States of America and was called the American Revolution.

The urban rebellion/riots of the northern ghettoes dramatized the plight of the oppressed minority. It also showed the wide gap between

Chapter Eleven

common Black folk and the middle-class leadership of the civil rights organizations. This leadership along with their white sponsors attempted to down-play the impact of urban rebellions. They argued that the rebellions were only the actions of a lawless criminal element in the Black community. Thus most of the Black population denounced these rebellions and saw no utility in the actions of those that rebelled. This so-called fact was disputed, note the following quotation.

"Riots are generally viewed by Blacks as a useful and legitimate form of protest. Survey data from Watts, Newark, and Detroit suggest that there is an increasing support, or at least sympathy, for riots in Black communities. Over half the people interviewed in Los Angeles responded that the riot was a purposeful event that could have had a positive effect on their lives." [65]

The urban rebellions were testimony that the civil rights movement had failed. Thus the critique by Black militants that Blacks in America were colonial subjects gained wide acceptance. The critique and evaluation of civil rights eventually led to self-defense as a tactic of liberation. The thinkers of the protest movement were very concerned about the violence Blacks were subjected to during protest demonstrations. Protest demonstrators following King and his philosophy of passive resistance were brutalized by white people, including law enforcement officials often. There was also no justice in the southern court room. So, Blacks began to organize self-defense units for Black survival, in so doing self defense became an aspect of nonviolence.

Historically white people have glamorized self-defense in a white context. During the settlement of the U.S., the killing of the Indians and the move westward was all a part of the white man's folk lore. But because of his inhumane treatment of the Black man white people are scared to death of Black people arming themselves for self-defense.

The most significant self defense groups were formed in Monroe, North Carolina, Oakland, California, St. Louis, Missouri and Mississippi. The Black Panther Party established in Oakland in 1966 became the most widely known. The Black Panther Party became a

Big Ralph

national organization and developed a ten-point program for achieving liberation for Black people.

The Black Panther Party has had a great deal of problems with law enforcement. "Studies of the police emphasize that their attitudes and behavior toward Blacks differ vastly from those taken toward whites. Similar studies show that Blacks perceive the police as hostile, prejudiced and corrupt." [66]

"In view of these facts, the adoption of the idea of self-defense is not surprising. Again, in America self-defense has always been considered an honorable principle, and the refusal to bow before police harassment strikes a responsive chord in ghetto communities, especially among the young." [67]

A further analysis of civil rights will help us to clearly understand certain dynamics. These certain dynamics are again the ongoing critique by the so-called militants. The assimilatonists within the protest movement had active white support. Those whites also often were involved in civil rights organizations. Also many of these whites felt that they should have ultimate leadership authority in many Black organizations.

The new Black radicals questioned the white presence in civil rights organizations. In 1966 SNCC excluded whites from leadership positions. Thus, we see a gradual move from the old civil rights principles to a new ideology. This new ideology was a liberation philosophy that viewed American Blacks within a global context. Black Nationalism was born and the Black militants and radicals now had a philosophical base. This philosophical base of Black Nationalism also conceptualized a world-view.

This world-view simply noted that white people and/or Europeans viewed the world regarding their interests. These interests often projected imperialism and the exploitation of people that were nonwhite. On the other hand, Black people came to view the world realizing that they had interests that contradicted with white people. Here they realized their particular history of oppression and related to other nonwhites who also had a history of oppression throughout the so-called third world.

Chapter Eleven

Meanwhile, white people in America continued to deny the existence of racism. Even when commissions sanctioned by the government to study racism released their findings, the attitude of white people was negative. "The most significant conclusion of the National Advisory Commission on Civil Disorders (The Kerner Commission) was that "white racism" is essentially responsible for the explosive mixture which has been accumulating in our cities since the end of WW II. Yet most Americans reply not guilty to the charge of racism." [68]

The so-called inferior status of Blacks is often used to justify racism. The racists believe that Black people are inferior with fewer human characteristics than white people. Thus, racism is justified. A slave master sitting on his plantation might have more justification to believe the myth of Black inferiority. But the white people today who still place stock in such myths, refuse to step into the future and still think they are on the plantation.

This is a crucial set of circumstances for a Black police officer who wanted to do the right thing. All these factors came to have a bearing on the particular philosophy developed by Assistant Chief Cothran.

Big Ralph

Chapter 12

Police Review: Detention v. Prevention

*Quartered, labeled and housed in way stations of corruption,
a detention that is akin to bondage,
Here comes the challenge, the philanthropist of society who
look to recapture and breed principles and values in the
parasites
of humanity, the sad songs, they could be happy songs.*

Throughout the 80's race relations in Chattanooga were up for review. In some respects, there had been progress but the basic problems were still there. A good idea of the on-going debate on race relations can be seen in the reporting of the local media.

The Chattanooga Times ran a series of articles (6) on race relations in 1981. The following titles of the six articles gives us some insight in reference to the concerns about the conflict between the races:

"Education Seen as Key Element In Race Harmony," "Attitudes Changing As Races Work At living Together," "Cultural Preferences Set Pace and Place of Races' Social Life," "Mingling Among Races Pauses At Church Door," Economics Believed To Be Key For

Big Ralph

Improved Race Relations," "Despite Steps Forward, Racial Distrust Remains." [1]

By 1983 Ralph H. Cothran became the first Black Deputy Chief in the history of the Chattanooga Police Department. [2] This was also a time when Ralph formalized his theories on prevention v. detention. Catherine remembers that Ralph believed that the police department could not do the job of prevention by itself. Ministers were a special group of people that Ralph sought out for help. He talked with the ministers and had gotten some promises, when they did not follow through on their promises Ralph felt discouraged. Big Ralph realized that crime in the communities was a concern of all people especially responsible ministers. The ministers in Chattanooga were slow to react. Catherine recalls that "regretfully and on a positive note that ministers like Rev. Caldwell have been publicized about an organized effort to confront the murders in the Chattanooga community. So some have begun to answer the call made by Ralph after he has passed away. "

Ralph was a policeman's, policemen. He believed in his work as a law enforcement officer and often said "his job was to put people in jail." He did just that and gained respect from his fellow officers. This respect was further based on Ralph's hard work, his dedication to the job and his honesty.

Honesty is not something guaranteed of all police officers. Police officers are human and some officers violate their oath of office and become dishonest. Ralph was not of this breed. Ralph also knew that Black officers were less likely to get away with dishonest practices than white officers.

I would be hard pressed to say with all certainty that Ralph was the only honest Chief in the history of the Chattanooga Police Department. It would be safe to say that Ralph was one of the most honest officers ever in the leadership ranks of the department.

In 1983 when Ralph became Deputy Chief, two leaders in the Black community were fearful that racial conflict would erupt in Chattanooga. Johnny Holloway was the president of PUSH and Walter Tate who was then the president of the Riverside PTA. Both Holloway and Tate were afraid racial tensions would explode during the summer. [3]

Chapter Twelve

In Chattanooga Black people had a poor relationship with the local police. In fact throughout America Black people historically have had a conflicting relationship with the police. So the police department in Chattanooga was no different from any other police department in the south or north.

Ralph Cothran had a significant impact on police brutality as he rose in leadership. The impact Ralph had on arresting the on-going abuse of authority in the Chattanooga Police Department is the hallmak of Ralph's tenure as a Chief. So let the scribes of man duly document that Big Ralph did what no other Chief had ever done. He mended the racial fences and brought down the ugly and prominent head of police brutality as a way of life in the department.

Many white people have always expressed racism in America. It only stands to reason that many police officers are also racist. Of particular concern in Chattanooga has been the death of Black people in police custody. A protest group was formed because of police brutality.

The Concerned Citizens for Justice was established in 1983. Lorenzo Ervin the president of the Concerned Citizens For Justice claims he was active in the fight against police brutality beginning in the 1960's. [4] The death of Wadie Suttles and the organized effort through the Concerned Citizens for Justice to advocate for the family of Wadie Suttles prompted on-going media coverage about Wadie Suttles and police brutality.

Another personality also became significant in Ervin's campaign against police brutality. Maxine Cousin was the daughter of Wadie Suttles who was allegedly murdered by the police in 1983. Due to her father's death Maxine Cousin became active nationally in the fight against police brutality. The following are some excerpts from a speech she made at Unified African Liberation Day Rally in Philadelphia:

"In 1983, My father was beaten to death in the city jail in Chattanooga. He was 66 years old and the first person who struck him was a Black man.

At that time, he was the fifth Black man to die in the custody of the police. Since then, within the last year, four Black people have died

Big Ralph

in police custody, including a 23 year old Black girl who was tortured for 19 hours and finally allowed to bleed to death.

From 1968 until right now, 31 people have died in the custody of the Chattanooga Police Department because of the department's violence. That's 31 people that we know of." [5]

Thus the Wadie Suttles case became the main focus of the Concerned Citizens For Justice. The publicity of the Suttles case gave Lorenzo Ervin and Maxine Couisins a platform to promote their community activism. In fact it is argued that both Ervin and Cousins used the Suttles case to promote their stature as community leaders. But who is Lorenzo Ervin? The Chattanooga New Weekly (A Black Weekly published from 1987-1994) notes the following.

"Is Lorenzo Ervin emerging as a new Black leader? This was the title of a recent article in the Chattanooga News Free Press. But recently Lorenzo Ervin has showed signs of a mental disability that may hinder him from becoming an emerging Black leader." [6]

The writer of the article, J. B. Collins (Chattanooga News Free Press) had implied that Ervin has a mental disability. Also it was noted that Ervin had been the most vocal person regarding the federal law suit that challenged the at-large Commission form of government. J. B. Collins raised a second question. Is Lorenzo Ervin mentally stable? One would also question the mental stability of Dr. Thomas Brooks who was Ervin's biggest supporter and source for economic resources.

For example Brooks who established his financial base as the leading abortionist in the Black community was intent, with the help of Ervin of becoming the number one Black leader in Chattanooga. Thus after the at-large suit was settled Brooks, and Ervin attempted to take over the leadership effort to establish the councilmatic districts for the city. While the baby killing Dr. Thomas Jefferson Brooks never has admitted to being mentally deranged, Ervin has.

"According to a deposition Ervin gave in federal court during the at-large lawsuit, Ervin admits that he is receiving $354.00 per month from Social Security for a mental disability." [7]

Chapter Twelve

Ervin has claimed that he is a political activist that emerged during the 60's. Because of his community organizing Ervin claims, he was harassed by the Chattanooga Police Department. Since he feared for his life Ervin said, he fled to Atlanta and hijacked an Eastern Airlines jet to Cuba. But Castro sent Ervin to Czechoslovakia where he was arrested by U.S. authorities and brought back to the U.S. to stand trial for air piracy. These charges resulted in a 14-year prison sentence.

Ervin was paroled under mysterious circumstances. For example the local police noted that the FBI had a closed file on Ervin regarding the stipulations of his parole. Evidently no where in his parole stipulations was there any clause that said Ervin was not to engage in community organizing and political agitation.

So as the at-large suit became settled and a 9-District Plan that allowed for four Black districts became a reality, Ervin and Brooks returned to Wadie Suttles. Again there were questions raised as to the sincerity of the people that continued to raise questions about Wadie Suttles and the Chattanooga Police Department.

The Chattanooga News Weekly once again attempted to bring some clarity to a tragic situation that was being manipulated for the political goals of Ervin, Brooks and Maxine Cousin.

"Editors' note: It has been six years since Wadie Suttles died in the custody of the Chattanooga Police Department. Suttle's death was tragic and has been publicized more than any death of its kind in Chattanooga. While blame has been placed on the Chattanooga Police Department looking at Wadie Suttles as a human being, there is enough blame to go around." [8]

Lorenzo Ervin a reputed jailhouse lawyer was fast establishing himself as a person that would sue anybody. Ervin not only filed lawsuits against the city in federal court but he also attempted to sue the News Weekly.

"In a recent Chattanooga Times article it was reported that Federal Judge R. Allan Edgar again dismissed a lawsuit filed against the city and city officials for the death of Wadie Suttles. Although many lawsuits against the city may be legitimate, it is virtually impossible for the city to be held accountable for the actions of all its subordinates." [9]

Big Ralph

The article also noted that there were at least four facts that most likely contributed to Wadie Suttles death.

"These tragic facts of Mr. Suttle's life show that the Suttles family apparently cared very little for Mr. Suttles during his last days. But after his death the family and other concerned parties attempted to present a picture of love, responsibility and care." [10]

The most important fact regarding Wadie Suttles is: "While Mr. Suttles was arrested for public drunkenness, he was not held under any bond. Any family member could have merely signed him out of jail for free." [11]

The News Weekly ran another article the next week. This article noted that some people benefited from the death of Wadie Suttles. "The following motives may shed light on why certain people have been in the forefront in advocating for justice in the Wadie Suttles case:

First motive: The economic motive: The Suttles family hope to receive a million dollars in compensation from the city of Chattanooga for the death of Wadie Suttles.

Second Motive: Local political activists like Lorenzo Ervin have attempted to gain headlines to promote their own political agendas.

Third motive: Exploitation by antidemocratic elements, historically communists and/or socialist organizations have exploited problems in the Black community." [12]

No doubt police brutality has been a problem in Chattanooga, but in the case of Wadie Suttles the people advocating for justice were just as bad as the people that killed Wadie Suttles. Here they lost sight of justice and merely wanted to promote their own private agendas.

Chief Cothran knew in 1989 when he was appointed Chief that there was a problem between the department and the Black community. Catherine remembers that Ralph felt he had a lot to offer as Chief, he was ambitious and optimistic. He was the first Chief trained in narcotics and vice and he could bring integrity and honesty to the department. This is what the Chattanooga Times said of Cothran's appointment.

"The naming of Cothran as Chief was seen by City Hall insiders as an effort to mend the Police Department's tattered Black community relations." [13]

Chapter Twelve

In 1990 Michael Holden who was a sergeant on the police force, shot and killed Lebron Earls a 27 year old Black man. The incident happened on Christmas day and involved the theft of a pack of cigarettes. Holden was fired for the incident but the District Attorney would not bring charges against the officer.

"Although Holden claimed that he was justified in killing Earls, Police Chief Ralph Cothran and police Administrator Ervin Dinsmore disagreed with Holden. "Officer Holden's shooting of Earls was too casual," Chief Cothran said.

Chief Cothran went on to say that Holden violated departmental polices governing the use of deadly force when he fired into Earl's car. Chief Cothran and Administrator Dinsmore also criticized Holden for shooting a misdemeanor suspect. It is alleged that Earls had only taken a pack of cigarettes." [14]

No doubt that Chief Cothran did the best he could to halt the cases of police brutality in the Chattanooga Police Department. In fact officers guilty of abuse of authority were disciplined and often removed from duty.

The ugly head of racism exists throughout society. The most publicized murder of a Black man by the police in Chattanooga was the death of Larry Powell. This tragic murder took place February 1993. The following are excerpts from the News Weekly concerning Powell's death.

"Larry Powell died last Friday after being stopped in North Hamilton County for suspicion of drunken driving. After pulling him out of his car, handcuffing him and putting shackles on his feet, the officers began to choke him with a nightstick even though he was not resisting arrest." [15]

Powell was not murdered by the Chattanooga Police Department and did not die in the city. The officers involved in Powell's death were from county law enforcement agencies. Two officers were from the Soddy Daisy Police Department and four were sheriff deputies from the county sheriff's department. Chief Deputy Jim Hammond in a response to the press during a press conference made it clear that the six officers in question did nothing wrong. [16]

Big Ralph

The Powell case caused the Concerned Citizens for Justice and Lorenzo Ervin too once again come to the forefront. The News Weekly reported the following:

"Saturday afternoon, February 27, 1993, the Concerned Citizens for Justice and the Ad Hoc Coalition for a Mass March on Chattanooga will hold a protest march and a demonstration at the Hamilton County Courthouse to demand criminal prosecution of all the officers in the recent death of Larry Powell.

According to one of the rally organizers, Lorenzo Ervin, President of the Concerned Citizens for Justice, the demonstration is necessary to put pressure on the County District Attorney, Gary Gerbitz and federal authorities, who are also supposed to be investigating the case at this time. Ervin said the Black community in Chattanooga-Hamilton county has watched 25 other persons lose their lives in the custody of local officials for over a decade, and no officer has ever been prosecuted. He said the Powell case is just one of many police brutality cases." [17]

The negative feeling toward the police is a reality that has caused concern throughout America. Conflict between the Black community and the police have often been the cause of riots and civil disturbances. Generally the Black community has asked for reforms including police review boards.

"According to the Kerner Commission and other studies, conflict with the police was one of the most important factors in producing Black riots. In short, anger, hatred, and fear of the police are a major common denominator among Black Americans at the present time." [18]

As conflict increased among the police and the Black community, so did conflict between the police and other protest groups. The first peace marches by students during the 60's were peaceful. The students we governed by the principles of nonviolence and they seldom had any conflict with the police. "But slowly incidents began accumulating, until by the spring and summer of 1968 protest marches frequently became clashes between protesters and the police." [19]

The question of violence has affected not only the Chattanooga Police Department but all police departments. No doubt unnecessary police violence compounds the conflict between the community and the police.

Chapter Twelve

"More fundamentally, the misuse of police force violates basic notions of our society concerning the role of police. Police are not supposed to adjudicate and punish; they are supposed to apprehend and take into custody. To the extent to which a nation's police step outside such bounds, that nation has given up the role of law in a self-defeating quest for order." [20]

The reality is clear, police have become hostile toward Blacks and have shown hostility toward protest groups. Those that have sought to examine the role of the police have had a basic concern. This basic concern involves why have the police reacted violently toward Blacks and protest groups?

Big Ralph noted that a police officers job is getting even more difficult. Training and other resources that would help prepare a police officer to do his job have been limited. For example many departments do not screen applicants with scrutiny. In this case many perspective officers with a psychological profile unsuitable for law enforcement are likely to end up on the police force.

One interesting phenomenon that results from the police interaction with protest movements involves the question of reform. Protest groups seek political and social reform. The police cannot solve political and social problems. Thus, conflict with the police around social and political issues often place the police in a so-called problem solving position.

On the average the new police recruit is not a cruel, savage racist. Most recruits are average young men and ladies who are decent citizens. One problem that limits the pool of positive recruits is the low pay scale. Thus, many recruits are undereducated. The complex problems of today pose a dilemma for many police officers that are not educated and have only a basic skill level.

Many social scientists argue that the stress of police work is compounded by lack of skills. Even the well trained and well-educated officer will encounter stress on the job. Those ill trained and less prepared will be hampered by stress to an even greater degree. Stress and pressure of police work lead to early retirements. Generally most officers retire when they are eligible.

Big Ralph

There are some arguments also that work force needs are greatly reducing training programs in some police departments. The logic of those responsible for police training is lost in the politics of the haves and the have nots. Meanwhile, this also contributes to the strained relationship of the police and the community.

Another problem that strains the relationship of the police and the community is graft and corruption. There are dishonest people throughout society. Law enforcement as an agency also has its share of corruption. Dishonest and crooked police cause a serious distrust of the police and a lack of confidence.

The conclusions of the police and police organizations about man are also important. For example how does the police view man? Professor Skolnick notes that the police have a "rotten apple" view of man. This "rotten apple" theory applies to human nature and the behavior of man.

The conclusions of those in law enforcement that accept this view of man are grounded in the theory that some individuals are evil. Thus these evil people make wrong choices and commit crimes.

Those that refute individuals that accept this theory argue that criminal behavior can adequately be blamed on an inherent evil personality. There are various other forces, described as social factors that contribute to crime such as poverty, lack of skills/education and discrimination. Therefore the failure to include these factors in the analysis gives the police a narrow view of human behavior and supports a prejudice attitude toward the masses of society.

During the contemporary period of protest movements the police have had a direct conflict with those that advocate social reform. Social reform to law enforcement agencies and individuals that accept the "rotten apple" theory means to be soft on crime. A conservative view of social programs like welfare also becomes a part of policemen's negative outlook toward the poor. Again most of the people grouped into the "rotten apple" theories are poor. They are also further identified as racial minorities that have historically had a particular antagonistic relationship with the dominant population in America.

Chapter Twelve

Thus for law enforcement officials to deny the social and environmental factors that affect the so-called under class is an on-going public relations and or professional dilemma. From a Black perspective the police in this instance are viewed as an enemy that comes into their community to abuse and assault them.

It is also important to further describe the law enforcement view of society. Law enforcement literature refute the existing social problems in society. They do not recognize legitimate dissent. They generally conclude that organized protest is a conspiracy and inspired by communists. Thus some contented people are misled and turned into hard headed agitators.

"Such an approach has serious consequences. The police are led to view protest as illegitimate misbehavior, rather than as legitimate dissent against policies and practices that might be wrong. The police are bound to be hostile to illegitimate misbehavior, and the reduction of protest remains to be seen as their principle goal. Such an attitude leads to more rather than less violence; and a cycle of greater and greater hostility continues." [21]

Skolnick describes this as the "agitational" theory. Thus, this theory of protest leads to particular circumstances and conclusions by the police:

"1. The police are prone to under estimate both the protester's numbers and the depth of feeling.

2. In line with the "agitational" theory of protest, particular significance is attached by police intelligence estimates to the detection of leftists or outsiders of various sorts. And also the indications of organization and prior planning and preparation." [22]

The confusion of law enforcement officials regarding the communist's threat is clearly seen in the views of the infamous and legendary founder of the FBI.

"J. Edgar Hoover (Sept. 18, 1968) stated to the Cox Commission "communists are in the forefront of civil rights, anti-war, and student demonstrations, many of which ultimately become disorderly and erupt into violence." [23]

Big Ralph

Skolnick further notes that there is a reason the police constantly claim that left wing agitators are a part of all protest movements. In this instance the police broadly define radical and/or leftists and basically for all practical purposes inadequately define the term. Thus these narrow minded law enforcement officers cannot and do not distinguish between dissent and submission.

The political involvement of the police is also a factor that affects the relationship of the police to the community. Often their careers are based on certain political actions. The police are also an extension of the legal arena.

The basic duty of the police is to arrest people that are violating written laws. The courts then have the responsibility to bring the person to trial and render a decision on the person's guilt or innocence. Many observers of police behavior note that the police believe (many police believe in the "rotten apple" theory) that those that they arrest are guilty and should be punished.

The militant behavior of the police results from a conservative view of society. Whether the existing, political apparatus (city government) supports these views, the police can and often resort to violence when they confront protest movements.

The police have advocated police review boards to offset police violence. The public feel that an independent board of citizens should review actions by the police that cause conflict among the citizens. On the other hand the police feel that they are isolated from the community. They feel that they have a job to do but the public is interfering with their authority.

Anyway police officers stick together and abide by an unwritten code of conduct. Good officer's cover-up for corrupt and bad officers who abuse authority and commit criminal acts. Various instances of misconduct especially police brutality has caused the public in many cities to ask for civilian police review boards. Meanwhile, the police in most communities have defeated all efforts to be examined by independent civilian review boards.

Chapter Twelve

The attitude of the police is a result of various factors. In summation we see that the police are an over worked and under paid group in our society. These same people are commissioned to do one of the most critical jobs in our society. But they are often undertrained and undereducated. Also, as noted earlier in this chapter most police have a conservative view of society.

"This view gives little consideration to the effects of such social factors as poverty and discrimination and virtually ignores the possibility of legitimate social discontent. Typically, it attributes mass protest instead to a conspiracy promulgated by agitators, often communists, who misdirect otherwise contented people. This view, disproven so many times by scholars and distinguished commissions, tends to set the police against dissident groups, however lawful." [24]

The judicial system also takes on some attitudes of the police. The courts also view those that are in the protest movement differently. The courts are sanctioned to protect the rights and liberties of it's citizens. Civil disobedience and civil disorder have caused a great challenge to the courts.

Professor Skolnick makes the following comment regarding the judicial system. "For the courts, the fundamental problem is that they are organized to do one sort of task adjudicating and in civil disorders they are asked to deal with the outcome of political conflict as if it were only a criminal matter. Under such conditions, they often become and are perceived as an instrument of power rather than law." [25]

The previously mentioned examples of police attitudes is something all police departments are confronted with. This was also true for Deputy Chief Cothran and the Chattanooga Police Department. Thus, the conflict between the races continued. For example Blacks continued to honor Martin Luther King and many white people felt too honor King with a national holiday was a crime.

"A day after the first holiday honoring King a Black family awakened to find a burnt cross in their yard. Over holiday weekend Klan members drove through Black neighborhoods playing Dixie." [26]

Big Ralph

The following year the outcry against police brutality was again in the news. "Concerned Citizens for Justice (Lorenzo Ervin) plan to march to protest police brutality. Call for nation wide economic and tourism boycott. Group claims Chattanooga Police Department have shot and killed 14 Blacks and eight whites since 1978. Police figures show nine people, five Blacks and four whites that have been fatally shot. Since February 1985 when the U.S. Supreme Court struck down a Tennessee law that permitted shootings to halt fleeing felony suspects, there has been one fatal shooting-city officer returned fire with white suspects-reports police." [27]

The police Department no doubt was affected by the public outcry against police brutality. "Fraternal Order of Police was concerned about inflammatory literature urging reprisals against the police. They asked the city Commission to review whether distribution of such material could be stopped." [28]

Ralph was not yet the Chief of Police. He was appointed Deputy Chief in 1983 and would not become Chief until 1989. Ralph had been forming his theories on prevention of crime for some time. Ralph was interested in wholesome programs for youth. He often said "that an ounce of prevention is worth a pound of cure." It is for sure that Big Ralph did not just want to lock up criminals, he wanted to prevent young men from becoming criminals. Thus, he began to develop various recreational programs. His greatest vision was to develop multipurpose recreational facilities in various inner-city communities.

While working as a narcotic's detective in 1969 Ralph saw the devastation of many young people. Many of these young people were Black males. He felt that something had to be done to help these young people choose something else besides crime and drugs.

Ralph had a fruitful background of working with youth programs. He had also been greatly influenced by Pearl Vaughn who was a legendary Center Director at Lincoln Park. Thus Ralph had a vision for youth programs that went back to his days as a youth.

The greatest vision Ralph had about youth programs was to use many school buildings that had been closed down. There were two

Chapter Twelve

schools in particular that Ralph wanted to develop into youth recreational complexes: Charles A. Bell in Alton Park and James A. Henry on the westside.

Ralph wanted to develop these two closed schools and sought to do so by going through the necessary political channels. Meanwhile Ralph organized a Police Athletic League and established Explorer Scout Posts for Chattanooga area youth. Regarding his vision for broad based recreational facilities he continued to look for support. There was some support on the City Council for Ralph's youth programs but there was no viable move to develop the schools for recreational outlets in the two communities.

Any way before we speculate on the attitude of dissent there is a glimpse of Ralph Cothran's vision. He wanted the schools developed on a grand scale. Since the physical buildings would allow plenty of space Ralph wanted the school equipped to provide an assortment of recreational activities.

Many recreational activities would be in the competitive sports, such as boxing. Also these community recreational units would be a proving ground to maintain on-going positive community relations. Here a police precinct would also be moved in the building.

The vision of recreational activities for youth in low-income areas was to Ralph a sure way to help prevent young people from entering into criminal activity. But his dream and vision were ignored. Why would politicians and other officials feel that recreation has no viable affect on crime prevention?

Historically in Chattanooga and in most cities in the U.S. recreation was seen as a deterrent to crime. Simply because if a young person spent most of his leisure time playing sports he would not have the time nor the energy to be involved in juvenile delinquency. This was not a guaranteed crime prevention method but it had tremendous impact on positive youth development.

Why would the city recreation department decide that viable recreational programs in inner-city neighborhoods were no longer needed? Most likely recreational facilities are needed more now than

Big Ralph

they were in 1950 and 1960. The contemporary age of protest for human and civil rights also caused city bureaucracies like Chattanooga to conclude recreation was no longer needed in the inner-city.

This is the same inner-city filled with youth related violence. Widespread drug use and the drug traffic have caused many young people involved in these activities to become armed with very dangerous firearms. They use these weapons on each other and on innocent people.

So why would a society faced with an epidemic of youth crime and violence conclude that prevention methods like recreation are outdated and useless? In Chattanooga the city recreation budget show large sums of money spent on recreational facilities and programs in affluent areas where mostly white people live. For example there is considerable funding for city golf courses. Very few Black people play golf. First of all Blacks don't have the leisure time nor the money to buy the equipment.

So the reality is that there is still money available for recreation in the city. The city officials don't feel that the inner city should have any viable recreational outlets. These are the same officials that complain about the high incidence of crime and violence in areas where many minorities reside.

Many times when white people in power come to possess a strange attitude about Blacks, they also seek some consolation in having a Black idiot share their views. During the latter 70's a Negro by the name of Eugene Medley became the manager of the Alton Park Housing Projects (which is the largest housing project in the city, incidentally all public housing units are now predominately Black in Chattanooga). Medley spoke at a Chattanooga Chamber Commerce luncheon one day and informed the white business community and other civic leaders that the Black kids in Alton Park would tear up recreational equipment.

This strange thinking in a community that houses a multitude of low income youth is destined for problems. Because, the young people will find something to do and in many cases it will be negative behavior. Meanwhile, the city warehouses tons of recreational equipment and

Chapter Twelve

have a no hope don't "give a damn" attitude toward Black inner-city youth. These are the same people that cry and complain about youth related crime and violence. Evidently the majority are saying build more prisons and jails and lock young people up for life with no chance of parole.

Ralph didn't believe that more prisons and jails were the key ingredient toward dealing with the youth. For example the DARE Program was established by the Chief to go into the schools to teach young people about drug prevention. In this case Ralph established a special department to handle this program. A group of hand picked dedicated and informed officers were selected to operate this program that is highly regarded as a distinct learning tool in the Chattanooga Public Schools.

Another unique idea was the creation of police cards. Police cards are similar to baseball cards and hope to render the same type of appeal and attraction to young people. The Chattanooga Police Departments police cards have the pictures of various officers and brief information. For example Chief Cothran's card noted: on the front a picture of the Chief, on the back is the address and telephone number of the Chattanooga Police Department and the Chiefs badge number. The bottom of the card notes personal information, like "Big Cheese" Ralph's nickname. "Chief says, stay in school, study hard, do what your parents tell you and just say no to drugs. Hobbies, reading and basketball.

The Chiefs' card along with other high ranking officers were prized cards to collect. Many officers down through the ranks had cards also. So kids could collect a variety of cards from the various personnel of the department.

Ralph also believed in outreach programs, especially outreach programs to the schools. Ralph really enjoyed talking with young people in various schools. He was often invited to share information about the police department at various schools. The special patrol units within the department caused a lot of excitement for the kids. So the Chief would always take members of his Mounted Patrol, Motorcycle Patrol and Bicycle Patrol to the various schools.

Big Ralph

Chief Cothran was one of the first police Chiefs in the nation to establish a bicycle patrol. This patrol was established in 1989 soon after he became Chief. All of the previously mentioned programs were designed to prevent crime. The bicycle patrol is additional evidence of police presence on the streets to prevent crime. Crime prevention is also revealed in another program that renders a police presence.

The idea of police precincts and/or substations within the community had been around for a long time. Chattanooga had never had police precincts until Chief Cothran took over the CPD. At first the Chief had problems with the mayor regarding work force needs related to the precincts. The mayor felt that police manpower could be best used patrolling the streets especially the affluent areas where white people lived.

The Chief was persistent and he fought back. Boone Hysinger (now known as Harriet Tubman Homes) was one of the most drug infested areas in Chattanooga. Harriet Tubman Homes is all Black and numerous crack cocaine dealers had virtually taken over selected areas of the housing project. It was also rumored that even the management of Harriet Tubman was involved in the illegal drug traffic.

The crack dealers who numbered from 10 to 20 people selling drugs at a time had established themselves on a corner entrance to the projects. They had also influenced three tenants to allow them to use their apartments to sell drugs. So the crack dealers sold drugs from the street, and rendered curb service as cars pulled up to stop and cop drugs twenty-four hours a day. Various apartments provided sanctuary for the drug dealers, where they replenished their supplies, smoked the drugs, hid drugs and rested from their round the clock drug activities. Of course the young women who resided in these units were crack addicts. They thrived on this trade of drugs, in so doing they were paid in drugs for the use of their apartments. Sex was also used to win favors for drugs from the drug dealers and those that bought drugs from the dealers.

But this entrenched drug traffic was halted and eliminated with the establishment of a police precinct in Harriet Tubman Homes. The housing units that were used to sell drugs were closed down and

Chapter Twelve

boarded up. The Crack dealers with no housing units for sanctuary and the presence of police within the housing units vanished.

Many of the theories and ideas conceived by Chief Cothran as he established various police precincts were carried over to other programs. The "Police/Community Partnerships" was established city-wide. This program took neighborhood by neighborhood and organized them to fight crime and deal with inner city problems.

In this instance Ralph definitely needed help from other agencies. He made a direct appeal to the ministers of the city. This appeal spoke of the crime and violence of young people. His appeal was all for naught. Since his death there is some evidence that some ministers are heeding his judgment. We will mention more about this in the concluding chapter.

Big Ralph

Group picture of first Black police officers 1948. Walter Robinson Black newspaper publisher and political leader with suit on.

New recruits in front of City Hall 1964, Ralph back row 2nd from left.

Chapter Twelve

New Officers 1964, Ralph back row 2nd from left.

Ralph at crime scene as patrol officer.

Big Ralph

The Big Three from left Ralph, Frank Newson, and Napoleon (Doughout) Williams.

Recruiting program 1974, Ralph 2nd from left.

Chapter Twelve

Stephen and Cyzanne at Uncle Gerald Patton's wedding August 22, 1970

David's graduation from kindergarten June 8, 1980.

Ralph & Catherine at Cyzanne's Graduation from Notre Dame High School May 21, 1981

Mrs. Bessie Cothran and David.

Big Ralph

Ralph & Catherine on vacation in Miami 1989.

Grand children Stefano & Natalia Christmas 1991. The son & daughter of Stephen Cothran.

Catherine graduates from Covenant College May 1994. Ralph back row from left Cornelia Willis (close family friend) and sister Barbara Patton.

Ralph hugs Rev. Andrew J. Bullard Jr. at his pastor Appreciation Banquet July 8, 1992.

Big Ralph talks with demonstrators outside City Hall.

Retirement party for Fire & Police Commissioner Tom Kennedy 3rd from left 1989. From left C.B. Robinson & Asst. Chief Ted Wheeler.

Chapter Twelve

Swat Team July 1987. Commander Sgt. Bill McCleary. Deputy Chief in-charge Ralph Cothran back row Center. Deputy Chief (communication) Ervin Dinsmore left back row. Commissioner Tom Kennedy 2nd row right.

Appreciation Party for Ralph when he was appointed Chief & Ervin Dinsmore appointment as Director of Public Safety in 1989. Ralph (L)& Napolean (Doughnut) Williams (R)

Big Ralph meets the media outside City Council Chambers City Hall.

School Patrol Officer of the year 1987. Chief Cothran on the left and Chief Peggy Bullard on the right.

Combat Pistol Team Winners September 3, 1987.

Neighborhood Watch Outing 51 South Crest Rd. August 1989.

Big Ralph

Chapter 13

The Leadership Ranks: Parallels Of Crime And Civil Rights

*Surely the goodness of human rights,
that should be known to all of mankind,
Oh the wretched soul of man,
To disobey the just and unjust, Oh, what is justice?
Imperfection is the son of man who turns the positive
into negative,
Hail the joy of blessings to those among them that
know the way to eternal life.*

When Ralph Cothran was appointed Chief in 1989 Chattanooga was also on the eve of another historical occurrence. The following year Chattanooga would make the change from a discriminatory commission form of government to a more democratic councilmatic form of government.

The first Black Chief in the history of Chattanooga would also see a democratic representation of Blacks on the new City Council. Thus Chattanooga seemed to be on the move. Certainly the Chattanooga Police Department was greatly improved with the appointment of Cothran to Chief. But politics is a game of roulette at times, and in Chattanooga since 1911 there has been a on-going effort to control the electorate.

Big Ralph

By and large those that control the electoral arena also have the economic power. In this case all of the dynamic aspects of life are manipulated by those that hold the reins of power in Chattanooga.

The Times stated that Cothran's "first task as Chief will be to improve officer's morale and mend any rifts between the community and the department." [1]

The Chief's vision was to build morale on the force and cause a positive reaction to law enforcement officers by the community. Then the community the Chief envisioned could become their advocates and help them in the fight against crime and drugs.

These were the things the new Chief was saying publicly to the press and to the people of Chattanooga. In reference to the Black community the Chief was anxious to get on with his new duties. Big Ralph was happy to inform Black people that now they had a friend and somebody they could trust in the Chiefs' office. He went to a lot of neighborhood meetings and listened to the concerns of all the people. He gained the respect of white people because he also sincerely saw the needs of the white community. As a great visionary Ralph had a vision toward police working with the community they served for a long time. Throughout his career he had a vision and throughout his career supporters also saw this vision.

Meanwhile, he got many letters and other forms of correspondence from many people in private and public life. Many letters responded to Ralph reaching a milestone or advancement in rank. The first letter is from a former employer. Ralph worked for Fillauer, a large drugstore while he attended high school. The following are a brief sampling of the letters, Ralph received throughout his career, they mark significant periods in his life:

Chapter Thirteen

Letter from local businessman George William Fillauer
March 30, 1973
Dear Lt. Cothran:
We were much pleased to read of your appointment to the FBI Academy. Our good wishes for you. I enclose an article on crime in this Weeks "Time" you will like to read it.
Sincerely
G. W. Fillauer

Ralph received many letters and cards when he became Deputy Chief. The following is a very interesting letter from a former professor at Cleveland State Community College.
May 24, 1983
Dear Ralph:
I was certainly pleased to learn of your appointment as Deputy Chief of Police of the city of Chattanooga. Little did I think during those years when you, Tom and Gene were in my class that you would practically be running Chattanooga. You should feel very proud of yourself because you certainly have done well. My sincere congratulations and best wishes.
Sincerely,
James M. Stubbs

A local radio talk show host sent the Chief the following note.
October 21, 1991
Chief Cothran,
I think you are doing a good job for our city. My parents appreciate your interest in the elderly and their safety.
Thank you
Earl Freudenburg

Ralph received support from a variety of sources. The following letter is very interesting. The letter was actually written to the Chief's wife but the writer made special reference to the Chief. The letter is from

Big Ralph

one of the elderly members of their church, Orchard Knob Missionary Baptist. The following is an excerpt that pertains to the Chief.
December 12, 1994
Dear Mrs. Cothran,
Please tell your husband and that I do keep up with his job activities and feel that he makes some sound basic decisions and I think a change is in the making because of his leadership if he just keeps the faith. For I am praying for him. I want him to be the one to change the crime ratio in the city.

Black leadership can make a difference. Continue to persuade churches and other Black social organizations to help. Valuable information is given in the adult Sunday school class to help one to make basic decisions in his work day or business activities. If not the young adult class I think any class will give added insight and better understanding of the scripture which will help you to continue to make right choices. Do find time to attend Sunday school.

The letter is from Mrs. A. B. Locke. In this letter Mrs. Locke is appealing to the spiritual side of the Chief. Catherine attends church and Sunday school on a regular basis but the Chief was a very private person and shyed away from public gatherings except work related activities.

No doubt Ralph was a very spiritual person in his own quiet way. His compassion for his fellowman caused him great anxiety. Catherine, his wife as a faithful member of her church and a serious Christian knew that God was the answer for any problems they faced. I say they because a law enforcement officer's wife is also affected by the stress of their job.

Catherine had over the years dealt with many problems that all police officers' wives are confronted with. But when Ralph became Chief he had more responsibility and she also was more affected by his job. The Chief's job was more stressful.

For example a Chief may have night calls at any hour of the night. Swat calls also may come at any time. For the record Big Ralph was very proud of the special units within the Chattanooga Police Department. The Chattanooga Swat Team was very special to him. Big Ralph also was proud of the Mounted Patrol, The Bike Patrol and the Motorcycle

Chapter Thirteen

Patrol. These units and other special units were made up of the elite on the force and Big Ralph took special pride in identifying the cream of the crop to serve on these units. The Chief was also called to duty whenever a police officer was injured on duty. Death notifications were also a part of police work that could bring on depression and anxiety.

Many problems Catherine faced were a part of the job and she clearly understood. But corrupt police officers who made harassing phone calls was something she never got used to. Many officers that resorted to making harassing phone calls had been disciplined or fired. Their family members were also a source of anxiety because often they did not understand the circumstances of the decision to fire an officer.

Making decisions was a big part of the Chief's job. Catherine knew that Ralph had a burning compassion for people. Thus, he constantly had anxiety over the results of his decisions. You could not please everyone but the Chief if he had his way he would have wanted everyone to be happy.

Catherine as a Chief's wife also witnessed on-going battles between the police top administration and low ranking officers who were dissatisfied for a variety of reasons. Catherine surmised that these problems are things you have to contend with when you are a wife of a Chief of police.

She also realized that the stress and anxiety that affected her husband also had an affect on her. Thus, Catherine was very concerned about Ralph's health. As a former nurse she had all the skills to help Ralph with his health problems. Ralph was a diabetic and needed insulin shots daily. [2]

Thus Catherine knew that they needed to do something that would help off set some problems they encountered. She noted to Ralph frequently that exercise, sports activity and vacations were some ways to fight the stress of police work. Catherine as a loyal and dutiful wife also tried her best to inform her husband that "the job is not your whole life."

Ralph loved to eat and drink, the stress of the job began to impact on him significantly when he became Chief. He suffered from diabetes and

Big Ralph

high blood pressure. Thus, Big Ralph's eating and drinking habits conflicted with these two ailments. He enjoyed drinking and Ralph eventually began to use alcohol to blot out the depressing aspects of police work. Catherine remembers that she began to worry and started praying a lot to gain strength to deal with this problem. She sought help and finally decided that there is nothing you can do no matter how much you love your husband if they do not seek help themselves and/or admit they need help. But Ralph put the city of Chattanooga before any health concerns. Thus, his need for help regarding the abuse of alcohol was not a priority. Catherine notes that "Ralph literally gave his life to Chattanooga." His personal health needs and family came after his concern for his job and the city of Chattanooga.

Ralph loved his job and he had a torrid love affair with Chattanooga. For example as previously noted in chapter 11, when Ralph completed training at the FBI Academy, they asked Ralph to stay on as a swimming instructor. He refused the offer because he wanted to come back to Chattanooga to help his city.

Meanwhile Chief Cothran carried a heavy burden on his shoulders. The stress and the anxiety would eventually cause other health problems. His dedication to duty placed his health far behind the call of being Chief and attending to, police work.

No doubt Ralph was a great thinker. He formed distinct theories over the years that are very interesting. I have already given a background discussion of various aspects of the civil rights movement. Also, we have shed some light on other social phenomenon that affect us over time.

It is one thing for me as a social scientist to view occurrences throughout the urban landscape of America. But for someone who has had a long career in law enforcement to review social phenomenon is truly a look on the other side.

Ralph had a particular concern about the plight of the public schools. Ralph strongly believed that public schools aided in forming the character of young people. Positive experiences in a public educational setting would be surmised as a deterrent to crime.

Chapter Thirteen

Ralph felt that the destruction of public education in Chattanooga and throughout America came in 1954. School integration ushered in a new era. This era resulted in more white control of Black schools and the rise of private schools to accommodate the multitude of white students who fled the public schools in droves throughout America.

Meanwhile the schools who now serviced a small percentage of white students left the predominantly Black schools to the buzzards. Truant officers were done away with to save money. White people took away certain services such as eye exams and dental care. A leading anti-Christ monster by the name of Madeline O'hara also lead the fight to take prayer out of the schools. Some states are fighting this issue and trying to bring prayer back to the schools. [3]

When Ralph was growing up there was an abduance of male teachers in the school system. Many of these teachers were promoted to the Central office. Also paperwork became more important than the students.

Meanwhile, no emphasis was placed on colleges producing more male teachers. If male teachers were more important they should have been paid more. There was an attack on athletics. The role models were taken away with the no pass no play law.

After integration the schools also ceased to sponsor all types of recreation. When Ralph first attended school there were recreational activities from tennis to card games too square dancing to swimming and not just basketball, football and baseball.

In summary the integration of public schools in America caused most white parents to send their children to private schools. For some reason public schools then for the most part became something other than educational facilities. The result of education becoming of minor importance in pubic schools definitely has affected the character and outlook of recent generations.

For example schools have historically been a very important institution in our society. So much so that parents have taken for granted that schools would combine forces with the home, in preparing young people for the trials and tribulations of life. The reality is that since 1954

Big Ralph

public schools in Chattanooga and throughout America for the most part have become social gathering places for young people. In turn (especially in the high schools) teachers just try to keep the students from exploding and creating uncontrolled discipline problems.

The civil rights movement began soon after the 1954 decision to integrate the public schools in America. So by 1955 the organized civil rights movement began breaking laws. Power in numbers (mass demonstrations) were used because the system was unable to handle it. This taught children that it was OK to violate the law if they don't agree with it.

So during the civil rights movement there was a direct assault on law and order. The SDS (Students For A Democratic Society) began to assault the police verbally, such as calling them pigs etc.

The result was that the enemy became the police, the protectors of law and order. When this happened, the police were so bombarded with keeping law and order that they began eliminating different departments to keep more soldiers on the streets. One of the first departments eliminated was Crime Prevention and Public Relations Divisions.

Meanwhile, the school system also began to cut down on what they felt were non essential personnel such as social workers, and psychiatric nurses. The onslaught of violence throughout America has been harmful to young people. Unfortunately children watch violence in their own families and on TV without counseling being given to them.

Community based, policing was noted by Ralph as a vital tool in positive community relations with the police force. Community based policing started over 40 years ago. Beat walking allowed the police to get to know the people in the community. During contemporary times a vast amount of modern technological advancements took the police off the beat.

Thus, the police lost an interaction with the community. Presently we are involved in a new phenomenon called community policing. This new phenomenon is nothing more than what was started over 40 years ago.

Welfare is another issue that has a direct affect on the poor. Welfare also has an indirect affect on those in society with wealth. Because those

Chapter Thirteen

conditioned to receive welfare will resort to crime if their welfare checks are interrupted. The policy makers have created a monster. Most welfare recipients are females with dependent children. If children are born a male has to be involved. The men who have impregnated welfare mothers are usually human beings that seek life by taking from others. It is for sure that if welfare ceases to exist these young men will resort to more crime of property. In answer to the question why I make the following point. The young adult men who rely on welfare for drugs, alcohol, food and shelter will commit crimes to gain these necessities if welfare no longer exist. It is for sure that many of these young men are habitual criminals and they will commit more crimes to survive in the event of a welfare crisis.

Ralph felt that we lost our direction in welfare. Because welfare was originally designed to help people get back on their feet. Welfare now penalizes people for trying to get off welfare. For example if you get a job the money is taken away.

Drugs and crime were also an area where Ralph formed some distinct positions. For example he noted that America fought a war over oil in the Middle East but we don't do anything about the people shipping cocaine into the U. S. Therefore the problem of drugs is not in the inner cities it is at the borders.

There is also talk and ongoing efforts to build even more prisons for the criminals that we have created. We are graduating criminals every day. What we really need is crime prevention. Some foolish people see crime prevention as a means to showcase well known athletes.

For example athletes are constantly giving inspirational speeches about their drug rehabilitation. These athletes should be ostracized and not allowed to do it. First a 30-day drug rehabilitation program for someone who has been addicted to cocaine over a year is ridiculous. No one can rid an addiction to any narcotic substance in that length of time. It takes over 30 days to become oriented to a drug rehabilitation program. Treatment for addiction problems ranges from six months to a year at least.

Our efforts toward crime prevention took a serious blow when prayer was taken out of the schools. Also, this was a serious assault on

Big Ralph

the church. Society blindly is tearing down things that can help us prevent crime. Consequently, our moral structure has been damaged severely.

Different church denominations are cutting down each other constantly. There is very little unity, and without peace there is no harmony. Finally television that most parents watch as much as their children promote violence.

Crime and violence are recorded daily in media sources throughout America. Many TV news broadcasts sensationalize violence to boost their ratings. Blacks are also killing each other at an alarming rate.

"For whatever reasons, and they are many and complex, large numbers of Black youngsters in America are on a rampage of killing. And they are killing mostly one another." [4]

Black people are not the only people committing violent acts that include murder. Crimes of violence extend throughout America and youth violence is on the rise. [5] As the issue of violence escalates to a frightening reality, theories on violence and studies seek to attack the problem.

So what is violence and can it be stopped? "Harvard University's educator and physician Dr. Deborah Prothrow-Stith says we live in a culture that celebrates violence." [6] A cultural tradition of celebrating violence and the priority of the law of man has no doubt helped escalate the problem of violent human behavior.

No one is immune to the madness of unbridled passion for blood and inhumanity. The movie industry is often accused of promoting violence. Here no one could argue against this position. The horror movies that thrive on the blood, guts and wild scenes are the worse. In these scenes of gore man truly celebrates violence and removes himself totally from the spiritual realm and enters the realm of hell and the devil.

American violence has also prompted studies of the safest colleges. "When choosing a college, you look at the cost of tuition, room, books and at the curriculum. Do you also check the crime rates?" [7]

There have also been studies that have focused on family slayings. "Eighty percent of murder victims are killed by acquaintances or

Chapter Thirteen

members of their own family, according to a Justice Department study." [8] The family often no doubt receives its share of the violence in America. Also, the family is also the source of prevention for many aspects of violence.

"Fathers must be involved in their children's lives to make a dent in social problems like teen pregnancy, violence and drug abuse, said Don Eberly, president of the national fatherhood initiative." [9] The sad commentary of violence and the leading cause of violence is depicted in the following excerpts from the editorial pages of the Chattanooga News Free Press.

"It is a tragic reality in modern American society that many of our people are willing, even eager, to spend billions of dollars to ruin their lives by using illegal drugs. With such a big money demand, there are plenty of crooks ready to provide an ongoing supply.

Since it's such big business, big criminal operations are involved in bringing in the destructive substances. And they are willing to corrupt many people on the way to the market, where foolish people impoverish themselves and resort to crime to buy what will bring their destruction." [10]

Drugs contribute a great deal to the statistics of violence. Often violent acts are committed at random in a callous disregard for human life. The second editorial notes:

"Nine-year-old James Darby of New Orleans lived as too many children and adults live today--in fear. He wrote to president Bill Clinton: "I want you to stop the killing in the city. I think somebody might kill me. I'm asking you nicely to stop it. I know you can do it." Unfortunately, Mr. Clinton could not--cannot. Nine days after writing his letter, James was walking home from a mother's Day parade when he was shot and killed. It was typical of crime in our streets--wanton, senseless, random vicious." [11]

The irresponsible attitude of young offenders was an ongoing dilemma for Ralph. He saw a drastic attitude change by the young generation. By 1989 when Ralph became Chief of police, he definitely had concluded that civil disobedience contributes to crime.

Big Ralph

Thus when a group of people seek to break laws for justice their attitude toward institutional authority is removed. Since the 1960's many people have been conditioned toward civil disobedience as an avenue to justice. In the process many people feel that it is all right to break the law in the interest of justice.

Some advocates of civil disobedience have said unjust laws are illegal. Thus, civil disobedience and demonstrations against these laws are justified. Despite the circumstances, civil disobedience has caused many people to develop an attitude of disrespect for law enforcement. This attitude often extends to other criminal behavior.

No doubt that the civil rights movement had a positive impact. But the results of a society conditioned to disobey the law and defy the police is an ongoing concern for law enforcement. During the days of civil rights struggle, Blacks felt victimized by white racism. Thirty years later Blacks accused other Blacks of racism.

When Ralph was appointed the first Black Deputy Chief in 1983 [12] he was on good terms with his fellow officers. Ralph had been one of the founding members of the local Black Law Enforcement Association, but by 1995 the organization that he founded attacked him and the police administration.

"The Chattanooga Law Enforcement Officers Association noted that the present administration has a lack of concern for minority police officers. In a four-page document signed by members of its executive committee, the association charged that minorities are under represented and under utilized in the local department, that too few Blacks are named to responsible positions and that opportunities for advancement and promotions are kept from minority officers, hindering further career enhancement opportunities." [13]

Chief Cothran responded to these charges and the other concerns raised by CLEOA in an eight-page letter. (See Appendix C, the compliant letter written by CLEOA, letter from State of Tennessee Human Rights Commission concerning the Compliant and Chief's Cothran response to CLEOA). The City Council supported the Chief and noted that the charges of racism were unfounded and untrue. It is a

Chapter Thirteen

fact that racism exist throughout American society. But, the charges of racism raised by CLEOA were unjustified. Most likely many members that supported these charges wanted special favors and/or automatic qualification for advancement despite test scores.

Ralph was a very sensitive man and the charges of unfair treatment toward his fellow Black officers hurt him deeply. Anxiety and worry can take a severe toll on a police officer especially a Chief of police. Ralph loved Chattanooga and for years had placed the city before his health, his family or anything else. Thus when he was unjustly accused of wrong doing by any officer, it upset him.

Catherine remembers that Ralph had a great deal of stamina and was not easily upset. These were the days of Ralph's illness, he was slowing down, and his strength was limited. The ordeal of his fellow Black officers attack on his character and the charges of Black on Black discrimination greatly affected Big Ralph. Catherine recalls that " I would like to go on record as saying, if the intentions of the Black officers were to hurt Chief Cothran they certainly did."

Catherine would often tell the Chief that "you are not made out of iron." Yes, the Chief was also human and the accusations by his fellow officers took a toll on him. The Chiefs record will show how hard he worked to promote fairness between the races and between male and females on the force. He surely was not prejudiced.

By the spring of 1995 other charges surfaced. These charges were more serious because they were criminal. The Chief became aware of rumors that he was being charged with corruption by federal investigators. The charges of corruption centered on the misuse of funds allocated for drug investigations etc.

Ralph was very upset about the rumors, but he knew that he was innocent. As Chief he was supposed to handle the drug fund but this authority was placed in the hands of his immediate supervisor the Director of Public Safety, Ervin Dinsmore. Mr. Dinsmore's immediate supervisor was the mayor, Gene Roberts who took a hands on approach to his administrative responsibilities toward the police department.

Big Ralph

Also Ralph knew that he was Black and that perks open to white Chiefs would not be open to him. Ralph was also honest. This was not a quality that had any precedence in the Chiefs office, or in the office of Commissioner of Fire and Police under the old Commission system of government.

So to try to get to the bottom of the charges Ralph conceptualized a historical development of the circumstances. The following is his recollection of the events leading up to the charges of corruption.

"The first meeting, I had when I took over as Chief in 1989, was with my boss who was then Commissioner of Fire and Police and two agents from the Drug Enforcement Association. We talked about developing a Drug Task Force. They wanted to be in charge of the operation. In this we mutually agreed that drugs were the major problem causing all the crime.

I assigned two Chattanooga Police officers to DEA to work under their supervision. Shortly after that the FBI agent in charge came to my office and asked to work with us. We in turn assigned three CPD (Chattanooga Police Department) officers to work with him.

Later I was contacted by ATF. (Alcohol Tobacco and Firearms). They also wanted to work with us, I assigned one agent to work with them.

The addition of our men to the DEA doubled their size because they only had two agents. I thought the task force was a drain of man power. So I went to Knoxville and talked to the Chief FBI officer in the U.S. Attorney's office. I wanted to know-- if up the line was there one person in charge of all agencies. Within each agency the line of authority extended through their respective chain of command thus no single person controlled the task force.

I realized that everything went to the U.S. Attorney's office for prosecution. I concluded that if all agencies bring evidence to the U.S. Attorney, his office could work as a clearing house to bring all evidence and information together. Since all agencies are working independently, the U.S. Attorney can combine related evidence from different agencies and bring cases together for successful prosecution. The U.S. Attorney

Chapter Thirteen

agreed to do it. The Hamilton County District Attorney's office cross-trained a man to help him with the cases.

At this point I was pleased that the Task Force began to take shape. The FBI would pursue long-range cases, the top echelon of the drug trade. The DEA and ATF would handle the middle level drug cases. Finally the CPD would take care of street pushers and quick arrest cases.

The Task Force went along fine for a while and then it began to fall apart. At first we were one of the leading jurisdictions in the U. S. for the successful prosecution of drug cases.

One of our officer's assigned to the FBI began to cause problems. He had visions of taking over our narcotic's division and had a serious ego problem. We concluded that the man was a crook and was giving the FBI misinformation. Meanwhile, he was stealing drug money and creating bad blood among his fellow officers.

Dinsmore handled the money for the agent to operate. My job was to handle the information submitted by the different agents. After the operation called "Chatter Box" we found out that the agent in question was stealing money regularly. The auditors came out to check our books. We were not satisfied with the auditor's report and called in the TBI (Tennessee Bureau of Investigation) to investigate the situation.

We had previously called in the TBI to investigate gambling in Chattanooga. They had some successes and had called in the IRS several times. No one knew about these investigations except myself, Dinsmore and a U.S. Attorney.

The FBI eventually took over the investigation of the crooked officer and the stolen drug money. The accused officer began to tell different stories to the FBI to implicate others and to take the blame away from himself.

The FBI brought in an undercover agent to further investigate the case of the crooked officer. He investigated the case and found no evidence that anybody in our department was involved with the crooked officer and had done anything wrong. Eventually the other officers in the narcotic's division found out that the FBI undercover agent was investigating them. They in turn did not trust the officer and

Big Ralph

this created a poor working relationship. Also after the investigation was over the FBI left the undercover agent in Chattanooga to work with our department. Nobody trusted him and there was dissension within the department.

The coalition began to fall apart. Finally no agency wanted to work with any other agency. I meet with the U.S. Attorney's office and the FBI in Knoxville. They decided to call in all the bosses to try to get everybody to work together. I was not optimistic unless they got rid of certain people are transferred personnel.

Then came the rumors that I would be indicted for dealing in drugs or for some form of corruption dealing with drugs. I became very concerned about my character assassination. I felt that the source of the allegations was on Martin Luther King blvd. But I did not know who was bringing the information to people on M.L.K.

The DEA agents that worked with us retired. One of our officers that is honest was assigned to work with the DEA. This officer is now working in New Orleans. I felt that this agent could very well be the person to coordinate the Task Force and work with all parties.

Meanwhile I planned a meeting with the U.S. Attorney who was born in the Chattanooga area. I have the confidence that he will help solve the problem. I also believe that the rumors about my corruption could have come from a retired police officer. This officer hates my guts and has a daughter addicted to cocaine. Maybe we got to close to the big pushers and they started the misinformation.

I also believe that the big drug lords are giving us some people to keep us away from the top people. Our goal is to identify the people responsible for bringing the big supplies of drugs into the city. Chattanooga is not a town that cannot be cleaned up.

Presently I am working to bring the coalition back together. It seemed as if the idea of the Drug Task Force came from Janet Reno, but I believe that Bill Baugh a high official with the FBI gave them the idea.

One reason for the attack on my character is that previously there was always a Chief that would look the other way. Thus many people in Chattanooga still believe that the Chief of police is somebody you can

Chapter Thirteen

call when you get in trouble. But my job is to catch folk and put them in jail. So if you are not doing favors you are hated. So I am one of the most hated men in Chattanooga. But I don't give a damn, I have my family. I only want to clean up Chattanooga the best I can before I retire.

I do not plan to continue an investigation of the corruption rumors. I plan to continue to build the Task Force and fight drugs. Drugs are the cause of most of our crime. I also will not allow the crooks to get me involved in a turf battle or a preoccupation with the rumors of corruption. I plan to give the crooks a central place to discuss all of their plans and that place is the penitentiary.

The Task Force was loose knit. We need to be able to share information. Historically most local agencies felt that when they gave information to the FBI it went into a black hole. They never told you what they did with it and you never got anything back in return. That needs to change, we need to share both ways.

In conclusion Dinsmore and I played two separate roles. We confiscated money from various sources during drug operations. The people that deposited this money all work out of Dinsmore's office. My role was to organize the troops to go after the drug dealers." (Taped interview Chief Cothran by Carl Patton July 1995).

These were the last days of Chief Cothran. He had been stricken with diabetes some time ago and took daily shots of insulin. A few months later after the taped interview in July 1995 he was diagnosed with cancer. [13] By August of 1995 Dinsmore began to take over for the Chief as he began medical tests and treatment for his illness.

Catherine, the Chief's wife, has a disappointing testimony concerning the Chief's treatment. Catherine recalls that the chemical treatments speeded up the spread of the cancer. By November "Big Ralph" would pass on to eternal life in the Kingdom of Everlasting Peace and Paradise. His legacy was love of family and his great love of Chattanooga.

He was a God fearing man who literally gave his life for Chattanooga. Big Ralph put Chattanooga before his personal health needs. It is no doubt that Big Ralph was a true American hero and a great son of Chattanooga and a living testimony to honest law enforcement.

Big Ralph

Ralph Henry Cothran my beloved brother-in-law left the space of earth and entered the spiritual realm November 2, 1995. "It was a sad day at the Chattanooga Police Department after Chief Ralph Cothran lost his battle with cancer late Thursday. The Chief died around 9:50 p.m. at Erlanger Medical Center. He was diagnosed with cancer four months ago." [15]

Saturday the Times front page lead story noted that the Chief tried "to do the right thing at all times. "Criminals viewed him as enemy No 1, the top cop who lived to throw them in jail. But Cothran's giant size disguised his real demeanor, say friends and co-workers. He hated fights, physical or verbal. He preferred disarming confrontation with slow, quiet words and a straight forward gaze. Big Ralph even left his gun in the trunk of his car each night. He said he didn't want a gun in his house or around his children. Police officer's loved him because he tried hard to keep politics out of their work. Critics praised him for bringing sensitivity to a department under constant fire of racism. Community leaders say he brought back respect to the men and women in blue." [16]

The day after the funeral the Times and Free Press paid high tribute to "Big Ralph" again. "Tears mixed with laughter as friends, family and officials gathered to celebrate police Chief Ralph Cothran's "Homegoing" during funeral services Monday at Orchard Knob Missionary Baptist Church." [17]

On the same day the Times reported: "As the Orchard Knob Baptist Church choir clapped and rocked through the hymn I'll Fly Away, mourners dabbed at tears later, the police color guard led a riderless horse into National Cemetery. There, Chattanooga's police Chief, Ralph H. Cothran, was laid to rest." [18]

Mayor Gene Roberts in making remarks at the funeral noted that he worked with Cothran 25 years. "I never knew him to start a fight. He ended a few, though." Also making remarks was Eldridge Bell, former Chief of police in Atlanta and a long time friend of Chief Cothran. Chief Bell noted that the national organization of Black Law Enforcement Executives will honor the man who became Chattanooga's first Black Chief with the Ralph H. Cothran scholarship Fund."

Chapter Thirteen

Bill Castell a writer for the Chattanooga Times wrote a powerful tribute to Chief Cothran. The article was printed November 6, 1995, the following are some excerpts from the article.

Late October 1991 I had the opportunity to talk with Chief Cothran. He spoke of his love for Chattanooga and its people. He also spoke of how he wanted so badly to be able to bring the city's drug problem under control, and how he so often found his work personally rewarding.

He spoke not of drug busts or major arrests when talking of the rewards, but about young people that he had some how helped along the way to grow up and become good citizens, ministers in some cases.

Then (late October 1991) the media were heavily focusing on downtown crime, but though he doubted the veracity of some of the messages, he showed no animosity toward the messengers.

"The Public," he said "has given me the charge to make Chattanooga a better place to live and, as long as I'm here, I'm going to do it."

To many, his greatest contribution was the improvement of race relations in the city of Chattanooga. He went out of his way to improve the relationship of the police department with the community, especially the Black community.

This devotion to job didn't begin with his appointment as Chief. It started when he first pulled on his uniform as a rookie in 1964 and began walking a beat on what is today M.L.K. Jr. Boulevard. It was those 25 years of devotion that merited the eventual promotion to police Chief Ralph Cothran, the first of his race ever to hold that position in Chattanooga." [19]

As the city began to realize that the Chief was gone they sought ways to remember a man who truly loved Chattanooga and its citizens.

"Officer Pat O'Brien was presented the first annual Ralph H. Cothran Memorial Award. The late Chief Cothran was a strong advocate of the Epilepsy Foundation." [20]

The DARE (Drug Abuse Resistance Education) program had it's graduation ceremonies' January 25, 1996. The program was dedicated to the memory of Chief Cothran who established this program citywide.

The honors continued as the Hamilton County Commission got into

Big Ralph

the act. "It may be the most appropriate memorial for a man so often described as a gentle giant, a whole building. Acting on a proposal from Hamilton County Commissioner Sheila Harris, the County Commission Wednesday voted to name the new Emergency 911 building in honor of the late Chattanooga police Chief Ralph Cothran." [21] (The 9-1-1 Emergency Communications Center was dedicated September 1996. The Center was not named for Chief Cothran. "The lobby contains a memorial to Ralph Cothran, former Chattanooga Chief of Police and member of the 9-1-1 Board of Directors.) " This information was taken from a brochure printed for the dedication ceremonies of the 9-1-1 Center September 1996. There are also plans to erect a bust of Chief Cothran in the downtown Chattanooga Courts Building. "For having the distinct honor of being the first African American police Chief this city has known, a diverse committee of Cothran's friends and associates have announced plans to memorialize him."

Zack Wamp a young congressman from the 3rd District made a significant statement when he nominated Chief Cothran for the J.F.K. Profile In Courage Award. Congressman Wamp noted in his letter of recommendation that Black youngsters needed other role models instead of athletes and entertainers. He also noted that Chief Cothran's career was built on years of professionalism, hard work and integrity. [22] (See Appendix D Letter from Zack Wamp and recommendation from Mayor Roberts and the response from J.F.K. Profile in Courage Committee)

Most people would agree with Congressman Wamp regarding the integrity of Chief Cothran. The corruption scandal resurfaced again after the Chief had passed on. The Times reported--"Chattanooga Safety Administrator Ervin Dinsmore was called to testify before a federal grand jury Thursday about hundreds of thousands of dollars missing from the city's drug fund." [23]

The federal investigators noted that the rank and file members of the narcotic's division are not under investigation. Thus, the probe is centered on former officers and top officials in law enforcement. Earlier in this chapter and before his death the Chief made a series of statements about the missing drug money.

Chapter Thirteen

It is for sure also that because of racism by city officials Chief Cothran was not allowed the authority of his white predecessors. In this case the white administrators handled all the money. Evidently someone may have reason to try to implicate Chief Cothran to cover-up their misappropriation of the drug funds.

White racist have historically stolen money and typically attempted to place the blame on Black people. (For the record White racist are not the only people who steal money.) This tactic is not new and has been practiced every since Blacks were kidnaped and brought to America. But Chief Cothran was a talented investigator. It is for sure that in his last days of life on earth he dethroned who attempted to set him up and these people most likely also stole the drug funds.

Praise be to God Almighty that Chief Cothran had the strength in his last days to uncover the truth. Even in his death the investigation he spearheaded unfolds and the federal investigators will eventually find out the real crooks in the Chattanooga Police Department.

A few corrupt officers also cause other problems. Since the death of the Chief police abuse and harassment cases have reached an all time high. The Times reported "An internal report by the U.S. Department of Justice shows that City Police here rank among the worst in the country when it comes to citizen complaints about harassment and brutality. Armed with this study, officials; say the Justice Department could use a new law to conduct a thorough review of Chattanooga Police training, racial attitudes among officer and the effectiveness of the police Department's internal affairs division." [24]

No doubt that the city of Chattanooga has lost a great leader. As the police departments commanding officer Chief Cothran brought stability to the department. The department is now without leadership and the troops are on a rampage. During the years end that the Chief passed away the crime rate was down from the previous year. [25]

A prime example of the lack of leadership in the department since the death of Chief Cothran is an incident concerning the Muslim community. The local press reports noted that four to five young Muslim men were attacked by the police while they distributed Muslim literature in the 3600 block of Brainerd Rd. The incident occurred

Big Ralph

during the last of March 1996.

The Muslim (Nation of Islam) community in Chattanooga has been selling newspapers and have been visible to the public for years. Previously this visibility has caused no adverse reaction by the police. During Chief Cothran's tenure he made a point to understand all groups that made up the city's diverse population. Thus he had knowledge of what Muslims were taught in the Nation of Islam. Abdul Muhammad, Southern Regional Representative of the Nation of Islam came to Chattanooga in April and met with mayor and Public Safety Director Ervin Dinsmore about police brutality. Muhammad noted:

"We're the best citizens America has," he said. "We teach our people not to break laws. Not even to get a parking ticket. When we work for somebody, we give a full day's job. We don't lie. We don't steal. We don't kill. We don't drink liquor. We don't do drugs, and we don't smoke cigarettes." [26]

It is for sure that Chief Cothran knew that the Muslim community was law abiding. Chief Cothran was pleased with those that practiced law and order because he had a burning passion to lock up every crook he could lay his hands on. So a leadership vacuum has caused some indecision within the ranks but the entire department has not become totally irresponsible.

On the bright side is the stark and vivid reality of the legacy of Chief Cothran and what he stood for. This legacy is depicted in an article printed in the Times January 1996. The article notes that the bike patrol (which was established by Chief Cothran in October 1992) has been a significant tool in the project areas in establishing rapport with the youth.

Along with the bike patrol the Chief established police precincts in the project areas. The program is specially funded through the federal government. The Times noted that this program was briefly mentioned in the president's state of the Union address.

For example the program has decreased narcotics' arrests by 70% since 1991. That is when a determined coalition of police and residents prevailed to get funding for two police precinct officers and round-the-

Chapter Thirteen

clock beat officers assigned to some housing project streets. The bike patrol and police precincts have been previously noted as programs established by the Chief. The Times report is a clear testimony of the effectiveness of the programs. Thus, the legacy of Chief Cothran lives on.

Mayor Gene Roberts has played a significant role in law enforcement since he became mayor. He worked with the Chief for over 25 years. He was first elected as Fire and Police Commissioner in 1971, and was reelected in 1975. In 1979 Gov. Lamar Alexander appointed Roberts as Commissioner of the Department of Safety for Tennessee.

He came back to Chattanooga in 1983 and was elected mayor. Roberts began his fourth term as mayor in March 1993. Now Gene Roberts plans to retire. Mayor Roberts is a man who fought the change of city government to a more democratic system that would allow the Black minority equal representation. In the process he has paid off a group of Uncle Tom Black leaders to cover-up racism and manipulation of the Black electorate. This scheme of control is sanctioned by the elite economic power structure that control the pulse of Chattanooga.

No doubt Gene Roberts with his background in law enforcement has held a tight rein on the Chattanooga Police Department. It is a miracle from God that the Chief was still able to be effective in this atmosphere of racism. For example the city would not allow the Chief to have a computer in his home. Less than a year before he died the city installed a computer in his home but it was only capable of allowing the Chief to play a few card games, like solitaire. But the Chief noted that Director of Public Safety Ervin Dinsmore and the mayor had computers in their homes that would allow them access to information regarding the various city departments.

They must have thought that a Black man should not have access to information that could be pulled up on a computer hooked into the various city departments even if he was the Chief of Police. The Chief knew that if he could pull up information on the computer he could save himself a lot of time. But the mayor did not think so. So no matter what they say about the positive tenure of Gene Roberts, let's set the record

Big Ralph

straight. Gene Roberts was a plantation overseer for the elite element that control Chattanooga. If you are not familiar with the role and duties of plantation overseers go and read the volumes of literature on slavery.

Concerning Roberts impact on the police department the Times reports:

"It has never been a secret that Gene Roberts ran the Chattanooga Police Department from City Hall. He just extended his eight-year tenure as police commissioner. Now Roberts is retiring. In 10 months, the police force will face a new era. Already there has been no police Chief for more than six months, since the death of Ralph Cothran. And Public Safety Administrator Ervin Dinsmore is currently shadowed by a federal investigation of the department on his watch." [27]

Long live the legacy of the Chief. The days and times of man passes on. The last may come to be first and the first last.

Concluding Thoughts

Swept away and filled to heaven with messages for the good of mankind, comes verses of praise as we laud, glorify and magnify the Master of the universe the Ruler of the earth.

Eternal God, God of our Fathers, our Heavenly Father. We do give praise and honor to your holy name.

Our days have been well spent, but at times weary. Our faith is strong and everlasting, as is the love of our savior Jesus Christ.

Thank you for your mercy, Thank you for your kindness, for we are a people that often have found solace and peace in mis-direction.

Have mercy, O Lord that we find the straight way, the path that will render us truth, wisdom and knowledge of our ancestors and our place among the multitudes.

In our hearts, as hot as the blazing sun that shineth above, as the birds fly away, as the riders ride, we saw peace in your mercy and in the knowledge of you O Lord.

When we were locked out, hungry, thirsty and tired, we prayed and asked you, O Lord to forgive those that deceived and mistreated us.

Big Ralph

We have tried to be faithful, although
at times mis-informed, by those that work
for the enemies of Christ, but our faith is strong.

O Lord we have carried a burden like your son,
our savior Jesus Christ, down through time, we
have known the persecution of men, hence our
brethren have hung from trees of life.

To walk through rows of white soft sin,
dragging bags of blood sweat and tears,
but we looked to the sky and we saw the
North Star.

O Lord we the Black manchild still hear the cries
of our mothers, sisters and daughters heard through
the night, as lust filled the soul of those that bound us

We still prayed on, knowing that surely
God does exist, a just and merciful
God.

O Lord our master, our King on high
we will never forsake you because we are a strong
people on a journey, a mission of faith.

Down through the ages, from the beginning of time, our
brethren accepted the Messiah and some did not,
O Lord what confusion lies ahead?

We know that all people are special
unto you Almighty God that believe,
we come as always with humble hearts
giving praise and honor to you our Lord.

Conclusion

Through prayer and your written word
we will keep the lines of communication
open, for we want to be in touch with our
Lord

O Lord our God , Great Jehovah we call
your holy name, How long will this
wicked world last?

Man has lost sight of the law of
God, he is confused with the status
of man's law, he wanders like a lost sheep.

O Lord the wickness of man causes
him to seek a heaven on earth and
the worship of the idol, that are of
those days and times, of material wealth.

O Lord keep us strong to know that
the salvation of man, and his soul
is through the son and the Father
thus, the only way to eternal life.

O Lord we know that this is only the
first short leg of life's journey, we
know that everlasting life lies ahead.

No burden will be to great, O Lord,
we will make it to journey's end, no
matter how many doors that are shut

No power, no power, no power, on earth is great
enough to consume the Supreme power
of God, we are steadfast with the Master
our God the Father.

Big Ralph

The leg irons of life, the shackles of the
times, the clinging of iron and steel has
impacted strength not weakness, in
the way of the Lord

Hence our Brother went away to be
with Jesus, O Lord his life was not a
perfect life but a good life

Master you know he was a man of
God, he believed in your holy word
and your divine power

He was raised upon the teachings of
your word, he knew and accepted Christ as his
savior, O Lord do have mercy

May your mercy flow like the great
rivers of the world, to fill every cup,
runneth over

May your mercy extend like the great
sunshine, the darkness of night, that
you O Lord created.

Our hearts are not troubled, for we
know that there is always a
brighter day, we are patient
for the coming of that day

Because we know it is your decision
when we must come, O Lord we pledge
to come to you and not damnation.

Conclusion

Thank you for the revelation my Lord,
thank you for your daily and timely
blessings

We do pray with all sincerity and
with humble pride, in bowing down to
the Master of life the Lord God the
Creator of all things.
Amen.

Endnotes

Part One

Chapter One

1. Lerone Bennett, "Confrontation Black & White, Johnson Publishing Co. Inc., Chicago 1965, p .3.
2. Gerald Leinward, Editor, The Negro In the City, Washington Square Press, 1968, New York, p. 32.79.
3. Charles E. Silberman, Crisis In Black and White, Vintage Books a Division of Random House, New York, 1964, p. 75. The primary work Silberman consults concerning the parallels between Nazi concentration inmates and Black slaves is Stanley M. Elkins, Slavery A Problem In American Institutional and Intellectual Life, Univ. of Chicago Press, Chicago, 1968. Also see Kenneth M. Stampp, The Peculiar Institution: Slavery In The Ante-Bellum South, Vintage Books, New York, 1956.
4. Ibid., pp. 75-76.
5. Ibid. pp.76-77.
6. Ibid., p. 79.
7. Leinward, op. cit., p. 32.
8. Silberman, op. cit., pp. 79-80.
9. Ibid., p. 78.
10. Ibid., pp. 78-79.
11. Ibid., p. 82.

Endnotes

12. Ibid., pp. 85-86.
13. Ibid., p. 86.
14. Ibid., p. 86.
15. Ibid., p. 87.
16. Ibid., p. 87.
17. Ibid., p. 89.
18. Ibid., p. 90.
19. Ibid., pp. 91-92. Along with the works by Elkins and Stampp there are some other good sources that give a description of slavery. See Frederick Douglass, <u>Narrative of The Life of Frederick Douglass, An American Slave</u>, Doubleday & Company, Inc., Garden City, New York, 1963. The Douglass autobiography becomes most likely the most reliable book written about slavery by a former slave. Also see Booker T. Washington, <u>Up From Slavery</u>, Bantam Pathfinder Editions, New York, 1900. Washington's book is important because he was born into slavery in 1859 and does recall certain circumstances that occurred before slavery ended in 1865. The clear distinction between this work and the autobiography by Douglass is that Douglass was born into slavery in 1817 or 1818. He escaped from slavery as early as 1837. But in a clear contrast to Washington, Douglass, despite slavery did not accept an inferiority complex like Washington. Since both spoke out for leadership in the Black community their delivery exposed their interests and motivations. While Douglass was independent, strong and had the character of the field Negro, Washington was dependent, meek, and had the character of a confused Negro. <u>Black Abolitionists</u> by Benjamin Quarles, Oxford Univ. Press London, 1969 also gives specific information about slavery. Especially important is Quarles historical sketch of Black protest. Earl Conrad, <u>The Invention of The Negro</u>, Paul S., Eriksson, Inc., New York, 1966 is also an important work to review. Quarles gives a vivid account of how various circumstances caused the Black man to accept slavery and degradation and sub-consciously accept himself as a new and inferior race.

20. Lerone Bennett, op. cit., p. 25.

Big Ralph

21. Ibid., p. 25.
22. Ibid., p. 47.
23. Ibid., p. 51.
24. Ibid., p. 52.
25. Ibid., p. 54.
26. Ibid., p. 56.
27. Ibid., p. 57.
28. Ibid., p. 57.
29. Arthur C. Littleton & Mary Burger Editors, <u>Black View Points</u>, New American Library, New York, 1971, p. 25. Originally a "Letter to Harriet Beecher Stowe," March 8, 1853, published in <u>From Life and Times of Frederick Douglass</u>, DeWolfe & Fiske Co., 1892.
30. Ibid., pp. 25-26.
31. Booker T. Washington, <u>Up From Slavery,</u> Doubleday & Co., Inc., 1901, p. 154.
32. Ibid., pp. 154-155.
33. Ibid., pp. 155-156.
34. Ibid., p. 157.
35. Littleton & Burger, Editors op. cit., p. 32. Originally an article wrote by Washington that appeared in <u>The Negro Problem</u>, James Potts & Co., 1903.
36. Ibid., p. 32.
37. Ibid., pp. 32-33.
38. Ibid., p. 33.
39. Ibid., p. 42. Originally printed in The Douglass Monthly, V. 1863, pp. 833-36.
40. Ibid., pp. 42-43.
41. Ibid., p. 43.
42. Ibid., p. 54. Originally an article printed in "The Crisis," "The Immediate program of The American Negro," IX April 1915, pp. 310-12. Also see other writings by DuBois, <u>The World and Africa</u>, 1946, <u>Souls of Black Folk, 1903, and "Black Reconstruction, 1935.</u>
43. Ibid., pp. 55-57.
44. Ibid., p. 57-58.

Endnotes

45. Ibid., p. 58.
46. Ibid., p. 59. Originally an article written by DuBois printed in the Crisis XLI, January 1934, p. 20, titled "Segregation."
47. Ibid., p. 59.
48. Ibid., p. 60.
49. Ibid., pp. 62-63. Originally taken from The Philosophy and Opinions of Marcus Garvey, Frank & co., LTD., London, 1967. There are also several other works on Garvey. Edmond David Cronon, Black Moses: The Story of Marcus Garvey and the Universal Negro Improvement Association, Madison: The University of Wisconsin press, 1955. The most important works on Garvey are found in a scholarly review of Garvey by, Adolph Edwards, P.T.O., Marcus Garvey, 1887-1940, London: New Beacon Publication, 1967, and Amy Jacques-Garvey, Garvey and Garveyism, Kingston: A. Jacques Garvey, 1963, a helpful account by his wife.
50. Ibid., p. 66.
51. Ibid., pp. 64-66.
52. Ibid., Amy Jacques-Garvey, editor, Philosophy and Opinions of Marcus Garvey, Atheneum, New York, 1970, pp. 29-30.
53. Joanne Grant, Editor, Black Protest-History Documents, and Analyses 1619 To Present, Fawcett Publications, Inc., 1968, pp. 59-60. Also see Herbert Aptheker, ed., A Documentary History of the Negro People in the United States, The Citadel Press, Inc., New York, 1951, pp. 19-20.
54. Ibid. p. 93. originally a speech titled "Speech Against Segregated Transportation," by Charles Lenox Redmond. Reprinted in "The Liberator," Feb. 25, 1842.
55. Ibid., pp. 96-97. Taken from the works of Charles Sumner "The Sarah Roberts Case Against Segregated Education" (Excerpts from "Equality before the law: unconstitutionality of separate colored schools in Massachusetts"), argued before the Supreme Court of Mass. Dec. 4, 1849.
56. Ibid., pp. 98-99.
57. Benjamin Munn Ziegler, Desegregation and The Supreme

Big Ralph

Court,"D.C. Heath & Co., 1958, pp. 37-42.
58. Ibid., p. 42. Also see Edward S. Corwin, and Jack W. Peltason ,Understanding The Constitution, Holt, Rinehart and Winston, Inc., 1964, p. 147.
59. Ibid., p. 42. Also see Corwin & Peltason, op. cit., pp. 148-156.
60. Corwin & Peltason, op. cit., p. 159.
61. Joanne Grant, op. cit., p.159.
62. Ibid., p. 159.
63. Silberman, op. cit. pp. 6,7.
64. Bennett, op. cit., p. 86.
65. C. Vann Woodward, op, cit., p. 6.
66. Joanne Grant, op. cit., p. 165. Also see "A Negro attorney Testifies Against Segregated Travel, 1883." Senate report on Labor and Capital, testimony, Vol. IV, p. 382 1883. Statement of J. A. Scott of Birmingham, Ala. In Walter L. Fleming, Documentary History of Reconstruction New York: McGraw Hill Book Co. 1966, pp. 446-47. First published by Arthur H. Clark, Cleveland, 1906-07
67. Benjamin Munn Ziegler, op. cit., pp. 49-56. Also see Joanne Grant, Editor History, Documents, and Analyses 1619 To Present, Fawcett Publications, Inc., 1968, pp. 170-173.
68. C. Vann Woodward, op. cit., p. 7.
69. Ibid., p. 17.
70. Ibid. p. 20.
71. Lerone Bennett, op. cit., p. 96.
72. Ibid., p. 97. Also see Ginzburg's, 100 Years of Lynchings.
73. Ibid., p. 104.
74. Ibid., p. 104.
75. Joanne Grant op. cit. p. 203. "National Negro Committee Criticizes Booker T. Washington" 1910. See A Documentary History of the Negro People in the United States, Herbert Aptheker, ed. New York: The Citadel Press, 1951, pp. 884-886. A printed brochure, Race Relations in the United States, 1910 in DuBois MSS.
76. C. Vann Woodward, op. cit., p. 85.
77. Ibid., p. 95.

Endnotes

78. Joanne Grant, op cit., pp. 207-209. "The Niagara Movement Declaration of Principles," 1905 statement probably drafted by Dr. W.E.B. DuBois, the founder of the Niagara movement.
79. Ibid. pp. 242-43. "National Negro Congress The Call" (From the original call to congress held in 1935. The congress adopted resolutions urging unionization of Negro women workers, desegregation of public accommodations and schools, protection of migrant workers, and anti-lynch legislation. They also approved resolutions against war and fascism).

Part Two   Chapter Four

1. Chattanooga Times, "Race War On Electric Car" June 19, 1905, p. 5.
2. Chattanooga Times, "Calm After Outbreak," August 6, 1927.
3. Chattanooga Times, "Could Affect 73% of City Schools County System Sees No Difficulty," May 18, 1954.
4. Chattanooga Times, "NAACP official Calls Decision Momentous," May 18, 1954.
5. Gerald Leinward, Editor, The Negro In The City, Washington Square Press, New York, 1968, p. 36.
6. Ibid., p. 37.
7. Benjamin Munn Ziegler, Editor, Desegregation And The Supreme Court, D.C. Heath & Co., 1958, p. 37.
8. Ibid., pp. 49-56.
9. Elton C. Fax, Contemporary Black Leaders, Dood, Mead & Company, New York, 1970, p. 87.
10. Ibid., p. 88.
11. Ibid., p. 90.
12. Joanne Grant, Editor, Black Protest, History, Documents and Analyses 1619 To Present, Fawcett Publications, Inc., 1968, p. 226.
13. Ibid., p. 267.
14. Ibid., p. 267. Also see Benjamin M. Ziegler, editor, Desegregation and The Supreme Court, D.C. Heath & Co., 1958. Note 13th and 14th amendments p. 42. Also see "Summary of Argument For Negro

Big Ralph

Children on page 68.
15. Ibid., pp. 269-270.
16. Chattanooga Times, "Negro Elks Forum Urges Prompt School Integration, August 8, 1955.
17. Ibid.
18. Chattanooga Times, "City School Board Plans Integration But Not This Year," July 23, 1955.
19. Chattanooga Times, "City Board Respects Law," July 24, 1955.
20. Chattanooga Times, "School Board Reaffirms Intention To Integrate: Plans Hearings Soon", October 13, 1955.
21. Ibid.
22. Chattanooga Times, "Group To Plan Racial Mixing In City Named," November 10, 1955.
23. Chattanooga Times, 'School Board Ends Parley, Tear Gas Tube is Dropped," November 16, 1955.
24. Chattanooga Times, "Segregationists Ponder 2 Actions," January 10, 1956.
25. Chattanooga Times, "City School Board megers Integration By At Least 5 Years," April 1, 1956.
26. Chattanooga Times, "Protest Given By NAACP Unit," April 4, 1956.
27. C. Vann Woodward, The Strange Career of Jim Crow, Oxford University Press, New York, 1966, p. 132.
28. Ibid., p. 135.
29. Ibid., p. 135.
30. Ibid., p. 136.
31. Ibid., p. 140.
32. Ibid., pp. 140-141.
33. Ibid., p. 170.
34. Chattanooga Times, "Sit-In Arrests Net 24 Negroes," May 17, 1960.
35. Chattanooga Times, "Lunch Counters Serve Negroes," August 6, 1960.
36. Chattanooga Times, "Mothers' Group Adds To Reward,"

Endnotes

November 11, 1960.
37. Louis E. Lomax, The Negro Revolt, Harper & Row, New York, 1971, p. 78.
38. Ibid., p. 78.
39. Ibid., pp. 79-80. Also see U.S. Civil Rights Commission report # 3 Employment 1961.
40. Ibid., p. 80.
41. Ibid., p. 81. Also see Robert C. Weaver, The Negro Ghetto, Harcourt, Brace & Co., New York, 1948, p. 261.
42. Ibid. pp. 81-82. Also see "Economic and Social Status of the Negro in the U.S.," Urban League, 1961.
43. Ibid., pp. 82-83.
44. Ibid., p. 83.
45. Ibid., p. 85.
46. Ibid., pp. 85-86.

Chapter 5

1. Arthur Littleton &, Mary Burger Editors, Black View Points, New America Library, New York, 1971. Excerpts from Leroi Jones, "Tokenism: 300 Years For Five Cents," Home: Social Essays, William Morrow and Co., Inc., 1966, pp-80-83.
2. Ibid., James Farmer, "Are White Liberals Obsolete In the Black Struggle," The Progressive XXII, January 1968, pp. 13-16.
3. Louis E. Lomax, The Negro Revolt, Harper & Row, New York, 1971, pp. 194-203.
4. Ibid., p. 196.
5. Littleton & Burger Editors, op. cit., pp. 95-100.
6. Ibid., pp. 97-98. Kenneth B. Clark, "The Present Dilemma of the Negro," The Journal of Negro History, LIII, January, 1968.
7. Kenneth Clark, Dark Ghetto, Dilemmas of Social Power, Harper & Row Pub., New York, 1965, pp. 22-125.
8. Ibid., p. 115.
9. Ibid., p. 117.

Big Ralph

10. Charles E. Silberman, Crisis In Black and White, Vintage Books A Division of Random House, New York, 1964, pp. 68-69.
11. Ibid., p. 71.
12. Ibid., p. 74.
13. Ibid., p. 74.
14. Lerone Bennett, Confrontation Black & White, Johnson Publishing Co., Inc., Chicago, 1965, pp. 113-114.
15. Lomax, op. cit., pp. 92-107.
16. Ibid., pp. 93-94.
17. Ibid., p. 95.
18. Lerone Bennett, op. cit., p. 185-186.
19. Joanne Grant, Editor, Black Protest-History, Documents, and Analyses 1619 To Present, Fawcett Publications, Inc., 1968. Excerpts from "Nonviolence and the Montgomery Boycott," Martin Luther King, Stride Toward Freedom, Harper & Brothers, Inc., New York, pp. 83-85.
20. Ibid., p. 281.
21. Ibid., p. 281.
22. Ibid., pp. 281-282.

Chapter 6

1. Chattanooga Times, "Board Will Not Integrate City Schools Next Autumn." June 13, 1958.
2. Chattanooga Times, "Negroes' Seek Admission To City White Schools Now." February 23,1960. Also see Chattanooga Times, "Board To Receive Written Demands."2/24/1960.
3. Chattanooga Times, "Negroes' Ask Integration Within City." April 7,1960.
4. Ibid.
5. Chattanooga Times, "Board Expected Federal Appeal." April 7, 1960. Also see Chattanooga Times, "Letson, Petersen Are Served Writs," April 9,1960.
6. Chattanooga Times, "Mothers' Group Adds To Reward," November

Endnotes

11,1960.

7. Chattanooga Times, "Board Asks Delay In Desegregation,." June 8, 1960. Also see Chattanooga Times, "Negroes' Effort To Broaden Suit Is Turned Down, " May 6,1960. And Chattanooga Times, "Jury Would Get 5 Issues In Suit," June 8,/1960.

8. Chattanooga Times, "Hearing July 20 For School Plea,." June 22, 1960. Also see Chattanooga Times, , Negroes Allowed Time To Respond," June 11,1960. Chattanooga Times, , "City Challenges Negroes Claims," July 9,1960. Chattanooga Times, "Negroes Dispute Claims of Board, " July 16, 1960 . And Chattanooga Times, Hearing Is Jan. 9," July 16,1960.

9. Chattanooga News Free Press, "Judge Darr's School Memorandum," October 22, 1960.

10. Chattanooga Times, "Appeal Weighed By School Board," November 23,1960.

11. Ibid.,

12. Chattanooga Times, "Day of Decision Is At Hand As School Board, Law Meet," November 27,1960. Also see Chattanooga Times, "School Board To Ask Darr To Approve Move," November 26, 1960. Chattanooga Times , "Darr Turns Down Elucidation Plan of School Board." November 30, 1960. Chattanooga Times,,"City School Board Will File Appeal of Darr Decision," December 2, 1960.

13. Chattanooga Times, "Jones Questions Board Sincerity," December 3, 1960. Also see Chattanooga Times,, "Board Seeks Stay In order For Plan," December 8, 1960. Chattanooga Times,, "Attorneys Fight Order Suspension," December 4, 1960.

14. Chattanooga Times, "City Denies King Hall At Howard," December 15, 1960.

15. Chattanooga Times, "Board Asks Integration Start In 1962" December 21, 1960.

16. Louis E. Lomax, The Negro Revolt, Harper & Row, New York, 1971, p. 86.

17. Ibid., pp. 88-89.

18. Chattanooga Times, "Sit-In Arrests Net 24 Negroes, " May 17,

Big Ralph

1960.
19. Chattanooga Times, "Sit-ins Resumed Numbers Limited," May 20, 1960. Chattanooga Times, "Lunch Counters Serve Negroes," August 6, 1960.
20. Lomax, op. cit. p. 138.
21. Ibid., pp. 144-145.
22. Ibid., p. 149.
23. Charles E. Silberman, Crisis In Black and White, Vintage Books A Division of Random House, New York, 1964. p. 142.
24. Arthur Littleton & Mary Burger Editors, Black View Points, New American Library, New York, 1971, p. 235. Martin Luther King, Civil Rights Leader, "The Negro is your Brother" Letter From The Birmingham Jail, 1963.
25. Ibid., p. 240.
26. Silberman, op. cit., p. 302.
27. Ibid., p. 303.
28. Chattanooga Time, "Appeal Rights To Be Heard on Integration Case Here," January 21, 1961. Also see Chattanooga Times, "Hearing Delayed On School Plan," 1/4/1961. Chattanooga Times, "Judge Assigned Schools Appeal," January 13, 1961.
29. Chattanooga Times, "Darr Voids Ideas of School Board on Desegregation," January 24, 1961. Also see Chattanooga Times, "Board To Appeal Darr's Judgment On Schools Plan," February 9, 1961.
30. Chattanooga Times, "Court Contests School Decision," Mday 13, 1961. Also see Chattanooga Times,, "Clergymen Seek Peaceful Change," February 15, 1961. Chattanooga Times, "School Hearing Set For Oct. 16," September 9, 1961.
31. Chattanooga Times, , "Negro Parents Ask to Enroll 11 In White School," September 14, 1961 Also see Chattanooga Times, , "Drop Race Bars Country Is Asked," September 16, 1961. Chattanooga Times, ,"City Announcing Its Plans Friday," September 28, 1961. Chattanooga Times, "County Will Act On Negro's Plea," September 23, 1961. Chattanooga Times, "Lookout Negroes Are Turned Down

Endnotes

By School Board," September 28, 1961. Chattanooga News Free Press,, "Ridge School Plea Denied," September 30, 1961.

32. Chattanooga Times, "Carmichael Says Parents Must Discuss Integration," October 2, 1961. Also see Chattanooga Times, "83 Negro Pupils Eligible to Be Integrated In 1962 Under City Board's Plan," September 30, 1961. Chattanooga Times, "City Maybe Asked To Advance Date To January," October 8, 1961.

33. Chattanooga Times, "Maturity Urged As Schools Move To Desegregate," October 5, 1961. Also see Chattanooga Times,, "Board Approves Intent Notices," October 12, 1961.

34. Chattanooga Times, "Negro PTA Group Asks Compliance," October 20, 1961. Also see Chattanooga Times, "Integration Plan For Chattanooga In Judges Hands," October 17, 1961. Chattanooga Times,, "NAACP Hits Plan For Integration," October 9, 1961.

35. Chattanooga Times, "Integration Plan For City Delayed," December 26, 1961. Also see Chattanooga Times, "Court Backs Darr On Desegregation of Schools Here, " November 14, 1961. Chattanooga Times, "The Cincinnati Ruling," November 14, 1961. Chattanooga News Free Press, "Negroes Back Mixing Order," December 19, 1961. Chattanooga Times, "Negroes In Plea To Desegregate," December 22, 1961.

Chapter 7

1. Letter from RHC, to his wife, June 20, 1960.

2. Letter from RHC, to his wife, December 2, 1960.,

3. Letter from RHC, to his wife, December 11, 1960.

4. Letter from RHC, to his wife July 1962.

5. Joanne Grant, editors, Black Protest, History, Documents, And

Big Ralph

Analyses 1619 To Present, Fawcett Publications, Inc., 1968, p. 439. Originally printed in Crisis In Black & White by Charles E. Silberman, Rndom House Inc., 1964.

6. Ibid., pp. 452-53. "A Position Paper on Race" by members of the Atlanta Project. Excerpts from a discussion paper by members of the Atlanta Project of the Student Nonviolent Coordinating Committee, presented to SNCC in 1966.

7. Ibid., p. 453-54.

8. Ibid., p. 456.

9. Robert L. Allen, Black Awakening In Capitalist America, Doubleday & Co., Inc., New York, 1970, pp. 21-23.

10. Charles E. Silberman, Crisis In Black and White, Vintage Books A Division of Random House, New York, 1964, p. 131.

11. Louis E. Lomax, The Negro Revolt, Harper & Row, New York, 1971, pp. 116-117.

12. Ibid., p. 118.

13. Ibid., pp. 123-124.

14. Lerone Bennett, Confrontation Black & White, Johnson Publishing Co., Inc., Chicago, 1965, p. 219.

15. Ibid., p. 220.

16. Ibid., p. 221.

17. Lomax, op. cit., p. 233.

18. Ibid., p. 228.

19. Arthur C. Littleton & Mary W. Burger, editors, Black View Points, New American Library, New York, 1971, p. 236. Originally taken from Whitney M. Young Jr., Urban League Executive, "Crisis--Challenge--Change," Parks and Recreation, IV, April 1969, pp. 42-43.

20. Ibid., p. 265. Also see Whitney M. Young, Jr., Needed Now A Special Effort, To Be Equal, McGraw-Hill Book Co., 1964. Excerpts from this book was published in Black View Points and it depicts Young's domestic "Marshall Plan." This plan espoused by the Urban League seeks to reverse economic and social deterioration of urban families and communities and to develop the tools and understanding that will prevent such deterioration in the future.

Endnotes

21. Lomax, op. cit., p. 105. Also see Martin Luther King, "Showdown For Nonviolence," Look Magazine XXXII, April 16, 1968, pp. 23-35. In this article King reviews the question of riots as opposed to nonviolence. In essence King notes that less violence occurred over the course of the years during nonviolent demonstrations than in ten days of northern riots.

22. Ibid., pp. 89-90.

23. Arthur C. Littleton & Mary W. Burger, op. cit., pp. 295-296. Excerpts from Roy Wilkins, "Steady As She Goes," Keynote address NAACP fifty-seventh Annual Convention, 1969. Also see Jesse Jackson, "Black Power and White Churches, " Church in Metropolis, No. 16, Spring 1968, pp. 7-9. In this article Jackson adds clarity to the idea of Black separation and education. He also makes a creative apologist's statement on Uncle Toms. Also see Floyd B. McKissick, Three-Fifths Of A Man, MacMillian Company, 1969. Excerpts printed in Littleton & Burger, Black View Points, McKissick helps us further define relevant issues that concern our over-all interest. In this case McKissick notes the relationship of capitalism to the Black struggle. He also documents the different attitude of whites when Blacks are killed and when white people are killed.

Chapter 8

1. Louis E. Lomax, The Negro Revolt, Harper & Row, New York, 1971, p. 241.

2. Chattanooga Times, "Clam Transition Is Dunlap's Plea,"1/14/1962, Also see Chattanooga Times, "Ministers urged To Aid Transition," 2/6/1962. Chattanooga Times, "Desegregation Topic of Series,"2/10/1962.

3. Chattanooga Times, "Negroes Say Hostility Not Cause For Delaying Total Desegregation," 2/20/1962.

4. Chattanooga Times, "By Judge Wilson Court Expresses Belief In Ability of Chattanooga To Adjust to System," 3/2/1962. Also see Chattanooga Times, , "County Has Racial Plan On Schools," 3/9/1962. Chattanooga Times, "Hecklers Silent As County Voted School

Desegregation," 3/11/1962.
5. Chattanooga Times, "Pupil Choice Role Outlined In Court," 3/20/1962.
6. Ibid.,
7. Chattanooga Times, "Desegregation Without Malice Predicted Here," 3/12/1962.
8. Chattanooga Times, "School Change Orderly; 40 Negroes Are Entered In City's White School,." 8/30/1962. Chattanooga Times, "11 Negroes Enter At White Schools In County System," 8/31/1962. Chattanooga Times, "A Challenge Is Met," 9/6/1962.
9. Robert E. Allen, Black Awakening In Capitalist America, Doubleday & Co., Inc., New York, 1970, p. 25.
10. Ibid., p. 49.
11. Charles E. Silberman, Crisis in Black and White, Vintage Books A Division of Random House, New York, 1964, pp. 163-164.
12. Ibid., pp. 165-166.
13. Lerone Bennett, Jr., The White Problem In America, Johnson Publishing Co. Inc., Chicago, 1966, p.6.
14. Ibid., pp. 8-9.
15. Arthur C. Littleton and Mary L. Burger, editors, Black View Points, New American Library, New York, 1971, p. 240. Excerpt taken from Edward W. Brooke, "The Problem of Civil Rights," The Challenge of Change, Little Brown & Co., 1966.
16. Ibid., p. 276. Excerpts from Bayard Rustin, "Towards Integration As A Goal, "The American Federationist, LXXVI, Jan., 1969, pp. 5-7.
17. Ibid., p. 194. Excerpts from Kenneth B. Clark, "Fifteen Years of Deliberate Speed," Saturday Review LII, Dec. 1969, pp. 59-61.
18. Ibid., p., 200. Excerpts from Roy Wilkins, "The Case Against Separatism: "Black Jim Crow" News Week LXXIII, Feb. 10, 1969.
19. Ibid., p. 202. Excerpts from Nathan Hare Jr., "The Case For Separatism: Black Perspective," News Week LXXIII, Feb. 10, 1969.
20. Ibid. p. 362. Excerpts from Julian Bond, "Uniting The Races," Playboy Magazine, XVII, Jan. 1970, pp. 128-154. Also see James Farmer, "Education Is The Answer," Today's Education, LVIII, April,

Endnotes

1969, pp. 25-26.

Chapter 9

1. Chattanooga Times, "Zones Announced For all Schools In Desegregation," March 14, 1963. Also see Chattanooga Times, "NAACP Critical of School Board," March 29, 1963. Chattanooga Times, "NAACP Here Postpones Sympathy Demonstration," May 10, 1963.
2. Chattanooga Times, "Negroes' Denied Service At S & W," June 4, 1963. Also see Chattanooga Times, "S & W, 3 Krystals Reject Negroes, June 5, 1963.
3. Chattanooga Times, "8 Negroes Taken For Study At UC," June 6, 1963.
4. Chattanooga Times, "19 Schools Due To Desegregate," August 21, 1963. Also see Chattanooga Times, "Retain Dignity Mayor Implores," May 10, 1963. Chattanooga Times, "Ruling Seems To void Pupil Plan In City But No Conflicts Forseen," June 4, 1963. Chattanooga Times, "Mayor Says City Free of Discord," August 22, 1963. Chattanooga Times, "Bus Leaves Here With Delegation," August 28, 1963. Chattanooga Times, "Negroes Enroll In High School At Notre Dame," August 30, 1963.
5. Chattanooga Times, "Negroes Plead For Haste In School Desegregation," October 26, 1963. Also see Chattanooga Times, "Wilson Rules No Negroes at Kirkman Until Fall 64," December 22, 1963. Chattanooga Times, "Open Doors Now, Plea of Negroes," September 10, 1964.
6. Charles Silberman, Crisis In Black and White, Vintage Books A Division of Random House, New York, 1964, p. 297.
7. Ibid., p. 297.
8. Arthur Littleton & Mary Burger Editors, Black View Points, New American Library, New York, 1971, p. 348. Taken from Shirley Chisholm, "Black Is An Attitude," Address to student body Federal College, Wash. D.C., 1969.

Big Ralph

9. Ibid., p. 351.

10. Ibid., pp. 394-400. Taken from James Forman, "The Black Manifesto," Adopted by the National Black Economic Development Conference, Detroit, Michigan, April 26, 1969.

11. Ibid. p. 209. Taken from Maulana Karenga, "The Black Community and the University: A Community Organizer's Perspective," Black Studies In The University, Yale University Press, 1969.

12. Ibid., p. 210.

13. Ibid., 414-422. Taken from Leroi Jones, "The Legacy of Malcolm X, and the Coming of the Black Nation," Home: Essays, William Morrow & Co., Inc., 1966.

14. Ibid., pp. 424-430. Taken from Huey Newton, "In Defense of Self Defense," The Black Panther Newspaper, June 2, 1967. "Prison, Where Is Thy Victory?," The Black Panther Newspaper, July 12. 1969.

15. Ibid., pp. 432-436. Taken from Bobby Seale, "Other Voices, Other Strategies," Interviews with Julian Bond and Bobby Seale, Time, XCV, April 6, 1970, pp. 23-27.

16. Ibid., pp. 437-441. Taken from Eldridge Cleaver, "Revolution in the White Mother Country and National Liberation in the Black Colony," The North American Review, V, July-August, 1968, pp. 13-15.

17. Ibid., pp. 442-448. Taken from Stokley Carmichael, "Toward Black Liberation," The Massachusetts Review, VII, 1966, pp. 639-51.

18. Ibid., pp. 450-458. Excerpt from H. Rap Brown, Die Nigger Die, Dial Press, 1969.

19. Ibid., p. 110. Excerpts taken from Dr. Nathan Hare Jr., "Black Power"--It's Goals and Methods," Interview U.S. News & World Report LXII May 1967.

20. Ibid., p. 125. Excerpts taken from Malcolm X. "Message To The Grassroots," Malcolm X Speaks, Merit Publishers, 1965.

21. Ibid., p. 133. Excerpts taken from Malcolm's Last Answers and Interviews Racism, Harvard Law School Forum, Dec. 16, 1964.

22. Ibid., p. 134. Excerpts taken from Malcolm X. Interview 18 Jan. 1965, Printed in Young Socialist, March-April 1965.

23. Ibid., p. 134. Excerpts taken from Intermarriage and a Black State, From the Pierce Benton Show, taped at station CFTO--TV Toronto,

Endnotes

Jan. 19, 1965.
24. Ibid., pp. 152-155. Excerpts taken from Elijah Muhammad, "Help Self: What Must Be Done With the Negroes?, Message To The Black Man, 1965.
25. Ibid., p. 163. Excerpts taken from Roy Innis, "Separatist Economics: A New Social Contract," Black Economic Development, Prentice-Hall, Inc., 1969.
26. Ibid., p. 176. Excerpts taken from Stokley Carmichael, "Black Power It's Needs and Substance," from Black Power, Stokley Carmichael and Charles V. Hamilton, Random House, Inc., 1967.
27. Ibid., p. 179.
28. Ibid., p. 180.
29. Ibid., p. 181.
30. Louis E. Lomax, The Negro Revolt, Harper & Row, New York, 1971, p. 211.
31. Ibid., p. 212.

Chapter 10

1. Chattanooga Times, "Fire and Police Get 17 New Men," September 1964.
2. Chattanooga Times, "Intimate Knowledge of Negro Characters Has Been Big Help to Detective Gillespie," February 8, 1931, p. 6.
3. Chattanooga News Free Press, "Negro Says His Race Fares Better in South," October 31, 1947.
4. Chattanooga News Free Press, "Hoss Newell's Hoss Sense," November 1, 1947.
5. Chattanooga News Free Press, "NAACP Condemns Views of Newell," November 28, 1947.
6. Chattanooga Times, "Negro Policemen Returns To Beat," September 21, 1948.
7. Chattanooga Times, "Negro Policemen's Case is examined," September 21, 1948. Also see Chattanooga Times, "Policy I Adopted on Negro Officers," September 22, 1948. The City Commission

Big Ralph

adopted a resolution to deal with Black officers that arrest white people in the future. A Black delegation agrees with the suspension and concerns with white citizens that the rules that apply to Black officers are in the best interest of Blacks and whites.

8. Chattanooga Times, "Negroes Plead For Haste In School Desegregation," October 26, 1963. Also see Chattanooga Times, "Wilson Rules No Negroes at Kirkman until fall "64", December 12, 1963. Judge Wilson ruled that sound educational reasons unrelated to race make it undesirable and unwise to desegregate Kirkman Technical High School before the new term opens next fall. Also see Chattanooga Times, "Open Doors Now, Plea of Negroes," September 10, 1964. Here the NAACP called for full desegregation of all schools.

9. Letter from RHC to his wife, July 20, 1969.

10. Letter from RHC to his wife, July 21, 1969.

11. Chattanooga Times, "Federal Investigation of Bookie Turner," February 2, 1967.

12. Chattanooga News Free Press, "Federal Indictment of Commissioner Turner," February 24, 1967.

13. Chattanooga News Free Press, "Turner Relieved of Duties," June 9, 1967.

14. Chattanooga Times, "Resolution Passed By City Commission To Grant Power Over Chattanooga Police Department, June 10, 1967.

15. Chattanooga Times, "Turner Acquitted," October 19, 1967.

16. Chattanooga Times, "Law Commission For Full Probe of Police Force," October 26, 1967.

17. Chattanooga Times, "City Moves To Upgrade Negro Policeman's Role," April 19, 1968.

18. Chattanooga Post, "Grand Jury Asks Probe of Local Police Force," December 19, 1968. The Chattanooga Post was an afternoon paper and was published for about two years.

19. Chattanooga Times, "Black Ministers---$250 per month is paid each of Two Informers For Police Dept.," February 15, 1969. Also see Chattanooga Times "City To Retain Ministers at $150 per month each, Auto allowance of $100," February 20, 1969. Majority of city

Endnotes

Commission agreed to authorize Commissioner Turner to contract with Rev. Robert Richards and Rev. J. Lloyd Edwards Jr. for part-time special services to the fire and police depts. in helping maintain racial peace. See Chattanooga Times, "Richards, Edwards Reject City Investigative Jobs," February 21, 1969. Claim they are not informers, but have been working for peace in the community.

20. Chattanooga News Free Press, "IACP (International Association of Chiefs of Police) Advises City to Hire More Negro Policemen," May 4, 1969. IACP said a special effort should be made to recruit Black police from Chattanooga and surrounding areas. Also personal contact with such groups as the NAACP and colleges with substantial enrollment should be considered.

21. Chattanooga Times, "Black Police and Politics," September 19, 1969. White Policemen say most Negro officers off election day. The practice has existed for years.

22. Chattanooga Times, "County Awarded U.S. School Funds," January 6, 1965. Federal funds held up by Hamilton Co. for grade-a-year desegregation policy were released. The following newspaper accounts note the ongoing madness involving the desegregation/integration issue. Chattanooga Times, "1964 Gains Made In Desegregation," January 12, 1965. Annual report of School Board notes 955 attend on open basis. Chattanooga Times, "One Grade A Year," January 15, 1965. County schools to keep desegregation policy adopted earlier. Chattanooga Times, "Teachers Train In Desegregation," February 16, 1965. 75 attend 1st session of program to help improve classes. Chattanooga Times, " Wilson Orders Hearing on May 1 on plea for total Desegregation," April 10, 1965. Chattanooga Times, "Full Compliance In Desegregation Ordered by 1967," April 30, 1965. City County schools due action on grades 10, 12 this fall to keep aid, four levels mandatory. McConnell is critical of edict in view of ruling by federal courts. Chattanooga Times, "Board Maintains Speeding Change Bad for Schools," May 5, 1965. Says full desegregation a threat to quality education. Judge Wilson studies the case. While NAACP lawyers say time has come for opening of all classrooms. Chattanooga

Big Ralph

Times, "Teacher Groups Agree To Merge," May 19, 1965. White, Negro teachers in counties' system vote for unity. White and Negro teachers in the Hamilton Co. schools voted to desegregate their professional affiliations and consolidate in a single association at beginning of 65-66 term. Chattanooga Times, "City told To complete School Desegregation by start of 1966 Term," August 6, 1965. U.S. Judge Wilson cut three years off cities' desegregation plan. Chattanooga Times, "County Schools To Desegregate Grades 1-6, 1-10," August 20, 1965. Chattanooga Times, "Full Desegregation Seen As Fund-Getting Answer," August 27, 1965. Chattanooga Times, "School Openings Here, Elsewhere Free of Trouble," September 1, 1965. Negroes sign up Juniors Highs in city, they register 180 for the 7th grade. Chattanooga Times, "Desegregation Is Accomplished," November 10, 1966. City school board notes single system here after only five years. 27 of 444 schools in city now have biracial enrollment; seven are all white and 10 are all Negro. Chattanooga Times, "Negroes' Bring School Action," December 30, 1966. State city board still operates segregated education system. Chattanooga News Free Press, "42 of 103 Schools Here Desegregated," November 29, 1966. Chattanooga Times, "Schools Choice Is Now Altered," September 10, 1968. Boards' decision to close B. T. Washington school will eliminate need for freedom of choice. Chattanooga Times, "Opposes Busing McConnel Says," September 23, 1968. Supt. McConnel (County) is opposed to pairing of schools that would bring on busing of students outside their area to comply with federal guidelines that prohibit operation of an-all-Negro school.

Chapter 11

1. Chattanooga, Times, "Incidents of Racial Unrest Occurs Here a Second Night," July 24, 1980.
2. Chattanooga, Times, "Civil Rights Unit Will Meet Here," May 4, 1962.
3. Chattanooga, Times, "Picketing At Howard," Feb. 15, 1964.

Endnotes

4. Chattanooga Times (Boston special to the Times), "Mayors Convention Told Communication Excellent," July 28, 1967. Also see Chattanooga Times, "Equality Agency Will Open Here," Dec. 9, 1967. Branch of state office will work against discrimination under Tenn. Commission for Human Development.

5. Chattanooga Times, "Underwood Hits City and County on Job Policies," April 5, 1968. Job discrimination against qualified Negroes exist throughout Hamilton County government and token employment in the city was noted by attorney for NAACP." Also see Chattanooga Times, "King's Ideals Extolled at Rededication Rally," April 6, 1968. Mayor Kelly calls mass gathering and notes it is not a memorial but a service of rededication to the principles of equality, freedom of speech and nonviolence." See Chattanooga Times, "Poverty Marches Pass Night Here," May 31, 1968. Rev. Robert Richards offered refuge, food and rest to nine people on way to Washington---Poor People's Campaign. Richards is described in the article as a civil rights campaigner." See Chattanooga Times, "March Here Held Part of A Series, Nov. 18, 1968. "Wright says protests to continue over action in Avondale." Rev. Wright is the leader of a protest over rezoning in Avondale.

6. Chattanooga Post, "Open City Code," Feb. 25, 1969.

7. Chattanooga Times, "2nd Fire In Day Hits Home of Controversial Pastor," Feb. 11, 1969. Also see Chattanooga Times, "Charred House of Wright Razed," Feb. 20, 1969. "At the time of the fires' Wright said he suspected arson because of his recent human rights activities. No evidence of arson has been found." See Chattanooga Times, "Black Militants Describe Tactics To Take Over City," Feb. 3, 1969.

8. Chattanooga Times, "Picketing Is Set By Nationalists," Mar. 29, 1969. Plans for Easter boycott. Also see Chattanooga, Times "Negroes Picket 3 Stores Here," March 30, 1969. Easter boycott is begun led by Rev. H. H. Wright. See Chattanooga Times, "Reconciliation Meeting Set On City's Problems," Oct. 10, 1969. Meeting called by Jerry Welsh Asst. Director Model Cities Program said Chattanooga a city in trouble. Divisions between the rich and poor, Black and white. Statement asked

Big Ralph

Chattanoogans' to admit the city has social and economic problems." See Chattanooga Times, "Reconciliation Meeting Canceled, 5 Days of Concern Substituted," Oct. 14, 1969. "People worried about personal safety of those that will attend meeting." See Chattanooga Times, "Mayor Requests 125 Civic Groups Foster Good Will," Oct. 22, 1969. Mayor Bender sending out letters to 125 civic organizations making an urgent appeal for their help in creating an atmosphere of understanding and a spirit of good will in the community." See Chattanooga Times, "Racial Tensions in City Schools Seen Nearing Exploding Point," Dec. 21, 1969. "Brainerd High center of controversy because of the use of Confederate flag and the singing of Dixie. Tension also erupted between Black Riverside High School and the white City High School. Teachers and students tense in schools with white and Black students."

9. Chattanooga News Free Press, Equal Rights Failure Seen In Tennessee," April 14, 1970. Also see Chattanooga Times, "County Faces Race Problem, July 12, 1970. "Two problems county must address to improve race relations:

    1. Selection of a new member of the County School Board the body charged with over seeing the continuing integration of county schools.

    2. Questions concerning the possibility of mixed neighborhoods.

10. Chattanooga Times, "Panther Recruiter Says Strife To Last Until Blacks Recognized," May 25, 1971.

11. Chattanooga Times, "Groups Propose Programs To Aid Climate of City," June 9, 1971.

12. Chattanooga Times, "Walker Names Roy Noel To Community Relations," June 16, 1971. Also see Chattanooga Times, "Mayor Appoints Niedengeses To Head Committee on Community Relations," June 17, 1971. "Appointed chairman of Mayor Walker's newly created commission of Community Relations. Committee's work focused on whether or not a given situation is racial." See Chattanooga Times, "City Commission Receives Plea For Racial Climate Improvement," July 7, 1971. "Church groups asked city Commission to work in behalf of better racial climate. Urge passage of open housing ordinance." See Chattanooga Times "Mapp Urges Law on Open Housing," Aug. 8,

Endnotes

1971. "During radio talk show Mapp urges open housing. When criticized about busing as a part of city school integration plan Mapp said if there were open housing there would not be any need for busing."
13. Chattanooga, Times, "City School Board Denies Any Act for Furthering Race Segregation," May 8, 1969. Also see Chattanooga Times, "Whites Will Deliver A Manifesto Asking Schools End Segregation," July 24, 1969. See Chattanooga News Free Press, "City Schools Deny System Segregated," Nov. 25, 1970.
14. Chattanooga Times, "Wilson To Hear Evidence April 1st on Schools Here," March 8, 1971. "Seeks to learn if the city has a unitary system operating or pending. See Chattanooga Times, "Teachers, Staff Told To Expect Difficult Times," May 7, 1971. "School official testifies race plays no part in establishing pupil zones." See Chattanooga Times, "Some Busing For Schools Next Year, Franklin Says," June 16, 1971. "Busing plan opposed all over the city." See Chattanooga Times, "Blacks File Objections To Plan on Integration In U.S. District Court," June 22, 1971. See Chattanooga Times, "School Board, Cannot Please All Cooperation Needed," June 20, 1971. "Judge Wilson instructs city to submit a new plank of desegregation within 30 days. " See Chattanooga Times, "City School Board Asks Federal Court To Delay Assignment of Students," July 13, 1971. "Delay until fall of 1972. Faculty will integrate this year, a rehearing on the issue is sought." See Chattanooga Times, "But High Schools Are Tentative," July 27, 1971. "Judge Wilson approved school board's integration plan. Does not require full implementation of busing this fall." See Chattanooga News Free Press, "Baker Labels Busing As Phony Guise," Aug. 4, 1971. "Baker denounced as phony the busing of children under the guise of improving education by achieving social balance." See Chattanooga Times, "School Head To Seek $2 million In Federal Desegregation Funds; Fraction would Go For Security," Aug. 7, 1971. See Chattanooga Times, "City Hall March Against Busing Is Set ," Aug. 17, 1971. "Tri-state citizens council invite all white citizens opposed to busing to march on city hall." See Chattanooga Times, "Franklin finds Fault At Nixon," Aug. 18, 1971. "City leader says stand against busing

Big Ralph

adds to emotionalism. Nixon's recent order to government agencies discouraging the use of busing in achieving desegregation. See Chattanooga Times, "Dr. Bond Dislikes Mayors Request," Aug. 23, 1971. "Mayor Walker's request for presidential intervention to halt busing of children to achieve racial balance hasn't eased the task of school officials."

15. Chattanooga Times, "Highlights of Chattanooga School Desegregation History," Aug. 29, 1971. Also see Chattanooga Times, "First of City Schools Open Registration: Henry Says Everything Went Smoothly Sunday Declared Prayer Day For System," Sept. 1, 1971. Some white students enrolled at Riverside and Howard, 20 white students at each school." See News Free Press, "Only 30 Register At Riverside: 28 Others Enroll At Howard High," September 2, 1971. "Only 58 white students were enrolled at two formerly all Black high schools at the close of the two-day registration period." See Chattanooga News Free Press "Blacks Out Number Whites In City Schools For First time: Applies To all 3 Levels," Sept. 3, 1971. "Total 19,423, 10,230 Black and 9,092 white." See Chattanooga Times, " $372,970 Sought By :Unity Group For Integration," October 23, 1971. "Ask U.S. offices of Education for grant to work for grass roots harmony in the integration of the schools. See Chattanooga Times, "Rep. Baker Against Grant Requested by Unity Group," November 14, 1971. "Says Unity Group political organization, funds cut back to $57,000."

16. Chattanooga Times, "First Black Police Woman," July 9, 1971.
17. Chattanooga Times, "Police Insensitive To Go To School Approved In City," Oct. 27, 1971.
18. RHC to his wife Catherine, July 1973.
19. RHC to his wife Catherine, April 18, 1973.
20. RHC to his wife Catherine, April 1973.
21. News Free Press, "2nd Day of Tension Plagues Kirkman As Fights Averted," April 28, 1972.
22. Chattanooga Times, "Boycott of Store Laid To Panther's," June 4, 1972.

Endnotes

23. Chattanooga Times, "Coercion Illegal Davis Declares," June 9, 1972.
24. Chattanooga News Free Press, "Extortion Attempts Blamed On Blacks," June 16, 1972.
25. Chattanooga Times, "Black Panthers Say No Threats Have Been Made," June 26, 1972. Also see Chattanooga Times, "Four Blacks Arrested on Charges of Extortion Outside Food Store," Aug. 11, 1972. "Members of Black Panther Party arrested at Red Food Store on 3rd Street during boycott. See Chattanooga Times "Panther leader Is Indicted Here," Oct. 5, 1972.
26. Chattanooga Times, "1 Of 3 Found Guilty In Panther Trial," May 31, 1973.
27. Chattanooga Times, "VFW Club Refuses Admission To Black Marine," July 30, 1974.
28. Chattanooga Times, "Promotion Of 62 On Police Force Is City-Approved," August 28, 1974.
29. Chattanooga Times, "6 Groups Picket City Hall Here Asking Equality," January 1, 1975.
30. Chattanooga News Free Press, "Moore Jailed After Bid For Appeal Unsuccessful," Feb. 6, 1975. Also see Chattanooga Times, "State Argues Moore's Picketing Not Covered by 1st Amendment," June 3, 1975. Also see Chattanooga Times June 24, 1975, "Black Panther Leader Moore Paroled," The terms of his parole was for Moore to get a job or go to school and refrain from political activity for six months. Also Moore was not allowed to picket or boycott and was not permitted to solicit funds."
31. Jerome H. Skolnick, The Politics of Protest, Ballantine Books, Inc., New York, 1969. pp. 2-5.
32. Chattanooga Times, "Police Promotions Announced," October 1, 1980.
33. Ibid., p. 11.
34. Ibid., pp. 12-13.
35. Ibid., p. 13.
36. Ibid., p. 14.

37. Ibid., p. 15.
38. Ibid., p. 15.
36. Ibid., p. 15.
37. Ibid., pp. 15-16.
38. Ibid., pp. 5-7.
39. Ibid., p. 65.
40. Ibid., pp. 65-66.
41. Ibid., p. 67.
42. Ibid., p. 87.
43. Ibid., p. 87.
44. Ibid., p. 88.
45. Ibid., pp. 105-106.
46. Ibid., pp. 107-108.
47. Ibid., pp. 109-110.
48. Ibid., p. 127.
49. Ibid., pp. 128-129.
50. Ibid., p. 129.
51. Ibid., pp. 129-130.
52. Ibid., pp. 130-131.
53. Ibid., p. 131.
54. Ibid., p. 131.
55. Ibid., p. 132.
56. Ibid., p. 132.
57. Ibid., pp. 135-136.
58. Ibid., p. 136. "SNNC also issued a statement on Vietnam in 1966. A few months later, when Stokley Carmichael of SNNC brought the new direction of civil rights activists into the public eye with the slogan of "Black Power," it became clear that a shift of major importance had occurred." p. 137.
59. Three Books by Frantz Fanon are very useful in exploring the variables of colonialism, especially the psychological affects of colonialism on indigenous people. Frantz Fanon, The Wretched of The Earth, Grove Press, Inc., New York, 1963. The entire book is important to explore but the chapter "On National Culture" (pg. 206) is very useful

Endnotes

for the purposes of understanding culture in a colonial context. Also see Frantz Fanon, A Dying Colonialism, Grove Press, Inc., New York, 1965. Colonialism and how it affects a colonized people is discussed throughout the book. The work is centered on Algeria but the conclusions on colonialization can be applied to most colonial situations. Also see Frantz Fanon, Black Skin White Masks, Grove Press Inc., New York, 1967. Especially look at chapter 4 "The So-Called Dependency complex of colonized peoples, pg. 83. There are other works that also shed light on this question. Kwame Nkrumah, Neo-Colonialism, The Last Stage Of Imperialism, International Publishers, New York, 1965. Also the highly noted work by Walter Rodney, How Europe Underdeveloped Africa, Howard University Press, Washington, D.C., 1974.
60. Op. cit., pp. 141-142.
61. Ibid., p. 147.
62. Ibid., pp. 152-153.
63. Ibid., p. 153.
64. Ibid., p. 179.

Chapter 12

1. See Chattanooga Times, Sept 28, 1981--Oct. 3, 1981.
2. Chattanooga Times, May 17, 1983, "Kennedy May Name McCutcheon, Cothran to Head Police Department." In the afternoon paper an article noted that Cothran had been named Deputy Chief. See Chattanooga News Free Press, May 17, 1983, "McCutcheon Named New Police Chief. Ralph became a Deputy Chief after 19 years of service. The next year Ralph and some his of old friends celebrated 20 years of service. See Chattanooga News Free Press, Black Officers Celebrate 20 years Of Service," September 16, 1984.
3. Chattanooga Times, "Two Black Leaders Fear Discontent May Lead To A Long Hot Summer," July 1, 1983.
4. Chattanooga News Weekly, "Lorenzo Ervin Speaks Out," Aug. 7-14, 1987.

Big Ralph

5. The Burning Spear," I Know There Are Folks Negotiating On Our Behalf Who Have Absolutely No Idea What We Want Because They Don't Even Talk To Us It's The Black Bourgeoisie," (Unified African Liberation Day Rally, Philadelphia May 23rd.) June 1987.
6. Chattanooga News Weekly, "Who Said Lorenzo Ervin is Emerging As A New Leader in The Black Community,? Nov. 9-15, 1989.
7. Ibid. p. l, 13.
8. Chattanooga News Weekly, "Let Wadie Suttles Rest In Peace-- Sharing The Blame: The Tragic Life And Death of Wadie Suttles," Dec. 14-20, 1989.
9. Ibid., p. 15.
10. Ibid., p. 15.
11. Ibid., p. 15.
12. Chattanooga News Weekly, "Who Are Those Who Benefited From The Tragic Death of Wadie Suttles?" Dec. 21-27 1989.
13. Chattanooga Times, "Dinsmore Picked As Commissioner: Cothran Is Chief," July 29, 1989.
14. Chattanooga New Weekly, "District Attorney Sends Signal: It's Open Season For Racists Cops To Kill Blacks In Chattanooga," March 7-13, 1991.
15. Chattanooga News Weekly, "Sheriffs Department Maintains Deputies Did Nothing Wrong In The Murder of Larry Powell," Feb. 11-17, 1993.
16. Ibid., p. 1.
17. Chattanooga News Weekly, "March And Rally To Protest Police Brutality Planned For Chattanooga," Feb. 25-Mar. 3, 1993.
18. Jerome H. Skolnick, The Politics of Protest, Ballantine Books, Inc., New York 1969, p. 242.
19. Ibid., p. 245.
20. Ibid., p. 249.
21. Ibid., p. 262.
22. Ibid., p. 262.
23. Ibid., pp. 262-263.
24. Ibid., pp. 288-289.

Endnotes

25. Ibid., p. 324.

26. Chattanooga Times, "Hixson Family Awakes "To Find Burnt Cross In Front Yard," Jan, 22, 1986. Also see Chattanooga Times, "Unity Group Continues the Quest of Martin Luther King," Jan., 10, 1986.

27. Chattanooga Times, "Group Sets Protest, Boycott To Protest Alleged Brutality," March 31, 1987. Also see Chattanooga Times, "Blacks Push Unity As Key To Progress," Feb. 7, 1987. Unity and action stressed by H. H.. Wright (Action Coordinating Council) concerning deaths of two Black Hamilton County prisoners and the wounding of another. Also see the Times article that gives specific information on the person who is the lead organizer for the march. Chattanooga Times, "Civil Rights March Planner Hijacked Plane To Cuba In 1969," April 1, 1987. ":Lorenzo Ervin was convicted of air piracy and kidnapping Feb., 25, 1969. He was sentenced to two life terms. Paroled in 1983, conditions not released."

28. Chattanooga Times, "FOP Asks Review of Literature alleging Racism, Police Brutality," Aug. 5, 1987. Also see Chattanooga Times, "Local Clergy, Civic Officials urge End To Bigotry At Unity Meeting," Feb., 20, 1988. Also see Chattanooga Times, "Citizens Review Board Pushed," Feb., 19, 1993. "The aftermath of the death of Larry Powell DUI suspect citizens seek review board. Board should have supeona power, to refer cases directly to the grand jury."

Chapter 13

1. Chattanooga Times, "New Chief Aims To Improve Morale, Image of the Force," July 29, 1989. Also on the front page see Chattanooga Times, "Dinsmore Picked As Commissioner, Cothran is Chief," July 29, 1989.

2. Chattanooga Times, "Police Chief Aims to Arrest His Diabetes," November 23, 1989.

3. Chattanooga Times, "Governor Signs Bill For School Prayer," April 9, 1994. Gov. Kirk Fordice (Of Mississippi) signed into law Friday a bill to allow prayer at school and school events, as long as students initiate

Big Ralph

the worshiping. Also see Chattanooga Times, "A Divisive Issue," March 4, 1995. For another issue that clearly goes against the law of God. "Perhaps no single issue clearly divides Americans of all faiths more than abortion divides them. The U.S. Supreme Court's 1973 decision to legalize abortion crystallized the differences between religious conservatives and religious liberals in a way the civil rights struggle and Vietnam War did not, noted professor Robert Wenthrow in The Restructuring of American Religion.

4. Chattanooga Times, editorial by Bob Herbert, "Blacks Killing Blacks," October 21, 1993. See Chattanooga New Free Press, "Car Jackings Here On Rise: Old Crime With New Name," May 22, 1994. Chattanooga News Free Press, "Wolf, Green Families See Justice In Differing Lights," July 3, 1994. Chattanooga Times "Suspect Sought In Monday Slaying," August 2, 1994. Chattanooga Times, "Warren Arrested In Shooting Death,"" July 31, 1994.

5. Chattanooga News Free Press (from the Associated Press), "Oklahoma 13-year-old kills Intruder With 357 Magnum," July 21, 1994. Also see Chattanooga Times (from the Associated Press) "5 Percent of Teens have Tried Suicide," June 16, 1994. New York five percent of American teen-agers say they have tried to commit suicide and 12 percent say they have come close to trying, according to Gallup Organizations study. See Chattanooga News Free Press (from the Associated Press) "no Arrests In Miami Slaying By Street Mob," July 14, 1994.

6. Atlanta Journal, Atlanta Constitution, Q& A On The News, "To Halt Violence, We Can't Get Tired," July 2, 1994.

7. Chattanooga Times, "The Nation's Safest Colleges," July 13, 1994.

8. Chattanooga News Free Press, "Most Murder Victims Know Their Killers," July 11, 1994.

9. Chattanooga News Free Press, "Fathers In Homes Believed Answer To Many Problems," July 11, 1994.

10. Chattanooga News Free Press, "The Cocaine Air Force," July 1, 1994.

11. Chattanooga News Free Press, "A Sad Story," July 18, 1994. Also

Endnotes

see articles that describe the serious problem of guns and crime. Chattanooga Times, "Fight Against Guns Pushed," September 6, 1994. Also see Chattanooga Times, "Police Officer Takes Aim at Firearm use by Felons," March 25, 1996.

12. Chattanooga Times, "McCutcheon, Cothran Are Approved: Vandergriff To Head Patrol Division," May 18, 1983.

13. Chattanooga Times, "Council Panel Backs Cothran," July 19, 1995. Also see Chattanooga News Free Press, "Police Test Supervisor Quizzed," Feb. 13, 1979."Police Capt. Ralph Cothran, a supervisor of the recent testing procedure for the promotion of 38 master patrolmen, was cast in the role of defender of the procedure during the second in a series of meetings to study the tests and procedures.
The investigation was called at the request of Black leaders George Key, president of the local chapter of NAACP, and Lt. Paul Calloway, president of a local chapter of national police officers association which is predominately Black."

14. Chattanooga Times, "Dinsmore Filling In For Chief," August 8, 1995.

15. Chattanooga News Free Press, "Police Mourn Cothran Death, November 3, 1995. Also see Chattanooga Times, "City Chief of Police Cothran 57, Dies," November 3, 1995. Chattanooga Times, "City 'Mourns Gentle Giant," November 4, 1995. Also on page A3 "The Tough 'Job of Filling Cothran's Shoes," Funeral arrangements for Chief Cothran. See Chattanooga News Free Press, "Chief Cothran Services At Orchard Knob Baptist," November 4, 1995. Chattanooga News Free Press, "Big Shoes To Fill: Colleagues, Friends Praise Cothran's Professionalism," November 5, 1995. Chattanooga Times, "Services Today For Cothran," November 6, 1995.

16. Chattanooga News Free Press, "Tears, Laughter Mark Chief Cothran Farewell," November 7, 1995.

17. Chattanooga Times, "Friends Bid Cothran Farewell," November 7, 1995.

18. Chattanooga Times, "Cothran A Credit To Us All," November 6, 1995. Also see Times editorial "Gentle Giant Cothran Stirs Fond

Big Ralph

Memories," Jan 5, 1996. In this editorial the Chattanooga Human Rights and Human Relations Commission pay tribute to Ralph.
19. Chattanooga Times, "Beyond The Call," November 29. 1995.
20. Chattanooga Times, "Commission To Honor Cothran," February 8, 1996.
21. Chattanooga Courier, "Local Group Pays tribute To Police Chief Cothran," March 4, 1996.
22. Letter from Congressman Zack Wamp to Mr. Richard K. Donahue Chairman Profile in Courage Award Committee, March 14, 1996. See Appendix D for Wamp letter and response letter from Richard K. Donahue and a statement of nomination from Mayor Gene Roberts.
23. Chattanooga Times, "Feds Probe City Police: Inquiry focuses on mishandling of Drug Money," March 29, 1996. Also see Chattanooga Times, "Drug Fund Cash Flowed Wildly: Investigators Wonder Who Got The Money," March 30, 1996.
24. Chattanooga Times, "Police Rank 7 In Abuse Reports," April1, 1996.
25. Chattanooga News Free Press, "Crime Rate Down In City For 1995, December 24, 1995.
26. Chattanooga Times, "Muslim Cleric Warns Against Police Action," April 8. 1996.
27. Chattanooga Times, "Police Play Officer Friendly Project Precinct Make a Difference," January 25, 1996.
28. Chattanooga Times, "Time To Move On: Roberts Decides Against 97 Run, May 3, 1996. Also see related articles, "Biography Newsman, FBI Agent, Mayor," Pg. A3. "In His Words: The Past And The Future," pg. A 4 Chattanooga Times, "Mayor's Retirement To Bring Police Changes," May 4, 1996.

APPENDIX DATA

Appendix A: Chapter Five. Editorials, letters on segregation.

1. Letter to the Chattanooga News Free Press Editorial page June 30,1958 concerning segregation by Catherine Patton Cothran.
2. Other editorial responses to segregation Chattanooga News Free Press June 23,1958.
3. Response to Catherine's letter by Jerry Paul Perry, June 30,1958.

Appendix B: Chapter 11. Congratulation letters on promotion to Assistant Chief.

1. Walter Smart, Commissioner of Fire and Police, September 30,1980.
2. Roy Noel, Director of Equal Opportunity Office, October 3,1980.
3. H. Q. Evatt, Sheriff Hamilton County, October 1, 1980.
4. Jim Hammond, Chief Deputy Hamilton County, October 1, 1980.
5. Dalton Roberts, County Executive, October 7,1980.
6. Robert E. Brown, Director of Housing Management Chattanooga Housing Authority, October 8,1980.
7. Sullivan R. Ruff, Jr, Principal Howard School, October 15,1980
8. Gene Roberts, Commissioner of Public Safety State of Tennessee, October 6,1980.
9. Marilyn Lloyd Bouquard, Congresswoman 3rd District, October 10,1980.

Appendix C Chapter 13. Letters regarding controversy with Chattanooga Law Enforcement Officers Association. (CLEOA)

1. Letter written to Chief Cothran by Chattanooga Law Enforcement Officers Association June 5, 1995.
2. Chief Cothran's response letter to CLEOA, June 28,1995.
3. Cover letter to Carlton Parks from State of Tennessee Human Rights Commission regarding his compliant, April 3,1995.

Appendix D Chapter 13. Letters regarding John F. Kennedy Profiles In Courage Award.

1. Letter from Congressman Zack Wamp recommending Big Ralph for JFK Profile In Courage Award, March 6,1996.
2. Recommendation letter from mayor Gene Roberts.
3. Response letter from JFK Profile In Courage Committee, March 22,1996.

Big Ralph

Mixing Stand Hit
Negro Woman Takes Issue With N-FP Editorial

To The Chattanooga News-Free Press:
I am hoping that you will be liberal enough to print this criticism of an article which recently appeared in your paper. This is in reference to "What Now?", found on the editorial page of the June 13th issue.

Perhaps I shouldn't be, but I am somewhat abashed at Chattanooga's attitude toward the "segregation-integration" problem concerning public schools. I expected too much of what I call fair-minded citizens in Chattanooga. Alas, Chattanooga voices the sentiments of Faubus and Talmadge and other anti-desegregationists. But who would think that one would carry in her heart respect for the ideas and ideals of such states as Mississippi, Georgia and Arkansas.

I do not pretend to know the details concerning the origin of the 14th Amendment at this time, however, I do know that you are rationalizing by giving "good" reasons instead of real ones in reference to the May 1, 1954 Supreme Court ruling to outlaw segregation in public schools in America. I am sure that back of this prejudice, hate and bias is some love and understanding that seeks only half a chance to become known.

It is only logical (to use your term) in my opinion to think that naturally, integration should not be a forced thing, but carefully planned to a great degree. On the other hand it is absolutely disgraceful and outrageous for the following to have appeared in print: "Hamilton County should elect three state representatives and a state senator prepared to adopt sound, well reasoned and far-reaching laws for segregated schools.

"Hamilton Countians and other Tennesseans must elect a governor who will provide leadership for segregation."

Why do I speak, why do I criticize this article—because—yes, I am a Negro, one in 15 millions of an oppressed people. We do not have to have a "forced racial mixing," but then, on the other hand we should not keep living under the forced pressure of segregated public schools.

The lack of harmony in human relations is caused by a lack of understanding each other.

It is foolish to even think of closing schools to avoid integration.

Only until the day comes when you can think of people as people not as black or white, working and striving together according to individual tastes, talents and abilities will progress be made and the continuance of back-sliding and falling into a rut ceased.
CATHERINE PATTON.
17 Sawyer St.

Against Segregation
Writer Presents His Observation of Negro Race

To The Chattanooga News-Free Press:
First, I would like to commend you people on what I consider an excellent editorial policy, that of printing all kinds of letters, those which do not agree with you as well as those which do. This is truly in keeping with the ideals of free speech as we know them.

But it is also strange in view of some of your other policies. Naturally, in the question of segregation, you are as much entitled to your stand as anyone else and I respect that right, although I do not agree with it one iota's worth.

Being a native of Chattanooga, I was raised in an environment in which segregation was the accepted thing, past, present and future. Then, about eight years ago I gradually began to realize just what sort of deal the Negro is getting in the South. We have all seen them laying sewers, digging ditches, unloading boxcars, etc., and just about everything else to make a dollar. I have seen at firsthand the bigotry, prejudice, narrow-mindedness and injustice with which they are dealt.

If I were treated like one of them, day in and day out, I think I would either migrate north or do away with myself. I don't understand what they have to live for, anyway. Although crime and violence in any form are never justifiable, it is not hard to understand why they must sometimes resort to it. It is probably a case of crime" or "starve."

These people have been slaves since time immemorial. They lived in various forms of slavery in this country from 1619 until 1865, nearly 250 years. Now, nearly 100 years after their so-called "freedom," they are at the bottom of the economic ladder, many of them live in hovels and substandard housing and the white man has fixed it so that they will stay there. That is where they "belong"! If you, Mr. Editor, would think for five minutes of how you would like to trade places with them, I don't see how in the name of justice and humanity you could sit in your office and dictate such vilification of an unfortunate race, knowing that, except for the grace of God, your skin would be the same color as theirs.

To keep the record straight: I am not a Communist, not a "nigger-lover," and not a NAACPer. am a male white and an arch enemy of all forms of tyranny. I must ask you to withhold my name for obvious reasons. I also have children of grammar-school age.
ANONYMOUS.

Disagrees
Letter Says N-FP Not Facing Problem in Race Issue

To The Chattanooga News-Free Press:
You assume that the NAACP represents only the radical element of our Negro population. You assume that utter and eternal separation is desired by "decent" Negroes and "decent" whites, and is the single answer to the race problem. I fear you have not had the courage to face the true problem.

I do not pretend to understand all the problem myself. I believe, however, that you are unaware of the way most Negroes think and of what they need. I know, also, that in the hated NAACP and in smaller Negro groups toil some people who have faced the race problem with more honesty and courage than you have shown.

If democracy is to continue in our nation — this is the pitiless fact — integration must one way or another come about.

Why? Because most Negroes now, whether you will admit it or not, are forced — by dismal upbringing, by isolation from free communication with the majority group in education, by restricted job opportunities, by the white man's blind and vicious stereotypes—are made to be inferior, second-rate citizens.

There is no such thing as separate but equal.

The underlying cause for separation is that one group considers the other group hopelessly inferior. Separation thus only reaches and enforces more inequality. Such a condition is a fatal termite in democracy's foundation.

If we truly are concerned about our children's children, we must set about inventing and using new ways — not self-destructive ways to delay integration — but to bring about sensible integration.
JONATHAN FELIX.
(Chattanooga White)

CHATTANOOGA NEWS-FREE PRESS
Published Each Afternoon Except Sunday
ROY McDONALD, President and Publisher
EVERETT ALLEN, Treasurer
LEE ANDERSON, Editor
National Representatives — Shannon & Associates, Inc.; Creamer & Woodward, Inc.
Telephone AM 6-8111
MONDAY, JUNE 30, 1958

CHATTANOOGA NEWS-FREE PRESS
Published Each Afternoon Except Sunday
ROY McDONALD, President and Publisher
EVERETT ALLEN, Treasurer
LEE ANDERSON, Editor
National Representatives — Shannon & Associates, Inc.; Creamer & Woodward, Inc.
Telephone AM 6-8111
MONDAY, JUNE 23, 1958

Appendix Data

2508 East 5th Street
Chattanooga 4, Tennessee
June 30, 1958

Mrs. Catherine Patton
17 Sawyer Street
Chattanooga, Tennessee

Dear Mrs. Patton:

I read your letter last week in the News-Free Press, agreed with what you said, and decided it was high time that I wrote them also. For a long time I had been intending to. So this week the editors got my letter, and to my surprise, published it--in the June 30th Forum.

With that letter I used a pen name, Jonathan Felix. Because my father's name--except for his middle name--is identical to mine, and because my father does not at all agree with what I had to say, I decided that I must prevent any mix-up, and so I signed it as I did.

My letter was not nearly so good as yours, but I feel that I can no longer be silent. I was born and raised in this city, attended Central High, and went off to college at Berea College in Kentucky. Berea, which is an integrated college, taught me more than I ever expected to learn. While there, I for three years served on a committee which helped break down segregation that remained on the campus and in the town, and for two years I acted as chairman of that committee. Of course, I left the college after my graduation this January knowing that much remained to be done, but at least progress had been made, and I and others had been changed by our efforts. This September I plan to enter Union Theological Seminary in New York. At present I am spending much of my time while not working preparing for what lies ahead. And this leads to my reason for writing you.

Sincerely I desire and need to talk with Negroes who feel concerned with this problem of integration. I want to know and to help, but I--in my own home town--hardly know where to turn. What I am wondering is if you might suggest someone who would take the trouble to talk to me--anyone, anywhere that is suitable.

If you desire to reply, you, or anyone else, might either write me a note, or call my home. The number is MA 2-8228.

Thank you for any consideration.

Cordially,

Jerry Paul Perry

Jerry Paul Perry

P.S. Forgive me if your name is Miss.

Big Ralph

City of Chattanooga
OFFICE OF
WALTER W. SMART
COMMISSIONER OF FIRE AND POLICE

September 30, 1980

Mayor and Board of Commissioners
City of Chattanooga, Tennessee

Gentlemen:

    This is to recommend that Captains Ralph Cothran and Theodore Wheeler be made Acting Assistant Chiefs in the Chattanooga Police Department effective October 3, 1980.

                                          Respectfully,

                                          Walter W. Smart
                                          Commissioner

WWS:bmt

Good luck Ralph I know you will do a good job. Walter W Smart

Appendix Data

EQUAL OPPORTUNITY OFFICE

ROY C. NOEL
Director

ROOM 307 • 103 CITY HALL ANNEX
CHATTANOOGA, TN 37402
615/757-5277

October 3, 1980

Mr. Ralph Cothran
Chattanooga Police Dept.
3300 Amnicola Highway
Chattanooga, Tennessee
      37406

Dear Ralph,

Today Chattanooga is proud of you. You have lead the
the way for many young blacks yet unborn. History can
bare me out.

We know it has not been easy but you had what it took to
make the grade. I am prouder of you than you will ever
know.

Thank God for men like you that braces our race for the
long struggle in the future.

A Friend,

Roy C. Noel

"AN EQUAL EMPLOYMENT OPPORTUNITY - AFFIRMATIVE ACTION EMPLOYER"

Big Ralph

H. Q. Evatt, Sheriff

Jim Hammond
CHIEF DEPUTY

October 1, 1980

Chief Ralph Cothran
Chattanooga Police Department
3300 Amnicola Highway
Chattanooga, Tennessee 37406

Dear Ralph:

    I wanted to take a moment to offer my congratulations on your recent promotion to Chief. The task is a big one but with your experience in the department I know you can handle it.

    Ralph, I do not remember a time when there has been a closer working relation between city and county. I know that men like yourself who have come up through the ranks have helped develop this rapport. If I can be of any help to you, give me a call.

Sincerely,

H. Q. Evatt
Sheriff

HQE/chd

Appendix Data

H. Q. Evatt, Sheriff

Jim Hammond
CHIEF DEPUTY

October 1, 1980

Chief Ralph Cothran
Chattanooga Police Department
3300 Amnicola Highway
Chattanooga, Tennessee

Dear Ralph:

    I want to congratulate you on your recent promotion to Chief. I know it takes a big man to fill the shoes of a Chief and you are about the biggest man I know in the department.

    Seriously Ralph, I know you are very capable of dealing with the needs of Chattanooga Police Department and after watching the way you handled the recent riot problems, I have the utmost respect for your abilities. If I can be of any assistance to you in your new position, please let me know.

                                      Sincerely,

                                        Jim Hammond
                                        Chief Deputy

JH/chd

Big Ralph

HAMILTON COUNTY
OFFICE OF THE COUNTY EXECUTIVE
201 Courthouse
Chattanooga, Tennessee 37402

DALTON ROBERTS
County Executive

October 7, 1980

Mr. Ralph Cothran
Acting Assistant Chief
Chattanooga Police Department
3300 Amnicola Highway
Chattanooga, Tennessee 37406

Dear Ralph:

I want to take this means of congratulating you on your recent promotion to Acting Assistant Chief.

This honor is something you have worked hard for and richly deserve. And, of course, your reward for long and excellent service will also serve as an inspiration and incentive for many other black officers.

I am very happy for you. And I know you won't stop here.

Cordially,

Dalton Roberts
County Executive

DR/as

Appendix Data

CHATTANOOGA HOUSING AUTHORITY

BOARD OF COMMISSIONERS
CAROLYN P. HENNING, CHAIRPERSON
HERBERT P. DUNLAP, VICE CHAIRMAN
WILLIAM H. PRICE
WILLIAM H. WHITESIDE
GARTHA B. COKER

BILLY C. COOPER, SEC'Y.-TREAS.
AND EXECUTIVE DIRECTOR

TELEPHONE (615) 756-7171
505 WEST NINTH STREET
P. O. BOX 1486

CHATTANOOGA, TENNESSEE 37401

October 8, 1980

Mr. Ralph Cothran
Acting Assistant Chief
Chattanooga Police Department
3300 Amnicola Highway
Chattanooga, Tennessee 37406

Dear Ralph:

It didn't take the Chattanooga Police Department long to recognize your true worth. Sixteen years from the policeman on the beat to the Chief of Police is a rewarding payoff. You've worked hard, I know, and the new title is more than deserved.

I hope it will make you even happier, however, to realize that all of us here at the Chattanooga Housing Authority are delighted that you have been properly rewarded--CHIEF.

Our cooperation and assistance is yours, even without the asking.

CONGRATULATIONS!!

                        Sincerely yours,

                        CHATTANOOGA HOUSING AUTHORITY

                        Robert E. Brown
                        Director of Housing Management

REB:gcs

Big Ralph

HOWARD SCHOOL
2500 SOUTH MARKET STREET
CHATTANOOGA, TENNESSEE 37408
Telephone (615) 267-9589

MRS. MARY J. GEE
ASSOCIATE PRINCIPAL
SENIOR HIGH DIVISION

SULLIVAN R. RUFF, JR.
PRINCIPAL

HERMAN GRIER, SR.
ASSOCIATE PRINCIPAL
ELEMENTARY DIVISION

October 15, 1980

Mr. Ralph Cothran
Assistant Police Chief
CHATTANOOGA POLICE DEPARTMENT
3300 Amnicola Highway
Chattanooga, Tennessee

Dear Sir:

My heartfelt congratulations on your recent appointment to Assistant Chief of Police for the Chattanooga Police Department. I know how hard you have worked in this department and for our great city. This appointment or achievement is also an honor for our school since you are a graduate of this institution.

Since this is our Homecoming Week it would give us high honor and privilege to have you as Honorary Parade Marshal for our 1980 parade on **Friday, October 17, 1980.**

Again, on behalf of my personal family and the Howard family, CONGRATULATIONS!

Sincerely,

Sullivan R. Ruff, Jr.
Principal

Appendix Data

TENNESSEE
DEPARTMENT OF SAFETY
ANDREW JACKSON BUILDING
NASHVILLE 37219

GENE ROBERTS
COMMISSIONER

10-6-80

Dear Ralph,

Congratulations on your appointment as assistant chief. Yours was a good choice. You've earned the respect of all of your associates in the department. And you've worked hard on the job and in improving your professional credentials (Cleveland State, FBI Academy) so as to be ready to step ahead when the opportunity came.

Ralph, you have my best wishes for success. Indeed, I have no doubt that you will do well.

I know your family is proud of you. So am I. And pleased to be your friend, too.

Sincerely,
Gene Roberts

Big Ralph

MARILYN LLOYD BOUQUARD
3D DISTRICT, TENNESSEE

COMMITTEES:
PUBLIC WORKS
AND TRANSPORTATION
SCIENCE AND TECHNOLOGY
SELECT COMMITTEE ON AGING

Congress of the United States
House of Representatives
Washington, D.C. 20515

208 CANNON HOUSE OFFICE BUILDING
WASHINGTON, D.C. 20515
TELEPHONE: (202) 225-3271

230 POST OFFICE BUILDING
CHATTANOOGA, TENNESSEE 37401
TELEPHONE: (615) 756-4250

1211 FEDERAL OFFICE BUILDING
OAK RIDGE, TENNESSEE 37830
TELEPHONE: (615) 576-1977

October 10, 1980

Mr. Ralph Cothran
Acting Assistant Chief
Chattanooga Police Department
Amnicola Highway
Chattanooga, Tennessee 37406

Dear Chief Cothran:

    I would like to take this opportunity to congratulate you on your recent promotion to Acting Assistant Chief of the Chattanooga Police Department. I know you must be proud of this accomplishment.

    Again congratulations, and if my office can ever be of assistance, please do not hesitate to call on me or my staff.

    Best wishes.

Sincerely,

Marilyn Bouquard

MARILYN LLOYD BOUQUARD
Member of Congress

Appendix Data

Chattanooga Law Enforcement Officers Association, Inc.
3300 Amnicola Highway • Chattanooga, Tennessee 37406

06-05-95

Dear Chief Ralph H. Cothran,

We bring you greetings from the Chattanooga Law Enforcement Officers Association, a charter of the National Black Police Officers Association.

Chief Cothran, there are cares, needs, concerns and objectives that C.L.E.O.A. will be addressing in the months to come. We are very unhappy with the current police administrations lack of concern with minority police officers, (men and women). ▓▓▓ty. We feel that minorities should be represented in the police departments middle management process and positions with the same ratio as these percentages. Currently the Chattanooga Police Department is under utilizing minorities in the positions of Inspector, Sergeant, Lieutenant, Captain, Major, Assistant Chief and Deputy Chief. In addition, within the Investigative Services Division minorities are grossly misrepresented according to current data pertaining to the Chattanooga Police Department not limited to the Affirmative Action Plan for 1995 from the Equal Employment Opportunity Office headed by Moses Freeman. The department currently consists of:

RANK	WHITE	BLACK
Patrol officer	191	58
Inspectors	24	7
Sergeants	42	5
Lieutenants	23	7
Captains	17	4

No black Majors, Assistant Chiefs, or Deputy Chiefs

There are various training seminars and schools that certain offcers attend, but this information is kept from minority officers hindering further career enhancement and opportunities. There are also a number of divisions and departments within which minorities are currently misrepresented and under-utilized:

Dedicated To "Community Service"

Big Ralph

Chief Cothran, with current ~~gang activity~~ on the rise and the potential for gang related issues pertaining to the community, we (C.L.E.O.A.) are concerned about the need to address inner city school children on their social and economical status to become productive and successful citizens one day. Also, catering to the concerns of poor and less privileged children in the community to show them that someone cares about their well-being and progress. Currently there are no minority's actually in the field in the ~~[redacted]~~ which is ridiculous, especially when a high percentage of crimes are being committed by minority juveniles.

Chief Cothran, there are numerous ~~[redacted]~~ in the Chattanooga Police Department what minority are currently misrepresented by under utilization:

- Homicide - 2 Minority
- Narcotics - 3 Minority
- Fraud & Forgery - 0 Minority
- I.D. Section - 0 Minority
- Beer/Wrecker Inspector - 0 Minority
- Polygraph Exam - 0 Minority
- Warrants/Fugitive - 1 Minority
- Intelligence - 0 Minority
- Crime Prevention Bureau - 0 Minority
- F.B.I. Street Task Force - 0 Minority
- Traffic/D.U.I. - 2 Minority
- Mounted Patrol - 0 Minority
- Explosive Ordinance Disposal Unit - 0 Minority
- Burglary/Robbery - 4 Minority
- Juvenile - 1 Minority Supervisor
- Auto Theft - 2 Minority
- Arson - 0 Minority
- Child Abuse - 1 Minority
- Pawn Shop Detail - 0 Minority
- D.A.R.E. - 2 Minority
- PIO - 0 Minority
- Crime Stoppers - 0 Minority
- Vice - 1 Minority
- K-9 - 0 Minority
- Park Police - 0 Minority
- Auxiliary Police - 1 Minority
- Police Athletic League - 0 Minority

Even the percentage of minorities in the ~~[redacted]~~ does not reflect the appropriate numbers, especially evident by the fact the you have not employed a black female officer since 1988 (7 years ago). We need a minority recruiter for the Chattanooga Police Department too seek out qualified minority applicants and hiree's from certain minority institutions.

Appendix Data

Chief Cothran, we are looking for fairness and equality. Under the ~~constitution~~ of the United States of American we as minority Americans are guaranteed certain unalienable rights but we are not receiving these rights guaranteed us, we have not been getting our fair share of the privileges, promotions and decorations entitled to us by the constitution.

The administration should rise above dishonesty and deprivation in order to be effective. The ~~differences that we noticed between black and white officers is well known and has made throughout the history of the Chattanooga Police Department~~. Black officers are disciplined more severely than white officers who may commit the same offence, but their offence is subject to be overlooked. There also needs to be a sensitivity course required for police officers of all races, to help different cultural groups better understand each others background.

IN 1994 an ~~FBI Crime Analysis Report~~ was released stating that Chattanooga, Tennessee was ranked 22nd in the nation for violent crimes committed, surpassing New York City, per capita. There should be more preventative measures taken to change this appalling fact, but let's first recognize that there is a problem and unless its addressed it will not go away. We the Officers of the Chattanooga Law Enforcement Association are dedicating ourselves to this issue at hand to come up with a positive solution for a community problem.

We the members of ~~C.L.E.O.A.~~ are ready, willing and able to sit down and discuss these issues. We hope that you will give us the same courtesy and respect that's given to the ~~F.O.P.~~ and ~~P.B.A.~~ members. We are currently working with several community organizations and churches who share our interest. We are not attempting to take an adverse position with the administration, but if we cannot reach some type of compromise on some of our concerns, other avenues will have to be pursued.

Chief Cothran, due to the sever differences in our positions, and the obvious path that the administration has taken in the past, we are willing to help work with the administration in establishing new standards in which we, as minority officers, can be better utilized in the department.

Big Ralph

We hope to receive a timely response, if not we will consider this letter ignored.

Sincerely, The Executive Committee C.L.E.O.A.

Carlton B Parks, President

Carlton B. Parks

Derrick C. Stewart Vice-President

Derrick Stewart

Tetzel D. Tillery, Treasurer

Tetzel Tillery

Ponda D. Bailey, Secretary

Ponda Bailey

Corliss A. Cooper, Parlimentarion

Corliss A. Cooper

Lee R. Stewart, Sergeant at Arms

Billy D. Usher, Sergeant at Arms

B. D. Usher

cc: Honarable Mayor Gene Roberts
    Saftey Director Ervin L. Dinsmore

Appendix Data

new

June 28, 1995

Chattanooga Law Enforcement
 Officers Association, Inc.
3300 Amnicola Highway
Chattanooga, Tennessee 37406

Dear Officers and Members of CLEOA:

Where were you, CLEOA? Where were you when I needed you?

I received your letter dated 5 June 1995 and read it in amazement, even anger. This is the first letter I have received from CLEOA in the six years I have been Chief of Police.

I was one of the founders of CLEOA over 20 years ago, and my door has always been open to the organization and its members. Black law enforcement associations have contributed in Chattanooga and elsewhere to bettering the conditions of blacks and minorities within the police service.

Regrettably, though, this historic, positive association (CLEOA) is now filled with confusion, dissension and a vile misrepresentation of the truth. From my analysis, CLEOA is another good cause gone bad. It is a shame that this once positive organization is now manipulated by self-serving individuals who could care less about the public welfare and community service.

Many of the serious challenges I have faced as the first black chief of this department have had racial overtones. As an experienced police officer and having a great love for my hometown, I have always had a deep interest in positive community relations. As a minority I have always had an on-going interest in equality for all people, including personnel in this department regardless of race or gender.

It has been a major objective of my tenure as chief to upgrade the department in all areas. Six years down the road as chief I would argue that there has been a turnaround in how the black community views the department.

Big Ralph

This job has not been easy. I have received opposition from persons inside and outside the department. But I have continued my efforts to rid the department of actions and/or officers--whether white or black--that cause the community to look at the department in a negative way.

CLEOA, where were you when I confronted questions of police brutality and abuse of authority in the department?

Where were you, CLEOA, in 1989 when I sought to establish a Police Athletic League? The essence of Police Athletic Leagues across the nation is an attempt to extend positive community relations with law enforcement agencies. But did CLEOA step forward to participate? No! CLEOA did not respond even though I approved overtime pay for all officers involved.

Where were you, CLEOA, when the the D.A.R.E. Program was begun to reach children before they got to middle school? This program uses police officers as positive role models to encourage children to resist drugs and alcohol.

Where were you, CLEOA, when the department launched the clean-up of Harriet Tubman Homes? The Harriet Tubman Homes is a predominantly black housing project that was once a haven for drug dealing, drug use and crime. But I received no help or support in this clean-up effort from CLEOA which claims to have the interest of minorities as their rallying cry. But we made significant changes within Harriet Tubman with the assistance of well-meaning residents and organizations in the city. Presently we have a precinct in Harriet Tubman and the drug dealers have left or they have been arrested.

Where were you, CLEOA, when I asked for help and support to establish an Auxiliary Police force? But we still went forward with this program that resulted in the establishment of a Reserve Officers Corp.

Where were you, CLEO, when we established community policing which is one of the proven methods of reducing crime?

At this point I would like to respond to some particular concerns noted in the letter from my fellow black police officers.

Percentage of blacks hired based on population figures for Chattanooga-Hamilton County.

Appendix Data

1989 TOTAL FULL-TIME EMPLOYEES

	NON-MINORITY	**MINORITY**	**TOTAL**
TOTAL	397	99	496

MINORITIES COMPROMISED 19.9% OF THE TOTAL FULL-TIME WORKFORCE IN THE DEPARTMENT.

1995 TOTAL FULL-TIME EMPLOYEES (AS OF 23 MAY 95)

	NON-MINORITY	**MINORITY**	**TOTAL**
TOTAL	386	141	527

MINORITIES NOW COMPROMISE 26.8% OF THE TOTAL FULL-TIME WORKFORCE IN THE DEPARTMENT.

FULL-TIME EMPLOYEES HIRED FROM JANUARY 1, 1989 TO PRESENT.

	NON-MINORITY	**MINORITY**	**TOTAL**
TOTAL	148	86	234

36.7% OF ALL NEW-HIRES DURING THE PERIOD WERE MINORITIES.

UNIFORM CRIME REPORT INFORMATION FOR 1989 AS COMPARED WITH 1994.

MODIFIED CRIME INDEX	**1989**	**1994**	**DECREASE**
	15,848	14,299	1,549

THE MODIFIED CRIME INDEX DECREASED BY 9.7% DURING THE PERIOD. ALSO, OF THE REPORTED CATAGORIES OF CRIME, OUR DEPARTMENT HAS DEMONSTRATED A DECREASE IN FIVE (5) OF THE SEVEN (7) CATAGORIES.

ACCORDING TO CRIME STATISTICS RELEASED BY THE F.B.I., CHATTANOOGA, TENNESSEE WAS REPORTED AS HAVING THE LARGEST REDUCTION IN CRIME FOR THE ENTIRE UNITED STATES. THE OVERALL REDUCTION AMOUNTED TO 27% LESS THAN THE 1993 FIGURES. CHATTANOOGA IS RANKED 69TH IN THE NUMBER OF PART I CRIMES REPORTED PER CAPITA.

A BLACK FEMALE POLICE OFFICER WAS EMPLOYED ON 8 FEB. 91.

Big Ralph

Racial representation by divisions and departments.

ASSIGNED	MINORITY	TOTAL
HOMICIDE(2)	2	11
NARCOTICS(3)	5	15
FORGERY/FRAUD(0)	0	2
I.D.(0)	0	9
(2 MINORITIES WERE RECENTLY PROMOTED AND THEIR POSITIONS HAVE NOT BEEN FILLED)		
BEER/WRECKER(0)	0	4
WARRANTS/FUGUTIVE(1)	1	1
CRIME PREVENTION(0)	1	2
TRAFFIC/D.U.I.(2)	2	10
MOUNTED PATROL(0)	0	3
BURGLARY/ROBBERY(4)	6	27
JUVENILE(1)	1	4
AUTO THEFT(2)	2	7
ARSON(0)	0	2
CHILD ABUSE(1)	1	2
VICE(1)	1	2
PARK POLICE(0)	0	13
P.A.L.(0)	0	1
ASSIGNMENTS:		
POLYGRAPH EXAMINER(0)	0	1
F.B.I. SAFE STREETS(0)	0	3
E.O.D. UNIT(0)	0	4
PAWNSHOP DETAIL(0)	1	1
D.A.R.E.(2)	3	4
P.I.O.(0)	0	1
CRIME STOPPERS(0)	0	1
(PART TIME ASSIGNMENT)		
OTHER DIVISIONS:		
PUBLIC HOUSING SECTION	18	25
TRAINING	2	5
PARK RANGERS	6	8
PARKING ENFORCEMENT	2	7

Appendix Data

-5-

OTHER ASSIGNMENTS:	
INTELLIGENCE UNIT	THERE IS NO INTELLIGENCE UNIT
AUXILIARY POLICE	SERVES ON VOLUNTARY BASIS

PART TIME EMPLOYEES:	W/F	W/M	B/F	B/M	TOTAL
SCHOOL PATROL	10	2	17	2	31
-TOTAL MINORITIES	19 = 61.3%				
-TOTAL MINORITIES INCLUDING W/F	29 = 93.5%				

NOTE: THE FOLLOWING SCHOOL PATROL OFFICERS ARE FULL TIME.

-CHIEF, SCHOOL PATROL .... B/F
-CAPTAIN, SCHOOL PATROL .... W/F

	W/F	W/M	B/F	B/M	TOTAL
PARK RANGERS	0	2	1	2	5
-TOTAL MINORITIES	3 = 60%				
-TOTAL MINORITIES INCLUDING W/F	3 = 60%				

Affirmative Action

One cannot look at affirmative action in a superficial way. Historically, affirmative action was established to address problems of discrimination in various instances confirmed by minorities. These measures were established during an era when many minorities were virtually excluded from many areas of work. So affirmative action in 1995 is a totally different ballgame.

Throughout the nation affirmative action is under attack. Reverse discrimination cases are on the rise, and many high public officials are interested in dismantling virtually all measures of affirmative action. In the process some people (CLEOA) seem to think affirmative action means a free ride or promotion without qualifications and skill level.

The Chattanooga Law Enforcement Officers Association also notes that they are deprived of training opportunities. The training division consist of four sworn officers and one secretary. A black captain heads the training staff along with a black lieutenant, one white male inspector and one white female officer.

Well-trained officers are the life-blood of a police department. No doubt the knowledge and leadership ability of black law enforcement officers is well received for blacks to be placed in such a sensitive and crucial division.

> Gang related activity - we are in the process and have been sending officers to seminars on gangs. Each time the ratio has been 50% black and 50% white.

Ingrained in the statement by my long-time colleagues from CLEOA is that I have no interest in positive youth development in our city. I am upset by the erroneous accusations and misrepresentations of the facts. I am really angered by this untruth.

My record speaks for itself. My conceptualization of positive community relations makes special mention of the South; for example, the Police Athletic League, the D.A.R.E. Program and community-based policing which deals with community-specific needs. Also, we are well on the way to re-establishing the interest in community recreational facilities with boxing as a city-wide competitive sport.

> The head of the Juvenile Division is a black female.

> The U.S. Constitution and employment rights. On this issue CLEOA really just went overboard or they have not read the constitution. Many minority organizations (civil rights groups) note the constitution in championing the rights of minorities. I have no problem with this. I am black and I want equal rights and fair play. But in reference to employment rights, the constitution does not guarantee minorities or anybody else promotions and decorations.

> History of blacks in Chattanooga Police Department. CLEOA in this instance turns a valid statement into a falsehood. Yes, the Chattanooga Police Department has had a history of racism and unequal treatment of minorities. But most agencies, public and private, were discriminatory in America, especially in the South during the days of Jim Crow and segregation.

First of all, my appointment as chief six years ago is clear indication that the status of blacks as Chattanooga Police officers has changed considerably.

Appendix Data

During my tenure not only has the community as a whole come to view the police in a positive light. Minorities have also witnessed an increased upward mobility.

But this upward mobility is based on experience, skill, training, and positive results. Thus under my tenure promotions have not been based on race, gender, the good old boy approach or any other counter productive measures--nor will they be as long as I am chief.

Relationship to law enforcement organizations.

I have always extended an open door policy to all existing law enforcement organizations. Presently my black fellow officers of the CLEOA feel that I am discriminating against them. This could not be further from the truth.

Let me set the record straight. I created a promotional committee that was open to everybody from sergeant and above. I also placed no limitations on how many could participate. A black officer was established as the chairman of this committee. In so doing, this committee under his leadership, recommended to me how promotional procedures should be carried out.

Administrator Dinsmore, with my recommendations, presented these procedures to the City Council. They were approved in a gesture of concern and fairness by the City Council and cost the city more than $100,000 to implement. But since the CLEOA leadership is part of the old school (of unqualified blacks, token blacks) they did not follow through with the testing process.

In closing, one cannot make rules, regulations and break them for one group of people. I stand on fair treatment for everyone--black, white, male or female.

Sincerely,

Ralph H. Cothran
Chief of Police

RHC/vl

Big Ralph

STATE OF TENNESSEE
HUMAN RIGHTS COMMISSION
CENTRAL OFFICE
CORNERSTONE SQUARE BUILDING, SUITE 400
530 CHURCH STREET
NASHVILLE, TENNESSEE 37243-0745
(615) 741-5825

August 3, 1995

Chattanooga Police Department　　　　THRC Charge #4070395
3300 Amnicola Highway　　　　　　　EEOC Charge #25A951666
Chattanooga, TN 37406

The Tennessee Human Rights Commission (THRC) has received a complaint against your facility alleging discrimination. Tennessee law requires the THRC to investigate and pass upon complaints of employment discrimination based upon race, color, sex, national origin, religion, creed, age, and disability. This notification letter, as well as a copy of the referenced complaint, are being furnished to you pursuant to Tennessee Code Annotated, Section 4-21-302(b). A request for information is also enclosed. If jurisdictional, this complaint has also been filed under comparable federal law with the Equal Employment Opportunity Commission (EEOC).

A THRC investigator will contact you when the investigation begins. The EEOC plans to refrain from conducting an investigation at this time. All facts and evidence provided by you to the THRC will be considered by the EEOC when it reviews the THRC's final findings and orders. These final findings and orders will be given consideration by the EEOC in making its own determination as to whether or not reasonable cause exists to believe that the allegations made in the complaint are true. In many instances, the EEOC will take no further action. Regardless of whether the EEOC or the THRC investigates this complaint, both federal and state record keeping and non-retaliation regulation and laws apply.

Sometimes complaints are resolved without investigations if both parties agree to mutually acceptable terms. In this situation, no findings are reached by the THRC, and there need not be any admission of wrongdoing on the part of the Respondent. This procedure is called a negotiated settlement and may be accomplished at any time prior to the issuance of a determination on the merits of the complaint. If you wish to enter into negotiated settlement discussions, or if you have additional questions, please feel free to contact me at **540 McCallie Avenue, First Floor #W106, Chattanooga, TN 37402, or by calling (615)-634-6222.**

Sincerely,

Alice B. Ford
Investigator
Human Rights Representative

LL/rw

Enclosures:　Complaint of Discrimination
　　　　　　Request for Information -　　**Please furnish information to me at the above address within 3 weeks after receipt of this letter.**

Appendix Data

MAJORITY STEERING COMMITTEE
COMMITTEE ON SCIENCE
SUBCOMMITTEES:
ENERGY & ENVIRONMENT
BASIC RESEARCH - VICE CHAIRMAN
COMMITTEE ON
TRANSPORTATION & INFRASTRUCTURE
SUBCOMMITTEE
WATER RESOURCES & ENVIRONMENT - VICE CHAIRMAN
COMMITTEE ON SMALL BUSINESS
SUBCOMMITTEE
REGULATIONS & PAPERWORK
TVA CAUCUS

ZACH WAMP
CONGRESS OF THE UNITED STATES
THIRD DISTRICT, TENNESSEE

WASHINGTON OFFICE:
423 CANNON BUILDING
WASHINGTON, D.C. 20515
(202) 225-3271
(202) 225-3494 Fax

DISTRICT OFFICES:
6100 EASTGATE CENTER
SUITE 3400
CHATTANOOGA, TN 37411
(615) 894-7400
(615) 894-8619 Fax

55 JEFFERSON CIRCLE, ROOM 231-D
OAK RIDGE, TN 37830
(615) 483-3366
(615) 576-3221 Fax

March 14, 1996

Mr. Richard K. Donahue
Profile in Courage Award Committee
John F. Kennedy Library Foundation
Columbia Point
Boston, Massachusetts 02125

Dear Chairman Donahue:

Thank you for giving me the opportunity to nominate a man of utmost courage for the prestigious Profile in Courage Award. Chattanooga Police Chief Ralph Cothran left this life early, but not before distinguishing himself as an important public servant in the community where he lived and died.

In a time when it is increasingly important for young males, in particular African-American youths, to have role models other than professional athletes or musicians, Ralph Cothran's life represents the kind of hope that transcends race or socioeconomic status.

Chief Cothran's career was built on years of professionalism, hard work and integrity. The fact that Chief Cothran's record led to his appointment as the first black police chief in Chattanooga teaches the lesson that perseverance and merit do pay off, a lesson all young people need at this critical time. So many young people are not willing to set long term goals and stick with them over time.

The life of Ralph Cothran should go down in southern history as a life of love, dedication and most of all hope - as he leaves with all young people the hope that they can achieve any dream if they are willing to work patiently and keep their priorities in line along the way.

Warmest regards,

Zach Wamp   *Thank you!*
Zach Wamp
Member of Congress

ZW:hh

PRINTED ON RECYCLED PAPER

Big Ralph

NOMINATION OF RALPH H. COTHRAN

for the

JOHN F. KENNEDY 1996 PROFILE IN COURAGE AWARD

In 1964, Airman First Class Ralph Henry Cothran swapped his Air Force blue for the blue of his hometown police force. The similarity ended there.

Waves of great change were rising in the American South in 1964, but were yet a year away from the inner city district where Ralph Cothran was first assigned to patrol duty.

His was the A-1 beat, distinguished from the overlapping A beat by the color of the officer's skin and the reach of his authority.

Cothran was a strong, 6'7" black man. He could arrest African Americans, but if a white offender needed to be taken into custody the A car had to be summoned. Only a white officer could make that arrest.

Young officer Cothran--he was 26 then--knew this old style southern policing was about to end. He had seen the positive racial changes taking place during his four Air Force years. The racial barriers were coming down across the South, slowly yes, but surely too. And Ralph Cothran was determined to be in the vanguard of southern policing when black officers would at last begin to be valued, appreciated, and given the chance to contribute the full measure of their abilities to the job.

It occurred to Cothran that in the New South, which was in the process of becoming, capable black officers would exercise increasing influence in police affairs. There were changes aplenty he wanted to make within the department and in its dealings with the community, especially the minority community. He was determined to be a difference maker in policing.

Cothran endured a year of working the A-1 beat, of the separate and unequal policing it required. And then, in 1965, the flow of racial change reached the Chattanooga Police Department. Officer Cothran no longer had to call the A car to make an arrest for him. He could do it himself. Very soon thereafter black and white officers were patrolling together in the same car in the so-called "hot" beats.

Cothran moved ahead rapidly in this new and freer police environment. By 1969 he was a narcotics detective. Two years later he was a lieutenant. In 1974, after graduating from the FBI National Academy, he became a captain and commanding officer of the more than 70 uniformed and plainclothes officers assigned to the seven patrol districts (no longer "beats") which covered the central city portion of Chattanooga. Here Cothran supervised many of those same officers the old system required him to call upon in order to take a white offender into custody.

Appendix Data

All who worked for him learned quickly that Cothran bore no malice. Color made no difference. If you were right, he backed you all the way, community protest notwithstanding. If you were wrong, knowingly wrong, you then had a very big problem with Captain Cothran.

In 1972, a white supervisor had recognized the potential in Cothran and suggested to him that he would be chief of police one day if he would enroll in college and polish his administrative and academic skills. Dramatic procedural changes in the law were requiring ever higher education for police officers. The Law Enforcement Assistance Administration (LEAA) of that time made it possible through federal scholarship grants for thousands of law enforcement officers to go to college. Cothran was one who seized the opportunity. He graduated magna cum laude with a two-year degree in law enforcement.

Those who worked with him during the 1970's are the chief witnesses for the proposition that Ralph Cothran, by his example of leadership and colorblind fairness, made the transition to increasing black leadership within the police service relatively smoother in Chattanooga than in most cities.

Cothran's surehanded grasp of command resulted in his elevation to assistant chief in 1980, and to deputy chief three years later.

In these roles, Cothran emphasized the necessity of personal ties between police and residents of communities they serve. Men and women who know and trust police officers, talk to them. Crimes are thus prevented or solved, neighborhoods made more habitable, and those who live there surer that order reigns and civil life can, after all, flourish in the city. Cothran believed all of these things were possible where police practiced the human dimensions of their demanding calling. He never ceased to believe it and to provide his own example of how to do it.

When Deputy Chief Cothran became Chief Cothran in 1989, he launched his idea of "police/community partnerships", neighborhood by neighborhood, on a citywide scale.

He helped neighborhoods organize so that they would then work with the police and other city agencies to attack problems of crime, drug abuse, housing code violations, zoning violations, littered lots, abandoned houses and other problems common particularly to poorer neighborhoods.

He organized bike patrols for the downtown and appropriate neighborhoods, and set up police substations in public housing communities.

For young people he organized a Police Athletic League and established an Explorer Scout Post within the police department.

Big Ralph

He took a personal and active role in drug abuse prevention programs, held leadership positions in local and national organizations of black law enforcement professionals and served as deacon in the church into which he was born and baptized.

It was said of Chief Cothran that he created a commanding presence whenever he was, and not only or mainly because he was such a big man. Dignity was a part of his very presence. Maturity and thoughtfulness characterized his judgment. He was truly a walking billboard for leadership.

Police officers who served under Chief Cothran trusted and respected his judgment, whether in deciding an appropriate police response to a dangerous situation, or in handing down a decision in a disciplinary action.

Chief Cothran was a police officer in the highest sense of the profession. He believed along with a former Tennessee governor that the police are "servants of the people, not Lords over the people."

Ralph Cothran was in the prime of his professional life when he fell victim to cancer on November 2, 1995.

His enduring legacy, one suspects, will be that his vision of police/community partnerships not only ennobles both partners, it works.

sp

Appendix Data

John F. Kennedy Library Foundation
Columbia Point
Boston, Massachusetts 02125
Telephone (617) 436-9986
Fax (617) 436-3395

March 18, 1996

MAR 2 2 1996

The Honorable Zach Wamp
United States House of Representatives
423 Cannon Building
Washington, D.C. 20515

Dear Congressman Wamp:

The Profile in Courage Award Committee has received your nomination for Ralph Henry Cothran and would like to thank you for your recommendation. The Committee especially appreciates your strong interest and commitment to public service and the qualities of leadership and political courage that President Kennedy valued.

We hope that you and others like you across the country will continue to insist on these qualities in our leaders. Together, we can continue to make a difference and work for a better and stronger America in the years ahead. Thank you again.

Sincerely,

Richard K. Donahue
Chairman
Profile in Courage Award

RKD/dhl